Structural Social Work:

Ideology, Theory, and Practice

Robert Mullaly

Canadian Cataloguing in Publication Data

Mullaly, Robert P.
Structural social work: ideology, theory, and practice

Includes bibliographical references and index.
ISBN 0-7710-6673-2

1. Social service – Philosophy. 2. Social service. 3. Social case work. I. Title.

HV40.M855 1993 361′.001 C92-095513-4

McClelland & Stewart Inc.
The Canadian Publishers
481 University Avenue
Toronto, Ontario
M5G 2E9

Typesetting by M&S

The support of the Government of Ontario through the Ministry of Culture and Communications is acknowledged.

Printed and bound in Canada

Contents

Foreword

To be involved in social work education today is to feel a certain chill – it is the despair many students feel about the practice of social work as being inauthentic, as representing a chasm between rhetoric and reality. We wonder, perhaps, what they think of their professors, we who attempt to make the case for a radical, critical, or structural form of social work practice, in which there is some congruence between belief and action. Do they wonder whether we are lying to ourselves about the emancipatory possibilities of social work, whether we are guilty of bad faith? In *Being and Nothingness,* Sartre points out that "in bad faith it is from myself that I am hiding the truth." Is there a truth that we, the "radical professors," might be hiding from ourselves?

These are hard questions, which arise in an increasingly acute form as one response to the various crises – economic, political, and cultural – to which Robert Mullaly gives sustained attention in the early part of this book. As capitalism takes a new turn in its world-wide exploitation of people and nature, so we enter an epoch of massive transformation, an historical shift that involves the decomposition and restructuring of states, classes, and beliefs. Is the current political scepticism about whether the effect of state intervention can ever be predominately benign simply a manifestation of those "morbid symptoms" (including post-modern angst, perhaps) that Gramsci identified as characteristic of an interregnum crisis when "the old is dying and the new cannot be born"?

This book represents a compelling answer to these questions. It shows that we must see social work as situated within a set of contradictions that permit us to engage in a critical practice "against the state" while still invariably being involved in dominant structures intent on homogenizing and subordinating those who, as "problematic populations," confront a patriarchal capitalist state, culture, and economy.

The critical debate within feminist and left perspectives on social work at present concerns the question of whether an emancipatory practice is possible under the particular conditions of post-modern capitalism with its massive forces of cultural control that penetrate gender, class, and ethnic relations, and if it is possible, precisely how it is to be engaged in. *Structural Social Work* is strong in its optimistic answers to the questions this debate articulates, drawing on a now substantial tradition of radical political work in the social welfare field. Mullaly's book critically engages with this work, synthesizes it, and delivers prescriptions for social work that are realistic and based on forms of practice we know to exist today, even under the most unpromising conditions.

To read this book, however, encourages not only reflection on present possibilities, but also on the historical burden of social work: its origins in forms of domination. Before social work could be established as a modern profession, equipped with an appropriate panoply of institutional powers and techniques, certain preconditions were necessary: the identification of the object of its interventions and the establishment of its moral purpose. Historically, social work originated as a *relation between classes* based on a bourgeois commitment to the regulation of the poor. This class regulation began, in the nineteenth century, with a focus on the "deserving poor." As "madness" was separated out from other conditions afflicting subordinate populations and was, as Foucault shows, identified as the object for which psychiatry would eventually be created, so other categorizations subdivided populations within the submerged lower classes. With the emergence of the welfare state, poverty is no longer the absolute and invariable distinguishing mark of the "client groups," though it remains its most notable characteristic.

We can see now that working-class subjects, especially women, remained the principal objects of social work. They were to be influenced and their resistance was to be overcome by professional expertise. This expertise originated in the belief that the poor were among the "dangerous classes" who needed to be reformed in order to reduce deviance, disease, and chaos and advance civilized standards. Because institutional incarceration or segregation in their ghettos was unlikely to be successful as a preventative measure, moral intervention in the family was necessary to counter the spread of moral as well as physical disease. The ideal agents of this patriarchal intervention were to be found among middle-class women as the upholders of Victorian family morality. To establish itself as a worthy occupation and later a profession, social work had to clothe its moral intervention in the mantle of scientific rationality. It brought reason and organization to bear on unreasonand disorganization, and it couched its purposes in a new language – the language, initially, of casework.

To what extent, we might ask, do these origins, despite intervening social transformations and further changes in language, remain powerful determinants of the social work enterprise, a spectre haunting our struggle to create a new social work?

Structural Social Work shows us that we do not have to be overdetermined by this history, that we do not have to write off social work as so hopelessly ineffective in its contribution to social justice that we must resign ourselves to Foucault's ultimate pessimism and simply oppose social work as orthodox Marxists did before the contemporary radical social work movement began.

The power of *Structural Social Work* to engage the reader may be judged, perhaps, by my response to it as an old Marxist strongly influenced by feminists and post-modernists: I found myself in turn both agreeing and debating with the book. For me, there can be no more compelling reason for reading it than that it provokes us to a response, and so plays a significant role in furthering the practical and intellectual work necessary in the struggle to develop emancipatory forms of social work practice.

Peter Leonard
School of Social Work
McGill University

Preface

Although social work has always had a progressive element within its ranks, only since 1975, with the publication of Bailey and Brake's *Radical Social Work* and Galper's *The Politics of Social Services*, has a substantial literature, known as "radical social work," developed. This perspective challenges the hegemony of conventional social work theories of "person-reform" and "limited social reform."

The major difficulties with radical or progressive social work are that, so far, it has received inconsistent treatment in the literature and that it has not progressed significantly beyond critical analysis of conventional social work. Consequently, the radical social work literature may be characterized as fragmented, lacking a comprehensive framework, and underdeveloped with respect to converting its analysis into political practice.

The purpose of this book is twofold: (1) to clarify the clutter of radical social work literature by integrating its ideological context, its theoretical base, and its political practice; and (2) to advance the existing theoretical base of radical social work.

The means of carrying out this dual purpose is to focus on one particular school of radical social work, "structural social work." This school was chosen for several reasons. First, the term "structural" is descriptive of the nature of social problems in that they are an inherent, built-in part of our present social order. Second, the term is prescriptive, as it indicates that the focus for change is mainly on the structures of society and not on personal characteristics of the individual. Third, structural social work has more potential for integrating various theoretical concepts and political practices because it does not establish hierarchies of oppression but rather is concerned with all oppressed groups. Fourth, it is a dialectical approach to social work practice and, therefore, is more flexible than some radical approaches that get trapped within false dichotomies. Finally, most of the development of structural social work has occurred in Canada, where it is now assuming an increasing importance as a major social work perspective and theory.

Part I shows how and why current social work theory and practice are part of the larger "fiscal crisis of the state." It is argued that until social work articulates a social vision consistent with its own values, ideals, and beliefs, it will remain ineffective in ameliorating or resolving social problems. To articulate such a vision, the social work profession must engage itself in ideological analysis and become more cognizant of various theories of the state. These tasks are addressed in Part I.

The impact of the international economic crises of the 1970s and 1980s on the welfare state and on social work is examined in Chapter 1. To date, social work has been ineffective in dealing with the deleterious consequences of the larger fiscal crisis and, therefore, is itself in a state of crisis. This situation has resulted in considerable soul-searching within social work with respect to many of its comfortable assumptions about the nature of society, the nature of social problems, and the nature of social work practice. Considerable criticisms have been made of our present social order and our present social work practices, and there is a significant call for alternative models. The concept of paradigm is presented in Chapter 1 as a means to explore alternative models of society, alternative explanations for social problems, and alternative theories for social work practice.

Chapter 2 differentiates two social work perspectives – the conventional view and the progressive view. The former accepts our current social system; the latter seeks to transform it. This book adopts a progressive view: an alternative vision of society must exist in advance of practice as a necessary prerequisite to social transformation. An outline of such a vision is developed and articulated. Chapters 3 to 6 examine the ideologies of four societal paradigms (neo-conservatism, liberalism, social democracy, and Marxism), the explanation each offers for social problems, the ideal type of welfare system consistent with each paradigm's ideology and interpretation of social problems, and the nature and form of social work practice of each paradigm.

Part II presents the theoretical basis of structural social work. Chapter 7 compares and contrasts the four paradigms with each other and with the elements of the progressive social work vision outlined in Chapter 2. It is concluded that progressive social work is much more congruent with the socialist paradigms (social democracy and Marxism) than with the capitalist paradigms (neo-conservatism and liberalism). The remainder of Chapter 7 shows how structural social work is part of the larger radical social work movement and presents an historical and conceptual overview of structural social work. Chapter 8 discusses the fundamental components of structural social work theory – its conflict perspective, its grounding in critical theory, and its dialectical approach. The chapter closes with a discussion of the contributions made to structural social work theory by feminism and by anti-racist social work practice.

Part III outlines several practice elements of structural social work which are derived from its theoretical base. Chapter 9 focuses on carrying out social work practice within (and against) the system and Chapter 10 deals with the practice of structural social work outside (and against) the system. Chapter 9 discusses several structural social work practice elements to be used with service users that differentiate structural practice from conventional practice. This chapter looks also at how a structural social worker can survive in a workplace that he or she is trying to politicize and democratize. Issues and strategies of radicalizing the workplace while protecting oneself from reprisal are discussed. Chapter 10 considers several arenas for struggle outside the social services system where structural social workers can contribute to social transformation. It is argued in the final section of the chapter that structural social work is much more than a technique or a practice modality. It is a way of life.

Part I

In Search of a Paradigm

1

Crises and Paradigms

The Welfare State in Crisis

The welfare states in Canada, Great Britain, and the United States, like those of much of the Western industrialized world, are in a profound state of crisis and restructuring. The growth these welfare states had experienced since the Second World War has been curtailed in some jurisdictions, halted in others, and even reversed in still others. Most writers on the subject pinpoint the mid-seventies as the starting point of the crisis of the welfare state, a result of the larger crisis of the slumping international economy brought on by sharp increases in oil prices initiated by the OPEC cartel in 1973 followed by stagflation and economic decline.[1] This combination undermined general confidence in the mixed economy and the welfare state.

The rash of social legislation enacted after World War Two via the Beveridge Report in Britain and the *Green Book* proposals for Canadian post-war reconstruction, and before the war by the New Deal in the United States, marked for many the beginning of a new era, variously referred to as "post-industrial society," the "mixed economy," "welfare capitalism," or, more commonly, the "welfare state." The Great Depression had shown that, left on its own, a laissez-faire state could not function properly. The economic and social costs associated with cyclical recessions, the inefficiency and waste associated with unfettered monopoly development, and the political and social instability associated with civil unrest led to a profound transformation in the economy, in society, and in the role of the modern state. Indeed, World War Two was viewed by many in Canada as a fight for a better society than that which existed under the free market economy prior to the war.[2] From this historical context the welfare state represented a new deal or social consensus among government, capital, and labour whereby government would use public funds to provide a wide array of services and programs to protect citizens from many social hazards associated with a complex modern society.

As Mishra points out in *The Welfare State in Crisis,* the post-war welfare state rested on two pillars: the Keynesian economic component and the Beveridge social component.[3] Keynesian economic theory argued for state intervention to ensure a high level of economic activity and full employment. Beveridge called for state intervention to protect people on a universal, comprehensive, and adequate basis against those contingencies that were part of a modern industrial society and further argued that social welfare benefits were to be provided as a right to all and not as a form of charity to a few. Social welfare developed in most Western industrialized nations on the assumption that a harmonious relationship could exist between capitalism and the social welfare sector (thus the terms "mixed economy" and "welfare capitalism"). However, the OPEC crisis of 1973, slower rates of economic growth, government deficits, excessive unemployment, inflation, and high interest rates brought this assumption into question and discredited Keynesianism.

Keynesian economic theory first appeared to be in serious difficulty in the mid-seventies with the onset of stagflation. This combination of high inflation and high unemployment contradicted the major tenet of Keynesian economic doctrine – the supposed trade-off between inflation and unemployment. In the past, when unemployment levels were unacceptably high, governments would cut taxes and increase public spending to stimulate the economy and increase the number of jobs. Conversely, when the economy was overstimulated and dangerous levels of inflation occurred, the government would raise taxes and reduce public spending, thereby reducing inflation but also reducing employment. Since the mid-seventies, however, recession and soaring inflation have on several occasions tended to coexist and do not seem to be amenable to Keynesian intervention.

Keynesianism has been attacked on another front as well. Partly because of economic decline, governments now take in less revenue from taxes than they did in the past. At the same time, there is more need for government programs to help increased numbers of people hurt by inflation and unemployment. Part of the economic crisis is that expenses have exceeded revenues, thus creating more debt for many governments. Critics of Keynesianism contend that governments that continue to provide services at a cost higher than a country's economic growth invite a serious fiscal crisis of overload. Faced with mounting deficits governments could either raise taxes or reduce expenditures. Right-wing governments were elected in 1979 in Britain, in 1980 in the United States, and in 1984 in Canada. All three governments voiced similar priorities to deal with the economic crisis. Margaret Thatcher's

Conservatives in the U.K. stressed the values of "self-reliance"; Ronald Reagan's Republicans in the U.S. aimed "to get big government off the backs of people"; and Brian Mulroney's Progressive Conservatives declared that Canada was "open for business." All three governments chose to reduce expenditures rather than raise taxes, and all three targeted the welfare state as a major area of cost containment and/or cost reduction. As a result of these retrenchment policies the welfare state has been undergoing a "crisis of legitimation"[4] for the past decade.

The crisis of the welfare state can only be understood by seeing it within the context of the larger international economic crisis. Gough notes that from the end of 1973 until 1975 the world capitalist economy experienced a slump greater than any since the Great Depression:

> The combined GNP of the OECD countries fell by 5 per cent, industrial output plummeted, and world trade declined by 14 per cent. Unemployment climbed to a staggering 15 million in all OECD countries combined. At the same time inflation accelerated and the advanced capitalist world experienced a growing collective trade deficit.[5]

As Gough and other writers point out, the action of most (but not all) advanced capitalist governments has been to retreat from their post-war policies of state intervention and to return to the pre-war free-market philosophy. Keynesianism is being replaced by policies of monetarism, supply-side trickle-down economics, and fiscal and regulatory retreat. Riches writes:

> In response to this [international economic] crisis . . . rugged individualism, in the guise of neo-conservatism, fanned into life by Thatcher, in the United Kingdom, Reagan in the United States and the Fraser Institute and Premier Bennett in British Columbia, came to dominate economic and social policy thinking in Canada. . . . Neo-conservatism has been largely responsible for the collapse of the public safety net in Canada by rejecting Keynesianism and calling into question the legitimacy of the welfare state.[6]

In 1992 a special issue of the *Journal of Sociology and Social Welfare* devoted to an examination of the effects of Ronald Reagan's policies and programs on the American welfare state, Midgely outlines some of the efforts made by the Reagan administration to disengage the state from welfare.[7] In its first two years the Reagan administration imposed substantial budgetary cuts on social expenditures. By 1984 unemployment insurance had been reduced by 17.4 per cent, child nutrition programs by 28 per cent, food stamp expenditures by 13.8 per cent, and Aid to Families with Dependent Children (AFDC) by 14.3 per cent. In addition to these cuts, benefit levels were reduced and stringent eligibility requirements, which were put in place, prevented many needy people from receiving any form of aid. For example, nearly half a million families were eliminated from AFDC rolls and more than a quarter of a million had their benefits reduced,[8] and more than one million people lost their eligibility for food stamps.[9] Homelessness, the incidence of infant mortality, and hunger increased under Reagan as well. One of the conclusions presented in this special issue of the *Journal of Sociology and Social Welfare* is that although the American welfare state remains intact it is more fragmented, its effectiveness has been impeded, and a reinforced popular antipathy to new revenues for human services was cultivated by the Reagan administration.

The Thatcher government came to power in Britain in 1979, a year and a half before Reagan assumed the U.S. presidency. It was one of the earliest critics of the Keynesian-Beveridge welfare state and sought to retrench big government by reversing the advance of the welfare state and by giving market forces freer play in the allocation of resources and rewards. Like Reagan, Thatcher's anti-welfare rhetoric was greater than the actual welfare retrenchment effected by her government. However, as with Reagan also, the negative impact on the welfare state was considerable. Public housing in Britain received the most retrenchment, with completions falling to their lowest level in fifty years, rents more than doubling as subsidies were drastically cut, and over one million council houses (15 per cent of existing stock) being sold at an average discount of 44 per cent of their market value.[10] Minimum wages were deregulated and unemployment, caused by a recession along with the abandonment by Thatcher of a policy of full employment, rose from 4.5 per cent in 1979 to an estimated 13 per cent in 1985.[11] In the health field Thatcher increased user charges substantially, promoted privatization, and held down expenditures on services as a means of stimulating the growth of private medicine.[12] Commenting on the crisis of the welfare state in Great Britain, Gough states:

> Certainly the signs of crisis are everywhere to be seen . . . in the welfare field, social expenditure is being cut back whilst here and abroad a rising tide of criticism engulfs the major institutions of the welfare state. The goals of liberal education are questioned, social workers are vilified in the right-wing press, and a welfare backlash develops . . . .[13]

Although Riches has presented an impressive amount of evidence that led him to conclude that Canada's safety net (though never fully developed) had collapsed,[14] several Canadian writers have suggested that so far Canada has not followed the footsteps of Britain and the United States in attempting to dismantle the Canadian welfare state.[15]

However, this suggestion loses all validity when one examines those aspects of the 1990 budget that dealt with the Canadian welfare system. In 1990 alone the federal government ended its contribution to the unemployment insurance fund, increased the waiting period for unemployment benefits, and decreased the duration of benefits for many areas of the country; it reduced contributions to voluntary women's and Native groups; it cut back funds for social housing by 15 per cent; it froze transfer payments to the provinces for health and education; it capped funding for social services for three provinces; it froze legal-aid funds for two years at 1989 rates; and it "clawed back" family allowance and old age security payments from persons with annual incomes of more than $50,000.[16]

George and Wilding sum up the response of right-wing governments to the world capitalist economic slump:

> . . . social services are currently under attack by right-wing governments in a number of advanced industrial countries. The immediate and most obvious reason for the attack is that the collapse of economic growth means that increased public expenditure can only be financed through increases in taxation. Such increases are seen as economically and politically unacceptable . . . cutting back on social service expenditure seems to offer the best hope of curing the economy and avoiding political bankruptcy.[17]

The effects of governments cutting back social expenditures are obvious to all who either depend on or who work within social services. The very nature of the welfare state itself has changed. Government has relinquished its responsibility for assuring that many people's social rights are protected by reducing its involvement and by transferring much of its responsibility to the private sector. Voluntarism, privatization, and self-help are replacing many statutory programs, including the provision of basic, life-sustaining benefits and services. In other words, the welfare state is being transformed into a charity model such as existed in many countries before the Second World War.

In Canada, unemployment insurance and social assistance caseloads have increased while freezes on public-sector hirings have exacerbated the situation. The federal government has turned a blind eye to the evidence that the provinces are not living up to the terms, conditions, and spirit of the cost-sharing Canada Assistance Plan. Government retrenchment has led to the formation of depression-type soup kitchens, food banks, and clothing depots, while the number of homeless people continues to increase. Churches and voluntary organizations have had to pick up the slack. This is the current situation facing those of us who thought that the "fight for our daily bread" was over when the welfare state was put in place. The absurdity of soup kitchens and food banks should make us question an economic and political system that takes an enormous endowment of natural resources and immense human potential and converts them not into happiness, security, and abundance but into misery, want, and scarcity. The great irony of the welfare state crisis is that we seem to be returning to the very conditions that gave rise to the welfare state in the first place.

A major theme of this book is that the welfare state is a social construction based on subjective and ideological grounds, not on objective and scientific grounds. Evidence of this theme is that not all countries affected by the international economic crisis have responded in the same way. Mishra notes that although economic decline, stagflation, and rising budget deficits may constitute "objective" phenomena, the analyses, explanations, and interpretations of the phenomena are "subjective."[18] In other words, a crisis may constitute a set of objective circumstances but it includes a subjective interpretation. Such interpretations are defined in terms of ideology and group interests. The international economic crisis is an example as there were two different ideological responses to it – one from the right and one from the left. Right-wing governments have called for a return to a pure form of capitalism, including a lean if not mean social welfare system. The left has responded by maintaining or consolidating the welfare component of welfare capitalism. Each response "represents a different cluster of values and a different pattern of the distribution of power and privilege in society."[19] Britain, the United States, and to a lesser extent Canada fall within the first response. Sweden, Norway, and Austria are examples of countries that chose the second response.

The notion that interpretations of crises and problems are subjective phenomena defined in terms of ideology and group interests is crucial for students of social welfare and social work. Every Western industrial country has a social welfare state, but no two countries have identical welfare systems. There is tremendous variation in levels of expenditures, in goals, and in the form and administration of the welfare state of various countries. The welfare states of all countries exist to deal with social and economic problems. However, although the problems may constitute objective criteria, the interpretations and solutions of these problems are defined in ideological and subjective terms. In other words, welfare states represent socially constructed responses to social and economic problems.

Social Work in Crisis

The responses by right-wing governments to the economic crisis have also created a crisis in social work. The current restructuring of the welfare state means that the context for social work practice is changing. Commenting on the ideological and fiscal change occurring within the Canadian welfare state, Bracken and Walmsley claim that "A reduction in resources available for social work services places demands on social workers to provide 'more with less'."[20] In a 1983 special issue of the *Journal of Sociology and Social Welfare* devoted to Ronald Reagan's social policies during his first presidential term, Reisch and Wenocur comment:

> The events of the last three years have shaken many social workers from the reverie of technique and forced them to face the harsh dawn of government cutbacks in programs for human welfare, accompanied by increasingly sharp attacks on the premises and goals of the unfinished United States welfare state.[21]

This crisis in social work is manifest at all levels and in all areas of social work activity.

At the delivery level there have been cuts in social expenditure, increased categorization and targeting of programs, privatization of many public services, special investigations of welfare recipients,[22] imposition of user fees, and cutbacks in public-sector social work employment. Along with these changes social needs have increased because of demographic changes, changing social roles, and increased unemployment and underemployment.[23] The net effect is that it is now impossible to address the economic and social needs of increasing numbers of people in a meaningful way – particularly the poor, the deprived, and the most exploited, which include women and the unemployed. Not only does this situation make it more difficult for people in need, but it has made the job of social workers more frustrating as more time is spent on refusing clients' requests, absurd systems of priorities are worked out, better co-ordination is emphasized, and new anomalies are encountered "as small and isolated cuts begin to grow into a virus-like attack."[24]

On an employee level social workers are being affected by the society's priorities, which lie in industrial enrichment and public order rather than in the well-being of the general population.[25] To meet these priorities social workers are asked not only to sacrifice their own living standards through wage control but to police the casualties of unemployment, inflation, economic neglect, and policies that place private profit above human need. Higher caseloads, declassification of professional social work jobs, increased use of volunteers, and the use of consumers as providers of service all suggest a deprofessionalization of social work in that many traditional social work tasks and functions are now being carried out by professionally untrained persons.

On a professional level social workers have experienced an increasing loss of autonomy in the workplace. Although never totally autonomous, social work has experienced a tendency toward increased bureaucracy in recent years as neo-conservative policies made at the political level are passed down to social workers to implement. Often these policies violate our deeper impulses as human beings and contradict our professional beliefs and values. Galper has provided a clear analysis of how agency expectations often reflect the prevailing ideology of the larger society and, in addition to controlling client behaviour, control social workers' behaviour as well.[26] The use (misuse) of computers is an example of a recent management control method that reduces social workers' autonomy by monitoring their work to ensure that it is being carried out along certain prescribed and correct (as determined by the organization) lines. Often these prescribed activities are based on conservative notions of individual pathology or blaming- the-victim assumptions. This loss of autonomy has been labelled by one group of writers as the "deskilling and proletarianization" of social workers.[27]

Although the precise nature of the crisis of the welfare state and its attendant crisis in social work are recognized by many social workers, what is less obvious is any theory or strategy to deal with these crises. This has prompted the president of the International Federation of Social Workers to ask, "Faced with this state of affairs and these key issues – economic retrogression, governmental debilitation, and the economic/social development conflict – what is the role of the social work profession and what should be its strategies for dealing with the issues?"[28]

Even though the neo-conservative ideology of welfare (or diswelfare) offends the traditional social work commitment to compassion, to social justice, and to preserving the dignity and autonomy of individuals,[29] social work to date has been ineffective in challenging the crisis confronting it. Burghardt identified three of the most prevalent role responses of social workers to the present crisis: (1) the "neutral empiricist" who accepts the problems associated with the crisis as a given and only reacts when stringent cuts are made to popular but questionable programs dealing with the symptoms of cost containment – personal stress, family disorganization, and community breakdown – but that ignore the structural causes of these problems; (2) the "politically disengaged clinician" who cashes in on the crisis by opening a lucrative practice serving a largely white, middle-class population; and (3) the "impersonal dogmatist" who uses rhetoric and grandiose posturing as a substitute for understanding and demands mass action, which is meaningless because it is incongruent with social work's low level of existing mobilization.[30] In the absence of theory, strategy, or critical analysis, the social work profession has tended to adjust to the retrenchment of the welfare state rather than look for (and fight for) alternative measures. Haynes and Mickelson present some examples of this adjustment in the United States,[31] which are just as applicable in Canada. With the re-emergence of hunger and homelessness as issues, social workers have participated in establishing food banks, soup kitchens, and temporary emergency shelters rather than mounting large-scale campaigns to expand social assistance benefits and public housing. The effect of this action has been to institutionalize hunger, begging, and homelessness.

Several writers have presented reasons why social work has been unable to deal adequately with the present crises. Karger believes that the profession, before the crisis, thought that capitalism could be reformed and, therefore, was left unprepared to present any progressive alternatives to welfare capitalism.[32] Similarly, several other writers have cited its relationship to the dominant ideology as the reason for social work's state of inertia in trying out new perspectives and roles. This ideology-social work nexus was well articulated in the 1970s.[33] Burghardt thinks that part of the problem is found within the methodologies and practice frameworks taught to social workers. Too many of them contain abstract propositions for action such as "link the social with the personal" or "see the individual in his or her environment," yet they do not go beyond these declarations themselves.[34] Jones contends that the present crises are forcing social work to question some of its comfortable assumptions about the relationship between the individual and the state and the role of the state in securing the welfare of the individual, and that "a process of soul- searching has begun in social work."[35] Other writers are more specific about the content of this "soul-searching" and claim, as Corrigan and Leonard do, that "The inability of many social workers to act effectively derives in part from the fact that their analysis of the state and its welfare functions remains at a relatively undeveloped level."[36] Findlay reinforces this claim: "Unless social welfare workers comprehend the nature and role of the state . . . they cannot hope to be effective in the work of achieving a more humane society."[37] And Simpkin, writing on the deleterious effects of the welfare crisis on users and on social workers, concludes that "In order to understand how this [crisis] comes about and what we can do to resist it, we must examine social work in relation to the state."[38]

Some writers contend that social workers must not only learn about the nature and role of the state and social work's relation to it, but there must also be a reformulation of social work theory.[39] According to these writers this reformulation must include: (1) an explication of social work's ideology as a necessary step in knowledge building; (2) knowledge about the nature and role of the state and social work's relation to the state; and (3) transformational knowledge of how social work practice can contribute to changing society from one that creates and perpetuates poverty, inequality, and humiliation to one more consistent with social work's fundamental values of humanism and egalitarianism. This book represents one person's efforts in developing such theory.

The Concept of Paradigm

In recent years a growing number of writers have focused on ideology as their point of departure when discussing the state, social welfare, and social work. Djao, Drover and Woodsworth, George and Wilding, and Mishra have presented comparative analyses of ideological perspectives on the welfare state.[40] Pritchard and Taylor, Galper, DeMaria, Carniol, and Kerans have presented comparative analyses of ideological perspectives in social work.[41] Lowenberg and Carniol point out that, to date, social work has not been successful in reducing the social problems with which it deals.[42] Part of the reason, according to Lowenberg, is the eclectic theory base of social work; Carniol cites the "jumble of confusion" taught to social work students when it comes to ideological analysis.

The task of reformulating social work theory, then, is to bring some sense of order to the field of social work knowledge – to develop what DeMaria terms "meaningful patterns" from the present non- unified theory base.[43] A number of theories and ideologies focus on the state. There are several models of social welfare and various explanations of social problems. A plethora of mid-range theories of social work intervention may be applied differently according to whether one subscribes (advertently or inadvertently) to a consensus or conflict view of society. How is the social worker to make sense out of this jungle of ideas, theories, perspectives, practices, and ideologies, especially when schools of social work reinforce this jumbled confusion by not providing students with any unifying frameworks?

In an attempt to bring some sense of order and to establish meaningful patterns from the present morass of social work knowledge, the point of departure for this book lies in the concept of "paradigm." Thomas Kuhn's *The Structure of Scientific Revolutions* (1962) attacked the idea that scientific knowledge develops in a linear accumulation of facts and insights about natural phenomena. Struck by the amount of disagreement among scientists over the nature of their work and methods, Kuhn wrote:

> Attempting to discover the source of that difference led me to recognize the role in scientific research of what I call" paradigms". These I take to be universally recognized scientific achievements that for a time provide model problems and solutions to a community of practitioners.[44]

Kuhn, on his own admission, provided only a loose definition of paradigm. One writer found twenty-one different usages of the term in Kuhn's book.[45] Consequently, the use of the term "paradigm" has become almost faddish.[46] We speak of research paradigms, educational paradigms, paradigms of social welfare, sociological paradigms, and so on. In spite of the semantic conflict over the ambiguity of the term, the meaning ascribed to it by some writers would appear fruitful for the development of social work knowledge. A common meaning that appears useful for social work is that a paradigm represents a "taken-for-granted reality"[47] or world view that consists of "the entire constellation of beliefs, values and techniques shared by a scientific community."[48] This does not refer to the beliefs of an entire discipline, as Kuhn points out, but to those dominant within the discipline (or profession). In other words, a paradigm represents a specific type of cognitive framework from which a discipline or profession views the world and its place in it. This framework allows for an analysis of the relationship between the scientific thought of a discipline and the social context in which it arises. Paradigms are the "taken-for- granted contexts, within which one locates facts and methods and ascribes meanings to them."[49]

Each paradigm presented in this book is subdivided into four interrelated parts: an identifiable ideology; an analysis and explanation of social problems emanating from the paradigm's ideology; an ideal type of welfare state consistent with the paradigm's ideology and its interpretation of social problems; and the nature and form of social work practice consistent with the other three elements of the paradigm. Within each paradigm these constituent elements are, by definition of a paradigm, internally consistent and mutually reinforcing. An ideology serves as the foundation of any particular paradigm and determines the nature, shape, and direction of the other parts. The ideological values, beliefs, and goals of a particular paradigm determine the interpretation and causal explanations given to social problems, which in turn determine: (1) the nature and form of the welfare state established to deal with these problems; and (2) the nature and type of social work activities that occur within the welfare state.

Although more than one paradigm can exist at the same time within a discipline, one "dominant paradigm" always provides the discipline with a framework for viewing the world. This dominant paradigm also provides the criteria for selecting and defining problems for inquiry, guides scientific practice by providing models of laws and theories and their application, and is transmitted throughout the discipline by practitioners and in the textbooks used for schooling new members of the discipline. As mentioned above, members of a discipline often are not aware of the dominant paradigm as it tends to be the taken-for- granted reality. Because it is viewed as the only reality, phenomena that do not fit into the paradigm are often not perceived or are rejected as being metaphysical, as lying outside the boundaries of one's discipline, or as being too problematic to be worth the effort of considering.[50] In this way a paradigm can "insulate the community [discipline] from those socially important problems that are not reducible to puzzle form [of the paradigm], because they cannot be stated in terms of the conceptual and instrumental tools the paradigm supplies."[51] Thus the person who brings any anomaly to the attention of the discipline is to blame and not the reality (i.e., not the dominant paradigm).

How, then, do dominant paradigms change or become discarded? Kuhn contends that only when anomalies can no longer be explained away or when they become so numerically overwhelming does the discipline begin to explore the area of anomaly that has violated its "paradigm-induced expectations" governing normal practice.[52] This exploration ends when the paradigm has been adjusted to accommodate the anomaly or when the dominant paradigm has been discarded in favour of another. And, Kuhn asserts, this adjustment or exchange of paradigms is generally preceded and followed by periods of resistance.

According to Kuhn, development of a discipline occurs "when the profession can no longer evade anomalies that subvert the existing tradition of scientific practice. Then begin the extraordinary investigations that lead the profession at least to a new set of commitments, a new basis for practice."[53] Alternative interpretations are posed, which leads to a competition between the present dominant paradigm and the new revolutionary paradigm. "Each revolution necessitates the rejection (not without resistance) of prior frameworks and rules in favour of new ones. The new paradigm is not simply grafted on to the old one: acceptance requires rejection of the old. When the transition is complete the profession will have changed its view of the field, its methods and its goals."[54] Shifts of paradigms bring members of a discipline to see the world around them in a new light. To present an alternative paradigm is the ultimate revolutionary act.

Utility of the Paradigm Concept for Social Work

In view of the international economic crisis and the ensuing crises of the welfare state and social work, how does the concept of paradigm help social work deal with the crises it faces, including its own tangled web of ideological, political, and theoretical confusion? The thesis of this book is that the application of the paradigm concept can perform three major functions for social work in helping it to confront, understand, and deal with these crises.

First, as noted by Carniol, ideological critiques and analyses at the level of social work methods abound in the literature.[55] These critiques and analyses might be better appreciated, however, if they were presented within a comparative framework that not only compares ideologies but also allows the student to compare and contrast the different views of the nature of social problems, of social welfare approaches, and of social work practices emanating from different ideologies. The concept of paradigm should help the student make the connection between ideology and social work practice, that is, how an ideology largely determines the nature and form of social work practice.

Second, one of the purposes of the above-mentioned comparison is to become aware of alternative ways of integrating economic and human welfare than that which is presently being offered by neo- conservatives.[56] A major theme of this book is that our present social order is not the natural and inevitable product of some evolutionary process; rather, there are alternatives to what we presently have. Sweden, for example, is representative of a different paradigm than that which exists in North America, and it has demonstrated that an efficient market economy does not have to be constructed at the expense of social welfare. Hopefully, an awareness of alternative world views – paradigms – will open *everything* to challenge and change, including our present social order, our present structure of social services, and the nature of our present social work practice.[57] These things should not be predetermined by either present statistics or current power relationships. "The shape of events is determined by people, all of us, and by our willingness to understand and seek to change the world for the better."[58] Indeed, several writers have argued that an alternative vision is a prerequisite for meaningful social change.[59] Such a vision, if consistent with social work ideals, values, and beliefs, could provide a goal and a direction for social work. An articulation of such a vision is presented in the next chapter.

The third function that the concept of paradigm may carry out for social work is to enhance our understanding of the dynamics of change, especially fundamental change. DeMaria informs us that "The concept of paradigm, particularly the causal link between social context and knowledge, has a history in philosophy, sociology and political science. . . ."[60] For example, DeMaria attempts to show how Kuhn's view of scientific development is similar to the Marxist view of social change. He states, "Whether it be a social revolution in the Marxian sense or a scientific revolution in the Kuhnian sense, the dynamics appear to be the same, with the existing paradigm or the Marxist notion of epoch carrying within itself the potentiality for a new order."[61] Three examples of characteristics of paradigms that have implications for understanding the dynamics of social change follow. First, the fact that usually one paradigm (e.g., liberalism) is dominant over others means that it is the taken-for-granted reality of most people in society – including social workers. Second, only when the dominant paradigm can no longer explain away certain anomalies (such as stagflation) can a shift of paradigms begin to occur. And third, an acceptance of a new paradigm does not occur without resistance. Understanding these dynamics of change should help social work make a transition in its view of society, in its theory, and in its practice. These are a few of the tasks taken up in this book.

2

The Social Work Vision: A Progressive View

The purpose of this chapter is twofold: (1) to present an argument that social work needs an alternative vision of society that is more in accordance than our present society with the social, emotional, physical, and spiritual well-being of all people; and (2) to outline such a vision based on the espoused values of the social work profession. By itself, this twofold purpose is impossible to carry out because social work is not a unitary profession. There is no consensus within social work with respect to the ideal nature of society, or to the nature and functions of the welfare state, or to the nature and political consequences of social work practice. As the title of this chapter suggests, the analysis and discourse presented here are derived from the progressive wing of the social work profession as opposed to the conventional wing.

Conventional and Progressive Perspectives within Social Work

Social work has always had two major competing views of society, social welfare, and social work practice:[1] the conventional view and the progressive or critical view. The conventional view, which has always been held by the majority, is influenced by and reflective of popular beliefs and attitudes about the nature of the individual, of society, and of the relationship between the two. According to this perspective our present social order, although not perfect, is the best there is and it ought to be preserved. Society is viewed as comprising social institutions that serve the individual as long as she or he makes full use of available opportunities for personal success. This view acknowledges that social problems do exist, but it defines them in terms of personal difficulties that require social work intervention either to help people cope with or adjust to existing institutions or to modify existing policies in a limited fashion. Carniol, a progressive Canadian social work scholar, points out that the conventional approach is adopted by those who believe that our social institutions are responsive to and capable of meeting people's needs.[2] Obviously, the political function of conventional social work practice is such that by conforming to established institutions, it reinforces, supports, and defends the status quo. This is not to say that there is no disagreement within the conventional view. Most of the political debate about social welfare has been conducted within a liberal-conservative framework, with the former seeing more services as a good thing and the latter seeing fewer services as a good thing.[3] Neither liberalism nor conservatism questions the legitimacy of the present capitalist social order, however.

In contrast to the conventional view, the progressive or critical view does not believe that our present social institutions are capable of adequately meeting human need. Social workers with this view are quick to point out that in spite of a social welfare state and social work interventions that have existed for most of this century, social problems are not decreasing but on the contrary appear to be worsening. Twenty years ago there were no soup kitchens or food banks in Canada or emergency shelters to feed or house other than derelict populations. Today these residual means of meeting basic needs have become institutionalized. Progressive social workers will also point to the growing gap between rich and poor, to the worsening plight of traditionally disadvantaged groups, and to the social control functions of welfare programs and social work practice as proof that the present set of social arrangements does not work for large numbers of people. Although there has always been a progressive or radical contingent within social work it has been a minority voice. However, in recent years and in the face of the fiscal crisis of the state, its numbers have been growing, as have their challenges to the conventional view.[4]

Carniol has termed the present situation of a society with increasing inequalities, of a welfare state that has failed to bring about a just society, and of the alienation of social workers from their work "the social work crisis" and calls for a social transformation.[5] This is the ultimate goal of progressive/critical social work, and the pursuit of this goal is a major theme of this book. This is not to say that there are no disagreements within the progressive camp. For example, although the elimination of oppression and inequality may be a universal goal, feminists, Marxists, social democrats, visible minorities, and so on have often disagreed on the fundamental source of oppression and on the strategies to overcome oppression and inequality.

Need for a Progressive Social Work Vision

We have witnessed in the past decade an increasing body of social science writings criticizing our present social order because of its failure to provide satisfying levels of living for large numbers of citizens. These criticisms are important for social work because they identify and illuminate the sources and reasons for many of our social problems and show us what it is we are struggling against. However, although critical analysis may show us what we are fighting *against,* by itself it does not show us what we are fighting *for.* As Galper states, "We need more."[6] We need a picture or a vision of alternative social arrangements that we can work toward. We need a goal – a conceptualization of "a society in which every person is afforded maximum opportunity to enrich his or her spiritual, psychological, physical, and intellectual well-being."[7] As Nevitte and Gibbins note in their discussion of social change, "A preference for social change in the abstract is meaningless."[8]

We have just passed through a period of history where societal visions or utopian models of society were not widely discussed. With the post-war welfare state in place and financed by an ever-growing economy, many believed that society by a process of evolution had reached its pinnacle.[9] However, the fiscal crisis of the state and the legitimation question of the welfare state have cast shadows of doubt on this notion. Presently, many of our comfortable and cherished assumptions about the nature of our society and its ability to genuinely respond to human needs are called into question. We seem now to need visions of alternative societies. "Given the dire [social] condition of the planet, it is . . . urgent that we formulate alternatives which are at once radical, comprehensive, and practical."[10] Without such alternatives or visions there is a danger that we will become victims of distorted notions of justice, well-being, and solidarity, thus denying many people their rightful place in society.

Because social work often deals with the casualties and victims of society, it, too, must become involved in questioning our present social arrangement. Given social work's belief in the inherent dignity and worth of the person, it must ask itself what type of society best promotes this ideal. Given social work's belief that people have a right to develop fully and freely their inherent human potential and to live productive and satisfying lives free from domination and exploitation by others, it must ask itself what type of social arrangements best accommodates these values. In other words, what type of society best promotes the values, ideals, principles, and beliefs espoused by the social work profession? What is the vision that social work should pursue?

Unfortunately, it would be impossible to reach consensus on such a vision of society. A major obstacle to developing and articulating a universally accepted social work vision is the existence of the two incompatible views of current society, social welfare, and social work. Not even a common value base or a professional code of ethics is enough to unify the profession with respect to the co-existing conventional and progressive views. The Canadian Association of Social Workers' (CASW) Code of Ethics (1983), as noted by Woodsworth, consists of "competing, even conflicting philosophies,"[11] and has been described by Lundy and Gauthier as "an amalgam of competing ideologies that are at times contradictory and even antagonistic to one another."[12] The contradictory nature of the welfare state (i.e., its social care and social control functions) is expressed within the Code of Ethics in that ideas of conservatism, liberalism, and collectivism are all represented.

If social work's espoused values were to be used to formulate a social work vision, the nature and form of that vision would differ depending on whether a conventional or progressive view was used. As indicated previously, the viewpoint taken here is progressive. The following discussion of social work values embodies that part of the social work duality that challenges rather than supports the status quo.

The Fundamental Values of Social Work

Values consist of beliefs, preferences, or assumptions about what is good or desirable for people. They are not assertions or descriptions of the way the world *is*, but rather how the world *ought to be.* Values do not stand alone but exist in systems of thought and are organized in such a way that they have a relative importance to other values. Fundamental or primary values represent ideals or goals that a profession attempts to achieve, that is, the end product. Secondary or instrumental values specify the means to achieve these goals or desired ends.

Because "[t]he profession of social work is founded on humanitarian and egalitarian ideals,"[13] these must form the cornerstone of social work's ideal society. Fundamental values cannot be compromised by such notions as economic individualism and/or competitive capitalism. If we do not have a society based on humanitarian principles then we have a society based, in whole or in part, on principles of inhumanity. If we do not have a society based on egalitarianism then we have a society based, in whole or in part, on principles of inequality. If we have a society based, in whole or in part, on principles of inhumanity and inequality then our secondary or instrumental values of social work – acceptance, self-determination, and respect[14] – are meaningless since there must be consistency between our primary values and our secondary values. Otherwise, how could a profession be true to itself if it is based on contradictory and inconsistent values?

Humanism

"Humanitarianism" tends to be used interchangeably in the social work literature with the term "humanism." While some writers contend that there are differences between the two terms,[15] others contend that the popular use of the term "humanitarianism" means the practice of the doctrine of humanism.[16] The latter usage will be adopted here, and henceforth the term "humanism" will be used since most of the reference material for this chapter employs this term.

A definition supplied by the *Dictionary of Philosophy* describes humanism as "a system of views based on the respect for the dignity and rights of man [*sic*], his value as a personality, concern for his welfare, his all-round development, and the creation of favourable conditions for social life."[17] This view recognizes that the individual should be the focus of all societal decisions. A society based on humanism would not only recognize the universal nature of human need but would actively seek to provide to everyone conditions conducive to physical survival, mental health, self-respect, dignity, love, a sense of identity, the opportunity to use one's intellect, and happiness.[18] Such a commitment must be based on social equality, co-operation, and collective orientation,[19] and consideration of all economic decisions ought to be based on their implications for human welfare.[20]

One writer has articulated his view of a society based on humanism as one in which: (1) each individual is seen as a person with inherent dignity and worth and not as an object with utility; (2) relationships among human beings are non-exploitative, co-operative, and egalitarian; (3) resources created by human beings through their labour are distributed so as to provide each person with the goods and services to meet his or her needs without denying others theirs; and (4) each individual has equal opportunities to develop his or her fullest human potential.[21] There is consensus in the social welfare and social work literatures that our present North American society does not contain these characteristics.[22]

Because some writers on the subject of the philosophy of social work have suggested that the values of social work are firmly rooted in humanism, we should be aware of the limitations of humanism. A common criticism of humanism is that it is ahistorical and does not consider the social context of people's lives – that is, it overlooks the implications of inequalities.[23] Certainly notions of "acceptance" in social work have been influenced by humanism in that social work practice often excluded concern for the material hardships of service users.[24] Psychoanalytic, client-centred, and family therapies focused on introspection, self-realization, and interpersonal dynamics rather than on the social context of people. An example of overlooking the material impoverishment and the social context of people is the fact that poverty was rediscovered in the 1960s by people other than social workers.[25]

Egalitarianism

Although there is more than one meaning ascribed to the term "egalitarianism,"[26] the one that forms part of a progressive social work ideology is that of "social equality." David Gil has written eloquently and extensively on the notion of social equality from a social work perspective. He argues that if we wish to establish a society based on social equality we need to explicate the meaning of this overused, yet elusive, concept. The central premise of social equality is that every person is of equal intrinsic worth and should, therefore, be entitled to equal civil, political, social, and economic rights, responsibilities, and treatment.[27]

Implicit is the belief "that every individual should have the right and the resources to develop freely and fully, to actualize his (or her) inherent human potential, and to lead as fulfilling a life free of domination, control and exploitation by others . . . ."[28] Social equality is a correlate of humanism, as the dignity of the person cannot be achieved if some people have control over others, have preferred access to life chances, or have more power concerning public affairs: "Genuine democracy, liberty and individuality for all are simply not feasible without social equality . . . ."[29] A society based on social inequality is based on the value premise that people differ in intrinsic worth and therefore are entitled to different rights and to as much power, control, and material goods as they can gain in competition with others. Humanistic ideals cannot be reached in such a society.

Social equality does not mean monotonous uniformity; rather, it aims at the realization of individual differences in innate potentialities, not at the division of available resources into identical parts for every member of society. The key element in arriving at a humanistic and egalitarian society is the development of a true collectivist spirit. This means taking seriously the fact that people form a social entity called a society when they live together. This does not mean uniform blandness or submission to the group, but it recognizes that decisions made in those areas affecting the whole must be subjected to collective thought and to collective action in the light of collective needs and resources.[30] Collectivism implies participatory decision-making, not hierarchical decisions made at the top and passed down. People should have a say in the decisions that affect any area of their lives – social, economic, political, the distribution of society's resources, and so on. This type of decision-making cannot occur in a society based on social inequality.

In sum, humanism (humanitarianism) and social equality must form the twin pillars of an ideal social work society. These fundamental values, not inequality, rugged individualism, and cut-throat competition, support the dignity and intrinsic worth of people. To realize these fundamental values society must be arranged according to the principles of collectivism, participatory decision-making, and co-operation and not according to the practices of exploitation, distribution of resources according to economic profit rather than social need, and hierarchical, elitist decision-making. A social work vision of society is based on the premise that the present set of social arrangements is not a natural phenomenon but is, instead, the result of person-made decisions. "People can be self-determining about social forms and can shape and reshape them to meet their current needs."[31] In other words, given the political will, a society can develop a social order that promotes human welfare. In addition to meeting people's individual needs, it is part of the progressive social work mission to promote this political will. Gil reminds us that social work practice cannot be politically neutral, "it either confronts and challenges established societal institutions or it conforms to them openly or tacitly. [Social work] practitioners should avoid the illusion of neutrality and should consciously choose and acknowledge their political philosophy."[32]

The Secondary (Instrumental) Values of Social Work

Social work's secondary or instrumental values stem from its fundamental values and contribute to the goals of humanitarianism and egalitarianism. "They dictate the ways the [social] worker should interact with others in carrying out professional activities so as to actualize the primary values, that is to achieve the desired ends or goals."[33]

Three secondary values highlighted in the preamble of the Canadian Association of Social Workers' Code of Ethics are respect, self-determination, and acceptance. The operationalization of these three values is assumed to contribute to the situation where the worth and dignity of people are realized. We affirm people's worth and dignity by showing respect for them, by allowing them maximum feasible self-determination, and by accepting their individualities.

Statham argues that these instrumental values are meaningless in societies based on economic individualism rather than on social equality:

> Social workers affirm their belief in the worth of each person by virtue of their humanity and see them as having needs in common, but the society in which they operate distributes rewards unequally, not because of faulty mechanisms which can be remedied by social work or reform, but because the allocation of rewards is intended to operate in this way.[34]

Do we not negate the respect we extend to clients in our interpersonal relationships with them if we accept a social order based on economic individualism with its inevitable consequences of poverty, homelessness, deprivation, and unemployment? By accepting a person's individuality are we also accepting her or his social and economic conditions? And how can we practise self-determination with people who do not possess the economic and social resources necessary for choices to be realized? Self-determination often has meaning only for those possessing the economic resources and social status necessary to implement choice. In a society based on inequality, self-determination is not possible for persons who are powerless "to resolve, by their individual efforts, the problems created, for instance, by inadequate income, housing, or by unemployment."[35]

It would seem then that social work's instrumental values are illusory if, as Biehal and Sainsbury suggest, "They are not seen in the context of people's lives – notably the context of differences in power."[36] It is not enough to show respect and acceptance for people and offer them choices restricted by their social position in society. Cries for acceptance of rights for people are empty slogans if the reality of power (to exercise rights) is ignored. Social work must also be concerned with realizing a society that promotes social work values rather than one that negates or compromises them. It would seem that only a society founded on humanitarian and egalitarian ideals could accommodate these secondary values. Surely, an imperative for social work is to work toward the establishment of a social vision based on its own value position.

A Progressive Perspective of Social Work Ideology

An ideology is a consistent set of social, economic, and political beliefs. It serves as the foundation and determines the nature and world view of particular social paradigms. Social work has historically been practised in an arena of conflicting beliefs. There has always been some degree of conflict between the social, economic, and political beliefs of the larger society and those espoused by the social work profession in general and by the progressive sector of the profession in particular. Social workers presently operate at the meeting place of the conflict between the dominant values of liberal capitalism and the dominant social work values of humanitarianism and egalitarianism.[37]

Many social workers also experience conflict within their own social, economic, and political beliefs. For example, social workers may subscribe to humanistic social beliefs about the dignity and worth of people but also subscribe to our present capitalist economic system based on competition and exploitation, without realizing the inherent conflict between their humanistic social beliefs and their capitalist economic beliefs. As well, many social workers may believe that self-determination is a laudable goal but will not question our present system of representative democracy where self-determination and meaningful participation are not options for large numbers of people.

Although social workers espouse many humanistic and egalitarian beliefs, insufficient attention has been paid to integrate these beliefs in any consistent fashion. Thus, an articulation of social work ideology must entail a delineation of specific social beliefs, economic beliefs, and political beliefs that are consistent with one another. Otherwise, the present hodge-podge of beliefs will continue to present conflict, inconsistency, and uncertainty to social workers in their everyday practice, and will do nothing in terms of informing social workers of the nature and form that society would assume if it were to be congruent with social work ideology.

Social Beliefs

David Gil has described in humanistic and egalitarian terms the nature of the ideal relationship between people and the society in which they live:

> All humans, everywhere, despite their manifest differences and their uniqueness as individuals, should be considered of equal intrinsic worth. Hence, they should be deemed entitled to equal social, economic, civil, and political rights, liberties and obligations. Societal institutions. . . should assure and facilitate the exercise of these equal rights, and the free, autonomous, and authentic development of all humans.[38]

In this view, people are considered to be social beings. John Friedmann contrasts this with economic individualism, which perceives people as independent, gratification-maximizing individuals with no social responsibility for others.[39] What distinguishes people as social beings from people as economic individualists is that the former view is based on the notion of community and the latter on the notion of the rugged individual. Whereas the economic individualist equates public well-being with the mere aggregation of individual interests, the social view of persons recognizes public well-being as a more complex construct made up of not only the aggregate of its members but the relationships among them as well.

Friedmann argues that the view of people as social beings is essentially moral whereas the view of people as economic individualists is essentially amoral.[40] As a social being a person is a thinking and feeling animal who stands in relation to others as a person. His or her recognition of the other person as one like him or herself establishes the manner in which their relationship will be fulfilled. People will treat others as they themselves would want to be treated. A society built on the image of economic individualism would be simply "a bundle of functional roles . . . superordinated, subordinated, or equal and either useful to you or not,"[41] a relationship based on a "suspicion of mutual exploitation."[42] In the economic individualist view the notion of the public well-being is arrived at by summing the individual utilities in the marketplace. The worth of a person is judged mainly by what he or she earns and/or owns. Community, which is the cornerstone of civilized life, is not possible with such an amoral foundation." Without community, there can be no justice, and without justice, life becomes brutish and destructive of both the self and others."[43]

In addition to its moral weaknesses, an economic individualist view ignores the realities of our modern industrial society.[44] For example, specialization and division of labour require people to depend on one another for provision of those goods and services they cannot provide for themselves; some contingencies, such as accident, illness, inflation, and recession, are beyond the control of the individual; and, if left on one's own, the individual tends to be overwhelmed by forces of which he or she is only dimly aware, which subjugate him or her to a role of decreasing importance and present problems with which the person has no means to cope.[45]

Economic Beliefs

In *The Politics of Social Services,* Jeffry Galper outlines a set of economic beliefs consistent with social work values.[46] He contrasts these beliefs with the present practices of our competitive and capitalist economy, which is based on the criterion of profitability. Galper contends that if we are to be successful in creating a world conducive to human well-being, then we must find a way to dominate, rather than be dominated by, economics. Neither the invisible hand of the marketplace nor the present partnership of government and big business ensures that social priorities will dominate economic decision-making.

Galper argues that in our present economic system goods are produced, decisions are made, and the number and nature of jobs available for people are determined on the basis of profitability. The consequences of this system are:

> an overabundance of goods that do not add up to a fundamental sense of well-being for most people, an absence of goods that we need but that are not profitable to produce, jobs that are destructive to people who hold them, a national psychology organized around

> competition and consumption, ecological destruction, and exploitation of large parts of the rest of the world to enable us to maintain our standards of material achievement. Human well-being is not, as it should be, the rationale for our actions.[47]

Galper contrasts our present economic system with one where all decisions of production are based on the criterion of human need. In other words, decisions about what should be produced and in what quantities, as well as when, where, and how, should be made according to their impact on our overall well-being. Galper uses two examples: (1) the decision to produce cars would not be made exclusively on the basis of their saleability but on the basis of such social criteria as the relative emphasis to be given to private versus public transportation, pollution, use of raw materials, safety, and the nature of the work experience for people; and (2) a new factory would be located not just according to the availability of raw materials, labour, and transportation, or for political gain, but according to the development needs of the various regions of the country.[48] An economic system consistent with social work ideals would assure each person full economic rights, and the distribution of wealth, goods, and resources would be much more equitable than presently exists.

In sum, to be consistent with social work ideals, the economic system must be rationalized from a social perspective. It must be viewed as the means to achieve those social goals to which social work aspires, not as an end in itself. Goods must be produced for their utility rather than their profitability, and consideration should be given to all the costs (social, economic, ecological, and so on) of production. Finally, the distribution of wealth, rather than following Social Darwinian notions, must be made according to social determinations – those factors that contribute to the well-being of all citizens, not just to those who own the means of production. These principles are, of course, contradictory to and inconsistent with the laissez-faire principles of our present liberal-capitalist economic system.

Political Beliefs

Social work subscribes to the democratic ideals of self-determination, participation, and an equal distribution of political power. In fact, much of social work practice is directed toward individuals and groups, helping them gain or regain autonomy and control over their lives. However, there are basically two methods by which democracy can be practised: representative democracy and participatory democracy.

We are all used to the representative form of government. Pateman describes and analyses this system of democracy:

> The characteristically democratic element . . . is the competition of leaders for the votes of the people at periodic, free elections. Elections are crucial to the democratic method for it is primarily through elections that the majority can exercise control over their leaders through loss of office. . . . The decisions of leaders can also be influenced by active groups bringing pressure to bear during inter-election periods. "Political equality" in the theory [of representative democracy] refers to universal suffrage and to the existence of equality of opportunity of access to channels of influence over leaders. . . . The level of participation by the majority should not rise much above the minimum level necessary to keep the democratic method working; that is, it should remain at about the level that exists in Anglo-American democracies.[49]

Although this model of democracy is relatively efficient in terms of the time it takes to make decisions, its weaknesses have been well documented in the literature.[50] (1) Political elites at times make decisions that are not responsive to the wishes of the electorate. (2) Interest pressure groups can gain some sectional advantage at the expense of more general welfare. (3) Unorganized sections of society may be ignored or exploited by powerful, organized sections. (4) The right to vote every few years is inconsistent with the notion of democracy. (5) Such a system promotes and relies on a considerable degree of passivity in the majority of people. (6) In the absence of participatory principles, those who make decisions will be those who have been most successful in getting to the top, which is an individualist and not an egalitarian practice. "Though democratic in the way it is chosen, representative government has been shown to be elitist in the way that it operates."[51]

By way of contrast, participatory democracy would produce a very different world.[52] It would "permit and encourage greater popular participation in non-governmental bodies like industry, trade unions, political parties, corporations, schools, universities and the like."[53] In addition, it would delegate a larger share of public power to local communities small enough to permit effective and meaningful general participation in decision-making:

> Participation in politics would provide individuals with opportunities to take part in making significant decisions about their everyday lives. It would build and consolidate a sense of genuine community that would serve as a solid foundation for government. The first and most important step is to recognize that personal self-development is the moral goal of democracy and that direct popular participation is the chief means of achieving it. When this is generally accepted, then society can get on with the largely technical job of thinking up new and better means for increasing popular participation.[54]

Table 2.1
Overview of Progressive Social Work Ideals and Beliefs

Social Beliefs	Humanitarianism (humanism) Community Equality
Economic Beliefs	Government intervention Social priorities dominate economic decisions Equitable distribution of society's resources
Political Beliefs	Participatory democracy (self-determination) in both governmental and non-governmental areas
View of Social Welfare	An instrument to promote equality, solidarity, and community Ideal = social welfare state or structural model
Principles of Social Work Practice (taken from the CASW Code of Ethics)	Treat people with respect Enhance dignity and integrity Facilitate self-determination and self-realization Accept differences Advocate and promote social justice

Surely, given social work's values and ideals with respect to egalitarianism, self-determination, and so on, participatory democracy rather than representative democracy is the preferred form of democracy.

Summary of Social Work Ideology

The amalgam of the above social, economic, and political beliefs comprises social work's ideology. Social beliefs are based on the person as a social being. Economic beliefs are based on the notion that human well-being is the major criterion for economic decision-making. And political beliefs are based on people having the right and the responsibility to participate in those decisions that affect their lives. Taken together, these beliefs constitute social work's ideology for progressive social workers (see Table 2.1). This ideology comprises an interdependent, consistent, and mutually reinforcing set of ideas and ideals that should underpin the type of society that best promotes social work's fundamental values of humanism and egalitarianism.

Social Work and Social Problems

All social work activity is concerned with social problems, that is, with alleviating, eliminating, or preventing social problems and the deleterious effects they have on people. However, although poverty, mental illness, and deprivation may constitute objective phenomena, the analyses, interpretations, and explanations of these phenomena are subjective. In other words, a social problem may be seen as a set of objective circumstances but it includes a subjective interpretation. Such interpretations are defined largely in terms of ideology and group interests. For example, the existence of poverty will be explained differently by a conservative than by a Marxist, the former attributing poverty to a defective individual and the latter attributing it to a defective economic arrangement (i.e., capitalism). The implication for social work is that the individual living in poverty would be treated in a punitive or remedial manner by a conservative social worker but would be treated as a victim of an oppressive social order by a Marxist social worker.

Although social work has a set of values generally considered progressive and humanistic, its definitions or explanations of social problems have not always been progressive or humanistic. Because social work has been reluctant to elevate the discussion of its values to a societal level, there has been no agreed-upon goal or product with respect to the type and form of society social work is seeking. In the absence of a publicly articulated social vision, social work falls victim to the prevailing paradigm. That is, in the absence of a vision social work has tended to accept the social order in which it finds itself as a given. This means that social work "theory and practice become accommodated only to that which is possible within existing organizational constraints."[55] With no alternative social order defined or articulated, social work becomes part of the existing social order, helping people to adjust to it or attempting to make small changes *within* the system rather than attempting to make fundamental changes *of* the system.

Social work, by being part of the present paradigm and in the absence of an alternative, tends to take on the prevailing definitions or explanations of social problems. And in the case of Canada and the United States, social problems have been defined mainly within conservative-liberal perspectives. Most indigenous social work theory-building has been in the methods or means of social work practice rather than in the goals or desired ends of social work practice. As long as social work avoids the task of articulating its desired ends or vision it will continue to treat objective social problems with the subjective prescriptions of the prevailing paradigm. To date in North America, most social work explanations of social problems and most social work interventions have been based either on "personal deficiency" (conservative ideology) or on "general systems – ecological" (liberal ideology) explanations of social problems.[56] Such approaches, of course, do not guarantee that social problems experienced by large numbers of people will be dealt with adequately or effectively. Radical explanations of social problems have not been a major part of social work theory to date because socialist/Marxist and feminist ideas and analyses have not been major parts of the prevailing paradigms in North America.

In sum, although social work espouses a set of values considered progressive, its approach to resolve social problems has not been progressive. In the absence of an articulated social vision or goal consistent with its value base, social work by default has accepted the mainstream definitions and explanations of social problems, which have come from the prevailing North American ideologies of conservatism and liberalism. The critical question arising from this situation is whether or not social work ideology (just explored in this chapter) is consistent with either conservatism or liberalism. Or is it more consistent with an ideology that does not prevail in North America? A related question is whether or not social work's progressive and humanistic ideology is consistent with or in conflict with its current theory base and practice.

The Ideal Social Welfare System – A Progressive View

Every industrial democracy in the Western world has developed a social welfare system to deal with the vagaries of the market economy. Although all states have policies of intervention, the forms of these interventions often differ, as do their purposes. Furniss and Tilton have aggregated the different forms of intervention into three models of social welfare states: the positive state, the social security state, and the social welfare state.[57] These models are described below in terms of the type of intervention employed, the groups in society benefiting from the intervention, and the vision of society that inspires each model. The first two models correspond to Wilensky and Lebeaux's typology of the residual model (the positive state) and the institutional model (the social security state).[58] The third model corresponds to Mishra's description of the structural model of welfare.[59]

The Positive State or Residual Model of Welfare

The main goal of the positive state is to protect the interests of business from the difficulties of unprotected markets and from potential redistributive demands. The policy emphasis is on government-business collaboration for economic growth. Business yields much of its market decisions to government in return for financial assistance at home and political support abroad. The positive state aims at minimal full employment, which is just enough employment to keep consumption up, labour costs down, and labour unions weak.

The preferred social welfare instrument is social insurance, which is consistent with economic efficiency and encourages proper work habits. As well, it functions as social control by tying people's eligibility for social insurance benefits to their participation in the labour market. The beneficiaries of the positive state tend to be those who, under conditions of laissez-faire individualism, prosper most readily. The vision of the positive state is not at all similar to that of social work. Rather, it is one of rugged individualism within the context of balanced economic growth and protection of business interests.[60] It is the model of welfare favoured by neo-conservatives. The United States best typifies this model.

The Social Security State or Institutional Model of Welfare

The key concept of the social security state is that everyone who is a casualty of the industrial order has a right to a guaranteed minimum of social security. This collective responsibility for individual maintenance recognizes that a society based on competitive capitalism cannot provide universal security and that it is the duty of the state to fill this void. Theoretically, it is possible to eliminate poverty by establishing the national minimum at an adequate level. The vision of a social security state is based on government-business co-operation, with the guaranteed national minimum financed by pursuing an economic policy of maximal full employment and public employment as a last resort. These economic and social policies are intended to be of direct benefit to every citizen and to overcome the limitations of social insurance provisions.

The social security state does not contain egalitarian social and economic ideals. The governing principle is "equality of opportunity" where all are equal in status before the law but unequal in material resources, life chances, and political power. It represents what Furniss and Tilton call "a modern and noble version of the Liberal ideal."[61] Great Britain (before Thatcherism) and Canada to a lesser extent typify the social security state.

The Social Welfare State or Structural Model of Welfare

Unlike the goal of minimalist-full employment of the positive state or maximalist-full employment of the social security state, the social welfare state has as its goal full employment. This requires government-union co-operation in the labour market. Equally important to the social welfare state are two other policies: environmental planning (in its most comprehensive form) and solidaristic wages. The former policy encompasses the regulation of property to preserve amenities, the prohibition of activities resulting in pollution, urban planning, and the development of new communities. In short, this policy represents an effort to inject collective and social values into a society founded on the good life of the individual. The purpose of the solidaristic wage policy is to counteract the tendency toward concentration of assets and income, to narrow differentials among groups of wage-earners, and to extract for labour a larger relative piece of the national income.

The social welfare state aims to promote equality and solidarity. It seeks more than a national minimum for citizens in that it attempts to achieve a general equality of living conditions. It substitutes public services, such as the public provision of health care, child care, and legal services, for social insurance programs. These services are available to all, not just to the underprivileged. The social welfare state rests on a vision of extending the locus of political and economic power and of increased citizen participation in all areas of living. It is similar to what Mishra calls the structural model of welfare.[62] Although no country at present typifies the social welfare state, Sweden best approximates it among Western industrial democracies.

In terms of its fundamental values of humanism and egalitarianism and its corresponding set of social, economic, and political beliefs, social work must reject the positive state because it violates most social work ideals. The social security state contains some humanistic elements but must be rejected by social work because of its lack of egalitarian ideals. The social welfare state, on the other hand, is most congruent with social work values, beliefs, and principles. Thus, progressive social workers must work toward and attempt to achieve this form of society if they are to remain true to their own ideals. However, the social welfare state or the structural model of welfare is not possible to achieve in our present society because it rests on a set of values contradictory to those of neo-conservative or liberal capitalism.

Conclusion

In this chapter the elements of a progressive alternative vision of society have been presented. The question for social work is, which of the existing societal paradigms is most congruent with: the fundamental values of humanism and egalitarianism; the instrumental values of respect, self-determination, and acceptance; a social belief of the individual as a social being; an economic belief whereby societal decisions dominate economic decisions; a political belief in participatory democracy; and a social welfare system that emphasizes equality, solidarity, and community? In other words, which societal paradigm is most congruent with the social work ideals and beliefs as outlined in Table 2.1?

3

The Neo-Conservative Paradigm

Conservatism

Conservatism is a set of beliefs that "springs from a desire to conserve existing things, held to be either good in themselves, or better than the likely alternatives, or at least safe, familiar, and the objects of trust and affection."[1] This view implies a distrust of sudden or radical change, preferring the maintenance of traditional institutions and processes that should only be modified with extreme caution. The political consequences of these beliefs are a suspicion of state interference, a sympathy toward property rights, and an acceptance of inequalities with respect to class, education, status, and wealth.[2]

The purest source of conservative principles is found in Edmund Burke's *Reflections of the Revolution in France* (1790).[3] Burke wrote during a time of turmoil (the 1780s) in France – a parliamentary system had been created, the Declaration of the Rights of Man was adopted, the last remnants of feudalism were abolished, the property of the Catholic Church had been nationalized, and the rationalism of the Enlightment had replaced tradition as the surest guide to human conduct. These changes occurred with lightning rapidity and caused Burke to predict correctly that turmoil and despotism would follow such a radical break from the past.[4] "The result was the emergence of a political faith that celebrated the beauties of stability and tradition."[5]

Burke's conservatism, an amalgam of economic liberalism (free market economy) and social conservatism (respect for the past and a hierarchical view of society), has been adopted by most Anglo-American conservatives.[6] Benjamin Disraeli, a late nineteenth-century Prime Minister of Britain, John Adams, second President of the United States, and John A. Macdonald and George-Étienne Cartier, two of the chief founders of Canada, are examples of heads of state who subscribed to the Burkean world of order, tradition, hierarchy, private property, laws, and customs. Conservatism in these terms is often found as the ideological foundation of conservative political parties such as the Conservative Party of Britain, the Republican Party of the United States, and the Progressive Conservative Party of Canada.

Conservatism was the dominant ideology in nineteenth-century Britain and North America, and although it started to wane in the latter part of the nineteenth century it remained dominant until the Great Depression of the 1930s, when many conservative notions fell into disrepute and were replaced by liberal ideals and beliefs, including a new economic theory developed by John Maynard Keynes and a new social policy direction as contained in the Beveridge Report of 1944. Following World War Two the state was seen as a force for implementing a more just and equitable society, and a growing welfare state represented the means of implementation.[7] The absence of a serious recession, steady economic growth, and full employment (with some national differences) made it seem that "the old order of capitalism with its crude dogma of laissez-faire, endemic business cycles of boom and bust and chronic unemployment had . . . been left behind in a major evolutionary advance"[8] and that acceptance of "The mix of values and institutions represented by the welfare state . . . symbolized the new social order."[9]

In light of such beliefs the events of the 1970s – the OPEC price increases, stagflation, the fiscal crisis of the state, and so on – came as a real shock and could not seem to be resolved by reformist liberal mechanisms and policies. Although never dead, conservative ideas and rhetoric have been revived as a way of explaining what had gone wrong with the mixed economy of the welfare state and as a guide to economic recovery and prosperity.[10] Political parties advocating conservative ideas and solutions have been elected in Britain (1979, 1983, 1987, and 1991), the United States (1980, 1984, and 1988), and Canada (1984 and 1988).

Neo-Conservatism

The resurgence of conservative ideas, policies, and rhetoric, along with an attack on the welfare state, has been variably referred to as anti-collectivism,[11] rugged individualism,[12] and the New Right,[13] but will be referred to here as neo-conservatism, which is more consistent with popular usage. Basing their economic and social views on the classical doctrines of laissez faire and individualism, neo-conservatives have called for a return to the values of the marketplace. Their solutions to the current crises are to attack government deficits by cutting profligate social spending, to rely on the private sector to restore economic growth, to eliminate or reduce the power of unions, to deregulate industry, and to limit the controls on multinational corporations.[14]

Resnick describes three different but complementary elements running through neo-conservative thought. (1) People's excessive expectations are seen as a threat to representative government. Hence, government's role should be reduced, rights diminished, and more traditional values such as authority and obedience reinstated. (2) The state should follow laissez-faire policies and reject government interventions; demand management of the economy should be replaced by supply-side economics; deregulation, privatization, and severe limits on government spending should be imposed; and balanced budgets should be the central goal. (3) Traditional concepts of morality and religion should be asserted to control the permissiveness of modern society, and school prayers, the sacredness of pregnancy, law and order, and anti-communism should be the four foundations of the good society.[15]

What, then, is new about neo-conservatism? That is, what are the differences between the conservatism of the last century and the first half of this century and the neo-conservatism of the 1980s and 1990s? Most writers suggest that there is little, if any, difference. Dickerson and Flanagan, for example, state, "We continue to use the traditional term conservatism because we see no fundamental change in ideology, even though popular support for conservative views has increased."[16] Mishra contends that the only difference is the context (i.e., welfare capitalism) and that the doctrine is the same: "Remove the context and the associated rhetoric and there is little that is new – that cannot, for example, be traced back to the classical doctrines of Adam Smith (individualism and free market) and Herbert Spencer (Social Darwinism)."[17] Most writers suggest that neo-conservatism represents a more sophisticated presentation of conservative doctrine rather than a different doctrine.[18] Rossiter[19] has identified some of the persistent philosophical themes of modern conservatism:

- the imperfect nature of people where unreason and sin lie under the mask of civilized behaviour;
- the natural inequality of people in mind, body, and character;
- the necessity for social classes;
- the need for a ruling and serving elite;
- the existence of a universal moral order supported by organized religion;
- the primacy of private property;
- the limitations of human reason, and the consequent need for traditions, institutions, symbols, and even prejudices.

Neo-conservatives have blamed much of the economic crisis on the welfare state. Mishra says, "It is one thing when economic growth stops . . . and governments find that they have to economize on social [expenditure]. . . . It is quite another thing when economic recession . . . becomes[s] the occasion for a general attack on the basic principles and practices of the postwar welfare state."[20] Neo-conservatives have argued that the welfare state has created both economic and social problems. Economically, the welfare state is too big and too expensive, and it is also inefficient because it allows (or encourages) workers to drop out of the labour market, thus depriving the economy of needed labour and increasing welfare costs at the same time. Socially, neo-conservatives argue that the welfare state has fractured traditional family life, eroded the work ethic, legitimated unearned leisure time without shame or penalty, and encouraged undesirable behaviour.[21] For example, such officials in the Bush administration as the Attorney-General blamed the 1992 Los Angeles riots that followed the "not guilty" verdict in the trial of the policemen who beat Rodney King on the liberal social programs of the Kennedy and Johnson administrations. Social expenditures were cited as encouraging too many inner-city black females to have children out of wedlock, and these children – the products of sexual abandonment without proper families – it was claimed, were responsible for the looting and rioting. To the neo-conservative, then, social welfare programs represent the cause rather than the cure for many social problems.[22]

A difference between traditional conservatives and neo-conservatives is that the latter group is much more sophisticated in its criticisms and attacks on the welfare state. Traditional conservatives were content to snipe at social programs from the sidelines, using clichés about welfare cheats, bleeding-heart social workers, and self-interested bureaucrats.[23] Right-wing think tanks such as the London Institute of Economic Affairs in Britain, the Hoover Institute in the United States, and the Fraser Institute in Canada have made serious proposals to restructure the welfare state rather than to eliminate it. Examples of such proposals are: to transfer as much welfare responsibility as possible from the federal government to lower levels of government and to the private sector; to transfer money from welfare to work programs; to encourage the involvement and participation of private citizens in the provision of many welfare services (i.e., set up food banks, soup kitchens, emergency shelters, and so on). Mullaly has argued that the current restructuring of the welfare state is occurring along class lines, with money being taken out of general welfare programs for the working class and redirected into fiscal welfare (i.e., grants, tax breaks, and so on for corporations and wealthy individuals) and into occupational welfare (i.e., perks and fringe benefits for the managerial and professional sectors of the working class, which are subsidized through the tax system). The result of this restructuring is a redistribution of social benefits away from those most in need (i.e., the poor) to those least in need (i.e., the wealthy).[24] The class nature of this restructured welfare state is, of course, consistent with the neo-conservative belief in hierarchy.

In sum, the differences between traditional conservatism and neo-conservatism lie in their different contexts and in the more sophisticated analysis and proposed changes of the welfare state developed by neo-conservatives. Rather than calling for the dismantling of the welfare state *per se,* neo-conservatives have achieved some success in restructuring it to their favour. What is not different between these two groups is their essential ideology – their social, economic, and political beliefs.

Social Beliefs

The central social values of neo-conservatism are freedom or liberty, individualism, and inequality.[25] Liberty is seen primarily as the absence of coercion. People must be as free as possible to exert themselves to the utmost limit of their abilities to the advantage of both the person and society. Any government promoting other social values that interfere with one's freedom is deprecated. Yet, if coercion is to be avoided, there must be sanctions against those who would use it. The state therefore uses the threat of coercion to avoid coercion by any individual. This institutionalization of coercion is perceived by neo-conservatives as benefiting everyone equally in spite of the stratified nature of society and the concentration of power within certain groups. Thus, one of the contradictions of a neo-conservative society is that coercion by the state is the instrument of liberty.

Individualism is a necessary correlate of liberty. One cannot exist without the other. The dominant theme of individualism is that the individual must have as much liberty as possible to pursue his or her own interests and to bear the consequences of his or her actions. If everyone in society adheres to the principle of the pursuit of self-interest without harming others, then society will run smoothly. Only when people fail to carry out their obligations or when government interferes with one's liberty do problems occur for the individual and for society. Individualism perceives people as imperfect beings who, therefore, must be controlled by sanctions and rules enforced by the state. Individualism also attributes a large role in the socialization of people to voluntary organizations and to institutions such as the family, the school, and the church. When these voluntary institutions fail in their socialization function the coercive role of the state is invoked.

Social equality and liberty are seen as contradictory by neo-conservatives. It is feared that equality of incomes from work will destroy people's work incentives and the social esteem that accompanies certain occupations. Politically, social equality would mean that powerful groups would have to share their political power, which could only occur through government coercion. To achieve social equality would mean interfering with equality of freedom (including the freedom to be poor rather than being coerced into affluence by the state). Equality of freedom is the only equality accepted by neo-conservatives and, in fact, is their supreme value. This equality of freedom is bound to produce material and political inequality. Thus, neo-conservatives support equality of freedom and social inequality. Obviously, these values foster a Social Darwinian "survival of the fittest" mentality that views any form of state intervention into people's freedoms as contrary to the laws of nature, leading eventually to an elimination of the fittest members of society and a proliferation of the weak and unfit.

Economic Beliefs

The fundamental economic values of neo-conservatism are laissez-faire economics, competitive capitalism, and private property accumulation. Descriptively, the term "laissez faire" (leave alone) refers to minimal government interference (as opposed to intervention) into the lives and activities of private citizens – especially in regard to their economic activities. The role of the state is to ensure the provision of the basic conditions for free competitive capitalism by maintaining law and order, enforcing contracts, protecting property rights, and defending the nation against attacks by other nations. It does not interfere in the economy by either holding back the successful or helping the unsuccessful.

Laissez faire is a prerequisite for competitive capitalism. Reference is often made by neo-conservatives to the natural laws of the competitive marketplace (laws of supply, demand, and price determination). A society that ignores or interferes with these natural laws will run into trouble, as surely as a person who ignores the law of gravity. Neo-conservatives believe that competitive capitalism, which is based on voluntary exchange rather than coercion, is the best model of an economic system.[26] The free market protects everyone's interests – the consumer, the seller, the employee, and the employer. The consumer is protected because he or she can buy from other sellers. The seller is protected because there are other potential consumers. The employee is protected because there are other employers he or she can work for, and so on. This whole economic process is carried out unfettered by any authority. If government were to interfere with this process by attempting to regulate and restrict competition, or to hamper the efficient and successful, or to help the inefficient and unsuccessful, the results would be to upset the delicate but perfectly balanced natural economic system. All society would suffer and be poorer for it. The best economic policy of government is to leave the economy alone.

One of the cherished freedoms held by neo-conservatives is the right to acquire, accumulate, and own property (land, material and natural resources, means of production, and so on) and to use one's property as one sees fit. Private ownership is not only consistent with neo-conservative social beliefs of liberty, individualism, and inequality, it is also the driving force behind the economic system. Private ownership provides the means for making profits and thus is the incentive in a competitive free market for persons to work hard to maximize their material and spiritual well-being. If people were not allowed to keep the fruits of their labour and to dispose of them in any fashion they wish there would be reduced incentive to work hard and the economy, as a whole, would suffer. Individuals are responsible to provide for themselves out of resources they manage to control. This notion forces people to attempt to increase their share of available resources, as any increase in property is perceived as an increase in material security and social status. To the neo-conservatives the appropriation of material resources is the fundamental principle around which a society's system of provision and the entire social order should be constructed.

Political Beliefs

The major political beliefs of neo-conservatism are: rule by a governing elite; subjugation of the political system to the economic system; law, order, and stability; and paternalism. Conservatives have always found the concept of democracy to be problematic. Politics to the conservative is restricted in meaning to the "art of governing," which is too important to be left to anyone but the most able and best prepared (who, of course, are inevitably members of the elite ruling class). To extend political rights to the masses is to run the risk of decisions being made by the wrong people, that is, by non-members of the established elite who are not legitimate rulers. The Family Compact of Upper Canada (Ontario) in the nineteenth century and the hierarchy of the Roman Catholic Church of Lower Canada, which dominated Quebec life well into the twentieth century, are examples of conservative ruling elites in Canada.

The belief in ruling elites is not a relic of political history but is used today by neo-conservatives as a political explanation of the economic and social crises confronting Western industrial societies. "A ruling class, unlike a democratically elected government, is expected to serve the interests of those who control the economy."[27] In a democracy political parties must compete with one another for votes. In this electoral competition excessive expectations are made on governments, pushing them further and further into being responsible for everything. The result, according to neo-conservative thought, is government overload: demands on government far exceed its capacity to meet them effectively. This situation is characterized by public expenditure out of control or by government itself being out of control, and it has been brought about by increasing democratization.[28] The neo-conservatives would like to see this process reversed or, at least, curtailed.

Neo-conservatives blame much of the current crisis on excessive government intervention and regulation. They would resolve this crisis by curtailing democratization of the political process (as mentioned above) and by depoliticizing the economy. If society is to benefit from economic activity, then, it is claimed, we must put up with the costs (e.g., unemployment, inadequate wages, questionable labour practices) of a free market. The role of government should be to protect, to support, to assure, and to enhance the workings of a free market. Government should not regulate, interfere with, or explicitly allow unions, professional associations, or other interest groups to modify the spontaneous workings of the market. Thus, although neo-conservatives believe in a strong central state, its sphere of activities must be restricted to such things as national defence and protecting individual rights and freedoms.

Neo-conservatives place a premium on the maintenance of a social hierarchy, and much of past conservative effort has been to conserve rather than reform the legal, political, social, and economic status quo. Originally there was a religious justification for such a perspective, but today there is a strong psychological attraction for conserving rather than reforming.[29] In other words, much of neo-conservative rhetoric is based on the psychological assumption that people have a basic need for security and will opt for a social system they are familiar with (even though it may contain many flaws) rather than take a chance on one they have not experienced and are unfamiliar with. Thus, much of neo-conservative political rhetoric is focused on law and order and preserving the old ways and values. Any change or reform is perceived as a threat to social stability and social continuity.

Another political belief of neo-conservatives is "paternalism for those whom society designates as not responsible,"[30] or, in Poor Law terminology, "the deserving poor." This form of government activity is seen as a necessary evil (the alternative is to let people die) rather than as a means to reducing inequalities. Although the risk of abuse is great (in terms of expanding the categories of people considered as not capable of taking responsibility for themselves), there is no avoiding the need for some degree of paternalism. The amount of assistance must be the lowest level acceptable to society. In return for this *noblesse oblige* the neo-conservative ruling elite would expect conformity and loyalty from its citizenry.

View of Social Problems

In accordance with its social, economic, and political beliefs neo-conservatism holds that people should provide for themselves by exercising their individual freedoms and choices in the competitive marketplace. In other words, everyone should provide for his or her own needs through work, savings, and the acquisition of property. Only those persons who do not carry out these obligations (the unfit, the lazy, and the inferior) encounter problems. And because these problems are of their own making, they do not deserve help from government or from hard-working, responsible, and honest taxpayers. In fact, neo-conservatives believe that helping those who fail to provide for themselves reinforces idleness and dependence on government and encourages others to avoid efforts to support themselves.

The neo-conservative view of social problems seldom considers structural or environmental sources of social and economic problems, but attributes such problems to individual weakness, deviance, or heredity. Social problems are viewed as personal problems and the focus is on the troublesome person or family. The problem is caused by supposed defects of the mentally ill person or the drug addict or the poor person or the criminal. The family is also seen as the source of personal problems because, consistent with Social Darwinian thought, unfit parents will produce unfit children. In other words, parents who are lazy, dishonest, and inferior will produce children with similar characteristics. Neo-conservative writer George Gilder contends that welfare programs and the decline of family values and traditional family patterns cause poverty, not sexism, racism, or unemployment, and that any cause-effect relationship between racism or sexism and poverty is a myth perpetrated by minorities and feminists.[31] In all cases, the view of social problems is the same. The individual is separated from society, and a biographical portrait of deficiencies is constructed and cited as the source of the person's troubles.

The above view of social problems is consistent with the "social pathology" perspective that was central to the thinking of early American sociologists with regard to social problems. Their work was infused with moral indignation formulated in terms of a medical model wherein many social problems are caused by sick or pathological individuals – that is, people who are defective, delinquent, dependent, and deficient.[32] The solution to social problems, according to these early sociologists, was to educate the pathological troublemakers in middle-class morality.[33] Coates has termed this perspective as the "personal deficiency approach," which he associates with conservative ideology, and contends that it has informed the diagnostic, functional, and psycho-social traditions in social work.[34] The impact that the larger social environment has on personal problems is not considered.

View of Social Welfare

George and Wilding explain how neo-conservatives are fundamentally hostile to a developed social welfare state.[35] Any provision of more than basic government services is believed to have unnecessary and undesirable social, economic, and political consequences. Socially, the more services the state provides, the more it weakens the traditional sources of welfare – the family and local voluntary organizations such as the churches. These sources will not only disappear over time, but so, too, will the individual's ability and willingness to provide for his or her own needs. Economically, neo-conservatives believe that government assistance, above a basic subsistence level, diverts human and capital resources from the productive sector, undermines work incentives, is provided inefficiently, and encourages consumption of unneeded services. Politically, social welfare undermines individual freedom, weakens public respect for government and the political process, and may lead to dictatorial regimes. In essence, the neo-conservatives see the "welfare state" as a misnomer because government intervention actually leads to a state of diswelfare.

The free market system, according to the neo-conservatives, is the main source and origin of welfare. Even social services should be delivered through the market by private commercial practitioners/entrepreneurs. The model or conception of social welfare most consistent with neo-conservative thought, and that has the free market as its central concept, is the residual concept of welfare.[36] This is based on the neo-conservative belief that social welfare programs (both private and public) should only come into play when the normal channels for meeting needs – the family and the market economy – break down. When these preferred structures of supply are not functioning properly or when an individual cannot make use of them because of illness or old age, a third mechanism of need-fulfilment is brought into play – the social welfare system. This is perceived to be a residual structure that attends to emergency functions only, and it is expected to withdraw when the two normal or regular structures – the family and the economic system – are again working properly. All social welfare assistance should be minimal and must not threaten or undermine the operations of the marketplace or erode wage-earners' sense of responsibility for themselves and their families.

Because of its temporary, residual, and substitute nature, social welfare often carries a stigma of charity and abnormality. This concept of social welfare formed the basis of the Elizabethan Poor Laws, which divided the poor into two groups – the deserving (dependent children, the elderly, the disabled) and the non-deserving (employable adults). The former group might have been eligible for residual welfare; the second group was not. That this model of social welfare is consistent with such neo-conservative values as individual responsibility, the free market, and minimal government intervention is readily apparent. The residual model of welfare is similar to the "positive state" model of social welfare[37] described in the previous chapter, where it was argued that it should be rejected by the social work profession because it is based on value premises diametrically opposed to those of social work.

Mishra contends that neo-conservatism challenges all persons who believe in an adequate and fair welfare state:

> . . . neo-conservatism is openly and unashamedly partisan and one-sided. It has forced upon the world of social welfare the realization that what we are involved in is essentially a contest over values, beliefs and interests rather than some objective necessity dictated by the economy. In breaking the consensus of ideas and practices over the welfare state it has thrown an open challenge to those on the side of social welfare to make an adequate ideological response.[38]

Social Work Practice within the Neo-Conservative Paradigm

Given: (1) such values as individual responsibility, inequality, survival of the fittest, and laissez faire; (2) a view of social problems as originating from individual weakness and deviance; and (3) a conception of social welfare as temporary, abnormal, and residual, the nature of social work practice within neo-conservatism would be one of control and coercion of people. Emphasis would be placed on getting people to accept their personal, family, and social obligations and not on social or environmental reform.

Because the nature of human beings is viewed as contentious, competitive, and self-absorbed, then social work must use coercive measures to make sure that people look after themselves. All other sources of assistance must be explored before a person would be considered eligible for any kind of financial help. A means test is an integral part of the residual model of welfare. Separation of the deserving poor from the non-deserving poor would be a primary function of social workers in a neo-conservative society. Investigation and monitoring of people's living, work, and financial situations would occur regularly to control abuse of social welfare programs. Because of the belief that social problems are mainly due to individual fault and deviance, then suspicion, moralism, and punitive attitudes would be qualities held by social workers. The primary task of social work under neo-conservatism would be to teach people how to do without the welfare state.

Individual behaviour within the neo-conservative paradigm is seen in a limited social context that would not likely extend beyond an individual's family. In other words, neo-conservatives might attribute problems to an individual's dysfunctional family, but it is not likely that the source of personal/social problems would ever be considered to extend beyond the boundary of the family. The dysfunctional family would not be viewed as a victim of the social order but as a pathological social unit. Social work with pathological families would consist of coercing, cajoling, and convincing individual family members to adjust their behaviours and to carry out their individual responsibilities to themselves, to one another, and to society. Threats of removing children and other intimidation tactics would be major tools used in working with families.

Rather than a focus on helping, social work would emphasize control of people's behaviour in order to remove any threat to the established social order. This is so because, according to the neo-conservatives, society can only function effectively and efficiently as long as everyone carries his or her own weight. Once the principle of individual responsibility starts to break down, the whole society is in danger of collapsing. If individual pathology cannot be controlled by social work, then it must be neutralized by other state mechanisms such as asylums and prisons.

One possible exception to the control and coercive nature of social work within the neo-conservative paradigm would be its treatment of the so-called deserving poor. Because a judgement has been made that the deserving poor are in need through no fault of their own, they would not likely be treated as punitively as their "non-deserving" counterparts. However, there is always the problem of determining who is deserving and who is not. As well, the history of the Poor Laws tells us that those judged deserving have always been numerically underrepresented. Even in working with the deserving poor, a social worker would be expected to exhort and cajole as much money and help as possible from the poor person's family for the maintenance of its unfortunate member.

Iatridis sums up the effects of neo-conservatism on social work:

> . . . neo-conservatism creates a special crisis for social workers because this ideology is the antithesis of social work theory, practice, philosophy, values, objectives, and commitments – of everything, in fact, for which the profession stands.[39]

Critique of the Neo-Conservative Paradigm

Neo-conservative thought forms much of the intellectual support for recent social policy in Canada, the United States, and Britain. An excellent overview of the criticisms of neo-conservative doctrine has been presented by Mishra[40] and is summarized here.

(1) Although there may be a grain of truth in many neo-conservative arguments there is a tendency to exaggerate this grain of truth and to generalize on the basis of insufficient evidence. For example, neo-conservatives often convey the impression that budget deficits have been occurring regularly since World War Two because of Keynesian economic practices when, in fact, it has only been since the recession of the 1970s that sizeable deficits have begun to emerge.

(2) Neo-conservative thought and argument vary in terms of theoretical sophistication but, on the whole, tend to be one-sided and based on highly selective evidence. For example, neo-conservatives often blame Britain's economic ills on its welfare state, but no mention is made of other European countries, such as Germany and Austria, with well-developed welfare states that also enjoy excellent economic growth, low inflation, and low unemployment. They are simply ignored.

(3) Neo-conservatives offer a one-sided view of how government functions. They criticize governments for not being decisive enough and for not taking quick action. They fail to see that government is not the same kind of undertaking as a business seeking profit. Hence, what may appear as government failure, for example, weakened authority because of greater democracy and more participation, may be government's success.

(4) Neo-conservatives possess an inadequate conception of the role of democracy and politics in modern societies. It was mentioned previously that neo-conservatives would like to see the capitalist market economy depoliticized as much as possible – that is, that elected governments should not be allowed to interfere in the market. This would be a reversal to the growth of the modern state and of citizenship that has been occurring over the past 100 years. It would negate the responsibility a democratically elected government has for the nation's well-being by not allowing it to exercise control and regulation over the economy.

Table 3.1
Overview of Neo-Conservative and Social Work Ideals

	Neo-Conservatism	*Social Work*
Social Beliefs	Freedom (from government coercion) Individualism Inequality	Humanitarianism (humanism) Community Equality
Economic Beliefs	Free market Competitive capitalism Private ownership	Government intervention Social priorities dominate economic decisions Equitable distribution of society's resources
Political Beliefs	Elite rule Depoliticalization of economic system Law, order, and stability Paternalism	Participatory democracy in both governmental and non-governmental areas
View of Social Welfare	Fundamentally hostile Ideal = residual model	An instrument to promote equality, solidarity, and community Ideal = structural model
Nature of Social Work Practice	Use of coercive measures to make people look after themselves Control people's behaviour Poor Law treatment of separating deserving from non-deserving Emphasize investigation and monitoring to prevent cheating the system	Treat people with respect Enhance dignity and integrity Facilitate self-determination and self-realization Accept differences Advocate and promote social justice

(5) Based on the values of individualism, liberty, private property, and inequality, neo-conservatism has little appreciation of the concepts of social justice and social integration as vitally important elements of modern, industrial democracies.

Conclusion

Table 3.1 outlines the major beliefs of neo-conservatism and contrasts them with the major beliefs of progressive social work. The only conclusion one can reach after examining the beliefs and ideals of each is that neo-conservatism and progressive social work are incompatible. The social, economic, and political beliefs of each clash with one another, as do their respective views of the welfare state. Although social work practice does contain coercive and controlling elements, these tend to be imposed by outside bodies such as the state and the authorizing agency. They are not self-directed functions of progressive social work. Neo-conservatism represents an updated version of a 200-year-old doctrine and contains several intellectual and scientific flaws. Its eighteenth-century assumptions about economic, human, and social behaviour conflict with those who are on the side of social welfare, and they represent the antithesis of progressive social work.

4

The Liberal Paradigm

Liberalism

Liberalism comes from the Latin word "liber," meaning free. It comprises a set of beliefs based on the assumption that there should be as much individual freedom as possible in any civilized society yet allowing for the existence of essential constraints.[1] Although liberalism developed as a coherent system of ideals and practical goals in the eighteenth and nineteenth centuries, it has a long and rich tradition.[2] It has roots in Greek philosophy and literature, in Roman law, and in several religious traditions, including Christianity, and was fostered by the Renaissance and the Reformation. It is the result of the convergence of a number of broad social and political trends and forces.

It is important to distinguish the older classical liberalism from contemporary or reform liberalism. Classical liberalism is similar to conservatism as both developed in the eighteenth and nineteenth centuries in Britain and Western Europe, and both used the same writers and thinkers for many of their ideas and theories.[3]

Whereas classical liberals saw the state in negative terms as a threat to individual freedom, reform liberals view the state in positive terms in that it can be used to promote freedom for those who otherwise might not achieve it. Great inequalities in market power make one person's freedom another person's oppression. Also, reform liberals view the state as a means to remedy some of the abuses of the free market, such as child labour, slum housing, tainted food, and so on.[4] Thus, economic freedom and the free market are not accorded the same primacy in reform liberalism as in classical liberalism.[5] Another major difference between classical and reform liberalism lies in the concept of equality that each holds. Equality to the classical liberal means only that everyone abides by the same rules (laws) and does not extend to a desire or responsibility to ameliorate inequality of wealth, status, or power. Equality to the reform liberal means equal opportunity. The reform liberal does not wish to eliminate inequality but seeks to reduce its excesses by using the power of the state to provide opportunities, such as public education and public health care, that would not be available to some people without government intervention. Thus, reform liberalism tries to modify the free market without abolishing it. Reform liberalism is the subject of this chapter.

Conservative thought and ideology helped to shape the welfare states from their inception in Canada, Britain, and the United States and continue to exert a great deal of influence today. However, the dominant paradigm that accompanied the emergence of the post-war welfare state in Canada and the United States, and to a lesser extent in Britain,[6] is liberalism. Although challenged by neo-conservatism today, liberalism is still the dominant social paradigm in Canada and the United States. In other words, North Americans live in liberal societies where both the social welfare state and social work practice have been influenced mainly by liberal ideology since World War Two. Therefore, it is crucial for the social work profession to be informed of, and to understand, the social, economic, and political beliefs that in large part shape our welfare state and determine the nature of our practice.

George and Wilding believe the term "liberalism" today stands for such a wide spectrum of political ideology that it has lost all meaning.[7] Instead, they use the term "reluctant collectivism." Djao follows the lead of George and Wilding and refers to liberalism as "modified individualism."[8] The term " liberalism" will be used in this book, however, because, as with "conservatism," it is more consistent with popular usage and is more widely used in Canadian social, economic, and political literature. Nevertheless, the terms "reluctant collectivism" and "modified individualism" are useful in distinguishing conservatism and liberalism and at the same time suggest what they have in common.

Liberals share many of the same values with neo-conservatives – a belief in freedom, in individualism, and in competitive private enterprise. However, liberals hold fewer absolute values in that they accept intervention into the economy on the basis of pragmatism and humanism. Their pragmatism is based on a conviction that although capitalism may be the best economic system, it is not self-regulating. It requires regulation and control to function efficiently and fairly. Their humanism is based on a recognition that capitalism is hurtful to many people. Concern for the human implications of capitalism led John Maynard Keynes and William Henry Beveridge in Britain and John Kenneth Galbraith in the U.S. to lead British and North American societies to reject conservative thought and to adopt the liberal paradigm.[9] Canadian social welfare writers responsible for the adoption of many liberal ideas with respect to the development of the

Canadian social welfare state were Harry Cassidy and Leonard Marsh, who both wrote during 1930s and 1940s.

Social Beliefs

The central social values of liberalism are essentially the same as those of the neo-conservatives. Both groups believe in freedom and individualism, and both are non-egalitarian. As mentioned above, however, liberals modify or qualify these values somewhat by pragmatic and humanistic concerns. For example, both neo-conservatives and liberals regard freedom as an essential value. However, neo-conservatives view freedom simply as freedom from the arbitrary power of governments, whereas liberals would include freedom from such social evils as unemployment, disease, and squalor in their concept of freedom. To protect this latter freedom would obviously necessitate some form of state intervention that would be unacceptable to neo-conservatives.

Individualism is a key value of liberals. All government action should have as its goals the maximization of an individual's pursuit of self-interest. The purpose of government intervention is to maximize individual welfare. It attempts to remove obstacles to self-sufficiency. Liberals would measure the total well-being of society by simply summing up the well-being of all individuals in that society. There would be no consideration of collective goals. Liberals do not speak of classes because society is viewed as a collection of individuals rather than as a class or stratified society. This individualistic view helps to absolve people from responsibility for the well-being of others in society. There is no obligation or responsibility for others. Anything done for others is carried out either on pragmatic grounds (i.e., it is more efficient or it will dispel social unrest) or on humanitarian grounds, which often leaves deprived or disadvantaged persons to the vagaries of charitable and paternalistic whims of others. People as social beings tend not to be recognized. There is little sense of community or collectivity, as society is viewed in an atomistic way comprised of individual, self-sufficient social entities.

Those liberals who do recognize that classes exist and that some classes fare much better than others in a capitalist society would contend that social and economic mobility is possible because of equal opportunity. In other words, some people in society may be suffering, but if they work hard and take advantage of the opportunities available to them they can get out of their present situation and move to a higher class ("socio-economic position" in liberal terms). Liberals accept inequality of circumstances because of their profound belief in equal opportunity, which means that we are all equal before the law. No one has any more freedoms or liberties than anyone else. Everyone has access to education, the job market, health care, social services, and so on. If a person fails in society it is because he or she did not take advantage of available opportunities. Liberals do not consider the possibility that some people in society, because of their social position and resources, may be in a better position to use these so-called available opportunities than others. To use an analogy, if one person has a fifty-metre headstart in a 100-metre race, it is not likely that the other person will ever catch up. The fallacy of the equal opportunity concept is that not everyone starts out at the same place in life. Therefore, some people have an unfair advantage and preferred access to these "equal" opportunities. Karger states, "The fallacy of the entire argument is that true equality of opportunity is unattainable in an unequal society."[10]

Although liberals are not egalitarians, they do think that inequalities should and could be reduced. Humanistically, liberals are aware of the ugliness of poverty and would seek to eliminate it, which is a different concern than the search for equality. Pragmatically, a wider distribution of income will: (a) increase aggregate demand, thus lessening unemployment, and (b) reduce social tension. From this point of view, however, egalitarianism destroys incentives, weakens social cohesion, and threatens the freedom of the individual.[11]

Economic Beliefs

The fundamental economic value of liberalism is competitive capitalism based on free enterprise, but with some government regulation. This type of economic system is often called a mixed economy as opposed to the neo-conservative's laissez-faire economy. Although both neo-conservatives and liberals subscribe to a capitalist economy, liberals do not share the neo-conservative belief that an unregulated free enterprise system works well.

Liberals have four major criticisms of capitalism.[12] (1) Capitalism is not self-regulating. Without state intervention it cannot solve the economic problems it has created for itself, such as cyclical recession, structural unemployment and underemployment, inflation, large discrepancies in wealth and income, and regional disparity. (2) Capitalism is wasteful and inefficient and misallocates resources. With each recession the productive capacity of nations is wasted as factories and people lie idle. If left by itself capitalism will result in private affluence and public squalor, which are morally unacceptable to humanistic liberals and politically dangerous, as public squalor can lead to crime, violence, and social unrest. (3) Capitalism will not by itself eliminate poverty and injustice. By its very nature (material acquisition, competition, survival of the fittest) capitalism produces and perpetuates poverty and inequality. (4) Capitalism leads to the interests of the economically dominant groups being identified as the national interest. These groups, for example, have convinced government and the people that industrial development, which is of interest to the capitalists, is really in the national interest. Consequently, giant corporations have little difficulty getting government to spend money on roads, technological development, research, and so on, while the care of the old, the ill, the poor, and others is neglected because no economically powerful group has spoken in their interests.

In spite of these significant criticisms of capitalism, liberals do not believe that it should be abolished. Rather, they believe it should be regulated because the faults of capitalism, in their view, are technical in nature rather than fundamental and can be made good by government action. However, liberals would still place limitations on this government action because they believe that: (1) once the technical problems of capitalism are solved the system will regulate itself; (2) capitalism is naturally superior as a source of initiative and liberty; and (3) government action, while necessary for freedom, is always a potential threat to freedom.[13]

Because liberals do not seek to change the given economic system, most of their interventions into the economy will be symptom-focused and ameliorative rather than structural. Fiscal and monetary actions will be designed to compensate for such instabilities inherent in capitalism as recessions, unemployment, and inflation, and will not be designed to overcome the systemic roots of these problems.[14] In other words, government intervention into the economy is intended to fine-tune it rather than change its basic nature.

Political Beliefs

The fundamental political beliefs of liberalism lie in representative democracy[15] and pluralism.[16] Liberals would argue that direct participation in the day-to-day business of government by the electorate is impossible. Rather, the essence of modern-day democracy rests in the popular control of elected representatives. Control is exercised through the competition of people running for office, selection by the people of representatives in periodic elections, limitations on the power elected representatives can exercise while in office, and removal of the incumbent representatives if they fail to perform to the people's satisfaction. In sum, the ultimate control within a representative democracy rests with the people who elect and hold accountable a representative government.

Representative democracy is based on the principles of free and regular elections, a broad suffrage, and the existence of a party capable of forming an alternative government.[17] A fuller discussion and analysis of representative democracy was presented in Chapter 2, where it was contrasted with the concept of participatory democracy. In addition, it was argued that social work ideology is more consistent with participatory democracy as a model than with the liberal choice of representative democracy.

According to liberals universal suffrage has led to a transformation of political systems in Western democracies from institutionalized ruling-class governments of the eighteenth and nineteenth centuries to open and democratic structures, where the ordinary citizen now has direct and immediate access to his or her elected representative. However, "modern society has become considerably more complex during the twentieth century and 'political power' has become more 'diffused' and more 'corporate.'"[18] In other words, governments are more involved in a whole range of issues and areas, and a host of competing interests and pressure groups have emerged whose purposes are to influence the decisions of elected representatives.

The above brings us to the second fundamental political belief of liberals – that in a representative (liberal) democracy political power is divided among competing interest groups so that no one group dominates another, let alone dominates the government. This view of political power is called pluralism. The government acts as an independent arbitrator of these competing interest groups, controlling their activities by a set of rules called the law through which it acts as the guardian of the public interest and of individual rights. Thus, it is claimed, no government can fail to respond to the wishes of its citizens because the individual is heard through his or her membership in particular interest groups and at election time.

Few serious commentators believe that liberal representative democracies are totally accessible. Some of the limitations of the pluralist view are: (1) as with any type of competition there will be winners and losers, so that the strongest and best organized interest groups will have their interests prevail over their counterparts; (2) not everyone belongs to an organized interest group; (3) some powerful interest groups may gain sectional advantage at the expense of the general welfare; and (4) the elites within the various interest groups may make decisions that are not responsive to the needs or wishes of the memberships.

View of Social Problems

Unlike neo-conservatives, liberals do not place the blame for social problems squarely on the shoulders of the individual or his/her family. "They accept the failure of the market to meet basic needs, the inability of the contemporary family to meet needs it supposedly met in the past and that economic growth will not, on its own, abolish poverty."[19] The imperfections of capitalism cause problems for some people, and this perception is different from the neo-conservative belief that the individual causes problems for him or herself. In other words, where neo-conservatives attribute social problems to weakness, deviance, or heredity of the individual, liberals attribute such problems to social disorganization inherent in an industrial, capitalist society.

Although liberals focus more on society as the source of social problems, the personal deficiency view is not dropped completely. Society is viewed as a complex whole consisting of individuals interacting within numerous interdependent social systems such as the family, the workplace, and the school. Liberals believe that these systems are based on consensus and have legitimate functions that contribute to the healthy functioning of society because they are expected to integrate individuals into the larger society.[20] They recognize, however, that the numerous interdependent social systems that comprise society are not perfect and may not adequately provide the resources needed for healthy functioning. The various systems may get out of tune with one another in a society that experiences urbanization, industrialization, technological change, migration, and so on. These movements or forces upset the equilibrium among systems and between people and social systems, thus precipitating social disorganization. In turn, this disorganization produces stress and personal disorganization – mental illness, alcoholism, family breakdown, crime, spousal and child abuse, even community disintegration.[21] Because social problems are caused by some systems being out of tune with one another, the solution to the problem is to fine-tune these systems and restore equilibrium. This may involve personal change and/or system change, but in all cases "such changes are accommodative to the status quo."[22]

From the disciplinary vantage point of social work, the social disorganization view of social problems is an improvement over the personal deficiency view held by neo-conservatives because it recognizes the role that society plays in creating these problems. The systems perspective of liberalism is found in most major introductory social work texts and in the curricula of most schools of social work. An outgrowth of this perspective is the ecological view of social problems, which assumes an "optimal goodness of fit" between the individual and society.[23] Thus, if personal disorganization occurs the social worker would try to change either the individual or a particular sub-system or both. This approach has contributed to a plethora of generalist and/or eclectic social work approaches. However, because liberals believe that our present liberal democratic social order, although flawed, is superior to all others, then any social change proposed by the liberal worker will be limited to fine-tuning the system rather than overhauling it. Any change will occur *within* the system and will not involve a fundamental change *of* the system. That is, after the change, liberal capitalism will still be intact.

In sum, liberals believe that social problems occur mainly because of instrumental or technical flaws in the capitalist system that cause personal disorganization for some people. They also believe that the capitalist system is the most efficient form of economic organization and must be preserved. Therefore, the response to social problems is not to alter the system drastically but to: (1) purge it of as many inefficiencies as possible by way of minor social reform (i.e., system-tinkering); and (2) purge it of injustices by tending to those persons who are hurt by the system.

This view of social problems is much more humane and benign than that held by neo-conservatives. Liberals believe that even when people conform to their roles in society and attempt to carry out their social responsibilities, they will sometimes experience problems because of events (technological and cultural changes, etc.) beyond their control. Thus, weaker members of society may succumb to the stresses they experience and will require care, cure, and protection. This approach to social problems has been termed "humanist liberal."[24] In spite of this humanistic aspect, liberals share two views with neo-conservatives with respect to social problems. First, liberals see individuals rather than social classes or social groupings as casualties of capitalism. Individuals remain the central unit of analysis rather than sexism, racism, and so on. Second, neither liberals nor neo-conservatives give a serious consideration to the possibility that the unequal distribution of resources in society may have a connection to social problems.[25]

View of Social Welfare

Liberals accept the social welfare state as an instrument for correcting and modifying the negative aspects of capitalism. They do not see the welfare state as a means for pursuing social equality or for promoting social or economic change.[26] Its role is to be reactive (i.e., to deal with existing social problems) rather than to be proactive (i.e., to use the welfare state to achieve greater equality or to extend democracy into areas outside of the political sphere).

A primary goal of a liberal social welfare state is to achieve for all citizens the "social minimum." This concept has been described by Leonard Marsh, architect of Canada's social security system, as "the realization that in a civilized society, there is a certain minimum of conditions without which health, decency, happiness and a 'chance in life' are impossible."[27] In other words, society should use the welfare state to guarantee a minimum income to purchase the basic necessities of life and to ensure that everyone has access to basic (minimum) levels or standards of health care, housing, and education. However, liberals do not believe that it is the responsibility of governments to provide more than a minimum. A social welfare system that has as its primary goal a social minimum was described in Chapter 2. It was argued that such a welfare system, termed the "social security state" or "institutional model," although containing some humanistic elements, must be rejected by progressive social workers because of its lack of egalitarian ideals. It does not seek to reduce inequalities above the social minimum, nor does it promote solidarity or attempt to extend social, economic, or political democracy.

The institutional conception of welfare is based on the assumption that industrialization and urbanization are natural processes of human progress,[28] and while they have brought higher standards of living to many people they have also brought disruption to some people who have had to bear most of the social costs of industrial progress. These people, it is argued by liberals, should be protected and compensated by state welfare programs. Unlike the neo-conservative residual conception of welfare, people in need are not considered to be lax, immoral, or irresponsible but are considered genuinely in need. Therefore, there is a reduced use of the humiliating means test, little suggestion of abnormalcy, and decreased stigma attached to social welfare programs. The institutional conception does not do away with family responsibility, but it recognizes that in a modern, complex industrial society families may need help in carrying out their obligations. Social welfare programs represent a first line of defence against the exigencies of a capitalist society, not a residual function. That is, the institution of welfare should take its place alongside all other social institutions in society rather than coming into play only after all other social institutions have failed. This view dispenses with moralizing about the shortcomings of people in need. In short, industrialization, urbanization, and the development of the welfare state are viewed as normal, logical, evolutionary, and inevitable processes in human progress. The purpose of the welfare state, according to this view, is not to change society but to make good for its defects.

Social Work Practice within the Liberal Paradigm

Because we in Canada live in a liberal democratic state most of our social work practice is determined by the values, beliefs, and tenets of liberalism. Galper argues that the greatest determinant of the kind of practice that social workers will engage in is the social-economic-political culture in which social work operates.[29] In other words, not only is the social welfare system a reflection of the larger society, so, too, is social work practice. Taken together they form a paradigm, and in the case of Canada it is a liberal paradigm.

The above is not to suggest that social work practice in Canada is based purely on liberalism. Social work ideology, itself, is another major determinant of the nature of social work practice. For example, social work generally subscribes to egalitarianism, and some of social work practice in Canada lies outside the liberal paradigm, especially that which seeks to transform the capitalist system. (Certainly, however, this is not yet an integral part of many social workers' practice.) Two other determinants of the nature of social work practice are historical continuity and competing paradigms. Canada was a conservative society before World War Two; thus, our social welfare system and our social work practice have retained some features of control and coercion. The paradigms competing with liberalism in Canada are neo-conservatism, which supports the retention of coercive social work practices, and social democracy, which seeks the transformation of Canada from a capitalist to a social democratic state. In spite of these other influences, however, social work practice today in Canada is primarily based on liberal values.

Social workers carry out basically three activities within the liberal paradigm: (1) personal reform based mainly on general systems theory; (2) limited social reform based mainly on the ecological model of practice; and (3) advocacy based on a pluralist view of society. The nature of these activities is determined by the liberal belief that social problems are caused by social disorganization, an undesirable but unavoidable outcome of capitalism. And because they can do nothing about the occurrence of social disorganization, social workers must focus their attention on its negative consequences.

One way of dealing with the effects of social disorganization is to take those people who have fallen out of the game and direct them back to the starting point. They must be counselled and helped to learn more effective methods and patterns of communication so that they can enter into and maintain healthy relationships in all areas of their life. Or, they must be rehabilitated or resocialized so that their attitudes and behaviour are more congruent with the expectations that society places on them. Or, they must undergo psychotherapy and have their ego defence mechanisms strengthened so that they can better cope with competing and conflicting demands imposed on them. General systems theory is widely used by social workers in this area because of its assumption that the system (society) is basically okay but that some people need help getting back into it or coping with it.

Another possible way of helping those people who are negatively affected by social disorganization is to try and make some changes in the person's immediate environment. Given that the capitalist system has some flaws, it may be possible to make minor reforms without affecting the working of the overall system. This could mean the removal of a family member, for example, in the case of family tension and dysfunction. Or it might mean a change in a public school's policy or program to better accommodate children from a disadvantaged group. Or it could mean some labour legislation to make work conditions less stressful. These changes are reactive, as they focus on the effects of social disorganization and not on its causes. Many would argue that the root cause is the capitalist system itself. The ecological approach is often used with this activity as the ecological model assumes that a "goodness of fit" or natural harmony exists between the person and society. What is not considered is that the system could be bad and that we are looking for a goodness of fit between a person and a bad system.

A third area where social workers within the liberal paradigm often find themselves working is that of advocacy. Much time and effort is expended by social workers in attempting to obtain programs, services, compensation, and/or recognition of various individuals and groups in society who are injured by the capitalist system. Promoting the well-being of the homeless by advocating for housing programs and lobbying government for job-protection legislation for minorities are examples of advocacy work, which again focuses on the consequences and not the causes of social disorganization. It is based on the pluralist view that society consists of competing interest groups, with some winning and others losing. The job of social workers is often to help the losers get back into the competition.

These three areas of social work are based on the belief that the liberal capitalist system is superior although it causes problems for some people. The job of social work is to work with capitalism's casualties for mainly humanitarian reasons. By doing so, social workers working within the liberal paradigm do not connect these people with economic structure, class, race, or gender. To make these connections we must look to paradigms other than neo-conservatism and liberalism.

Canada as a Liberal State

The political science literature reveals that there are three major political ideologies in Canada: conservatism, liberalism, and socialism.[30] There has been influence from other ideological perspectives, such as populism, progressivism, social credit, and nationalism, but these have not been as influential, as distinct, or as long lasting as the three major political ideologies. And, although Canada has three major political ideologies, they have not been and are not now of equal strength. There is agreement in the literature that the dominant and pervasive political ideology in Canada since World War Two has been liberalism[31]:

> . . . liberalism is not just numerically dominant [in Canada]. It dominates because it is the ideology of the dominant class: it has the full force of the state, church, media, and educational system behind it: it has been trained into all of us.[32]

For the most part all three major political parties in Canada are steeped in liberal ideology. The federal Liberal Party adheres to the beliefs, principles, and values discussed in this chapter. It has been the dominating and ruling party of the federal government of Canada for most of this century. The Progressive Conservative Party of Canada, although ideologically conservative at one time, and although it has adopted several neo-conservative policies under the Mulroney governments, is now essentially a liberal party.

> The national Conservative political party has been immersed in liberal ideology throughout that period [the past half-century], to such an extent, in fact, that it is indistinguishable from the national Liberal Party at the level of party policies and principles.[33]

Even the national New Democratic Party, which claims to be a social democratic political party, "has survived as a liberal reform movement, rather than as a fundamentally different ideological position."[34]

The fact that liberalism has been and is the dominant political ideology in Canada is of considerable importance as the context for the development of the Canadian social welfare state. As liberalism replaced conservatism as the dominant ideology of Canada beginning in the 1940s, Canada's social welfare state has gradually shifted away from a residual form toward an institutional form of welfare[35] (notwithstanding some of the regressive policies of federal and provincial governments in Canada in the past few years). Social policy and social welfare choices are limited or bound by the social, economic, and political beliefs of liberalism. Obviously, those who subscribe to an established dominant ideology will not purposely seek its transformation or undoing. In fact, the elite or dominant class will attempt to protect and strengthen the ideology they adhere to because, in so doing, they protect and strengthen their own positions in society. Thus, social policy in Canada does not threaten individualism, capitalism, inequality, or any other pre-eminent value of liberalism. In sum, Canada is a liberal society and its social welfare system not only reflects liberalism and its attendant values, it reinforces them as well.

Critique of the Liberal Paradigm

A few words must be said about the theoretical incapacity of the liberal paradigm to explain certain social, economic, and political phenomena in a liberal society. Marchak provides an impressive amount of data that reveal some realities of Canadian society that liberalism does not explain: there is poverty in the midst of affluence; there is evidence of interference in the political process by privately owned corporations; there is a persistent division of the population that liberals refuse to recognize as a class division but that otherwise is inexplicable; and the decisions of large corporations more profoundly affect the lives of people than do the actions of politicians. These empirical facts of a liberal society are not accounted for by liberal ideology.[36]

Liberalism accounts for differences among individuals in terms of quality of life as due to individual differences in talent or effort or due to imperfections in the system. According to liberals, the consequences of the former can be alleviated and the latter can be corrected or reformed. However, the evidence does not substantiate these beliefs[37] but suggests, rather, that there are consistent and persistent differences among identifiable groups in Canada with respect to wealth, power, and access to goods, services, and social institutions. The evidence also shows that these differences are attributable *not* to individual characteristics but to social characteristics such as ethnicity, gender, age, place of residence, and family of origin. The major criticism of liberalism is that it has failed to reform the system to correct the causes of these differences. Writing on the Canadian situation, Marchak articulates this criticism:

> Regional inequalities persist in spite of equalization payments; poverty persists in spite of a welfare system; the taxation system is finally unable to redress the considerable imbalances between the rich and the poor. These are puzzles that the liberal ideology, with its emphasis on individual achievement, equality of opportunity, a market-place for competing talents, and an openness to reform, cannot explain.[38]

A major criticism of welfare capitalism (i.e., the welfare state in a liberal-capitalist society) is that although it was set up to modify the negative impact of capitalism on people (i.e., humanize capitalism), it actually reinforces capitalism and thus, indirectly, contributes to many of the problems it seeks to eliminate. The reason for this is hardly surprising. The social welfare state is like any other social institution. It has been established within the social, economic, and political context of liberalism and is bound to reflect and support the context from which it comes and within which it operates. In addition to attending to the immediate needs of some people who are hurt by capitalism, it also carries out socialization, social control, and stabilization functions for the prevailing social order by reinforcing the norms, behaviours, institutions, and values of liberalism.[39]

> Paradoxically, then, implicit in the social services is the affirmation of oppression and exploitation of humans by humans, and the negation of equality of rights, responsibilities, and dignity and of genuine liberty and self-actualization for all. The social services are thus revealed not as part of the solution of issues of provision in our society, but as a factor in the maintenance of the human problems they pretend to treat and prevent.[40]

Table 4.1 compares and contrasts the ideals of social work with those of liberalism. The differences between the two sets of ideals are not as great as they are between neo-conservatism and social work. However, the differences and contradictions between liberalism and social work ideals are too great to be reconciled. With respect to social beliefs, although liberalism believes in a certain amount of humanism, it also subscribes to individualism and inequality, which contradict social work's beliefs in community and equality. And although liberalism subscribes to a limited amount of government intervention, it does not believe that society's resources should be distributed equitably among all citizens. Liberalism's belief in representative democracy and pluralism contrasts with the social work belief in participatory democracy. As a consequence of the above differences in ideals and values, liberalism holds a different view of the nature and purpose of the welfare state than does social work. Whereas liberalism perceives the social welfare state as a means of providing people with the social minimum, progressive social work believes the purpose of the social welfare state is to go beyond providing a bare minimum by promoting equality of living conditions, solidarity among citizens, and a sense of community.

With respect to social work practice it has been suggested here that: (1) a liberal society actually causes many of the problems that social work seeks to resolve; and (2) social work practice within liberal boundaries actually reinforces and perpetuates many of the inequities social work claims to be against. Thus, it seems that the social work profession should reject the liberal paradigm if it is to remain true to its own values, beliefs, and principles. This does not mean that social work should abandon the three basic social work activities practised within the liberal paradigm – personal reform, social reform, and advocacy. It does mean, however, that the limitations of these activities must be recognized and that another dimension of social work practice must accompany them. This other dimension, referred

Table 4.1

Overview of Liberalism and Social Work Ideals

	Liberalism	*Social Work*
Social Beliefs	Freedom Individualism Inequality (all the above modified by humanitarianism and pragmatism)	Humanitarianism (humanism) Community Equality
Economic Beliefs	Competitive capitalism with some government intervention (i.e., mixed economy)	Government intervention Social priorities dominate economic decisions Equitable distribution of society's resources
Political Beliefs	Representative democracy Pluralism	Participatory democracy in both governmental and non-governmental areas
View of Social Welfare	An instrument to modify negative aspects of capitalism Ideal = institutional model Provides a social minimum	An instrument to promote equality, solidarity, and community Ideal = structural model
Nature of Social Work Practice	Personal reform Limited social reform Advocacy	Treat people with respect Enhance dignity and integrity Facilitate self-determination and self-realization Accept differences Advocate and promote social justice

to in this book as structural or transformational practice, is the subject of later chapters.

Liberal Hegemony in Social Work

One of the characteristics of a dominant paradigm is that it is able to reproduce itself by socializing members of society into accepting the structures and social relationships it espouses. Literature and the media, for example, shape the thoughts and understandings of members of society. This socialization or reproduction is not necessarily a conspiratorial activity on the part of the ruling elite. However, it is only logical to expect that the people who run the media and people who write books and articles would reflect their world views and understandings of subjects in their work. Social work is no different. Most social work educators and writers in North America have been socialized not only into liberal societies but into a liberal view of social welfare and social work as well. Given this socialization, it should not be surprising that most of the social work literature in North America is accommodative to the liberal paradigm. A few Canadian examples are presented below to illustrate this point.

Three widely used introductory (and above-introductory) textbooks in schools of social work on the Canadian welfare state are Andrew Armitage's *Social Welfare in Canada,*[41] Dennis Guest's *The Emergence of Social Security in Canada,*[42] and Frank McGilly's *An Introduction to Canada's Public Social Services.*[43] Most social work students have been exposed to one or more of these texts (particularly Armitage and Guest, since McGilly's book is relatively recent) during the course of their studies. What do students learn about society, social welfare, and the relationship between the two by reading these books? In a word, students learn liberalism.

Although societal flaws are pointed out in each book, none of the three authors calls for a different social order. Carniol points out that Armitage analyses industrialization to show how it causes disorganization, which in turn brings about social welfare provisions[44] – in other words, a liberal view of social problems and social welfare. Four of the five themes in Guest's historical overview of the development of the Canadian welfare state are liberal notions and/or goals (the fifth theme explores the division of powers under the British North America Act): (1) the shift from a residual model of welfare to an institutional model is a laudable goal; (2) a goal of the Canadian welfare state has been to provide a basic minimum to all Canadians; (3) the cause of dependency has been redefined from one of individual fault to the consequences of industrialization and urbanization; and (4) a growth of citizenship status has occurred with the growth of the welfare state. McGilly writes unabashedly from a liberal perspective: ". . . the assumptions and predilections underlying this text may be characterized as *liberal, pluralist,* and *interventionist.*"[45] His stated definition of social welfare is "*society's struggle to keep up with the consequences of advancing industrialization.*"[46] As Carniol notes, such logic implies that social welfare services exist only "because of their humanitarian values, which are consistent with our society's desire to implement minimal standards of social responsibility."[47]

There are no Canadian introductory social work textbooks of the same stature as the social welfare texts discussed above. This means that Canadian social work students tend to be exposed to standard American introductory social work textbooks, which make prominent use of liberal approaches to social work, such as systems theory, ecological models, eclectic methods, and so on. The few Canadian textbooks on social work are similar in orientation (i.e., liberal humanism) to most of the American texts.[48] Shankar Yelaja's *An Introduction to Social Work Practice in Canada*[49] is framed in the ecological perspective, as is Lawrence Shulman's *The Skills of Helping Individuals and Groups,*[50] where the focus is on mediation (striving for a goodness of fit) between the individual and society. There is no questioning in these books of the fundamental nature of our present liberal-capitalist society or suggestion that social work consider a different paradigm.

In conclusion, social workers, like all Canadian citizens, are socialized into a liberal paradigm and because they work within a liberal social welfare institution their practice will reflect, protect, and promote the liberal view of how society should operate. Rather than challenging inequality or the capitalist system, which is based on inequality, social work in Canada has favoured large-scale government programs to compensate for the chronic and acute ills of an industrial liberal society and to ameliorate the resultant suffering. In identifying with liberalism the social work profession has accepted, almost uncritically, the notion that more and larger social service programs can overcome society's multiple social problems. Viewing social problems as technical matters rather than as political or moral problems, Canadian social workers have become planners, researchers, administrators, and front-line workers of ever-increasing social service bureaucracies. This approach to social problems, where more services and programs are seen as the solution to social problems, contrasts with the neo-conservative belief that fewer services and programs are needed. It also contrasts with the social democratic and Marxist belief that the issue is not one of more or fewer social services but of a different social order.

5

The Social Democratic Paradigm

Because social democracy and the next paradigm to be examined – Marxism – are associated with socialist ideology, a section on socialism precedes the discussion of social democracy. The major reason for including an overview of socialism is to dispel the following myths sometimes associated with socialism – it represents a single unified social doctrine; it is anti-democratic and totalitarian; and the recent events in Eastern Europe prove that socialism is unworkable and all but dead.

Socialism

Socialism to North Americans is probably the least understood and most misunderstood of all schools of political thought. The terms associated with the range of political and theoretical positions within socialism, such as anarchism, communism, Marxism, social democracy, and syndicalism, cause confusion. As well, part of our North American liberal/ conservative socialization is that socialism has been presented to us by the media, by our educational system, by our politicians, and by our other social institutions as totalitarian and atheistic. This is especially so in the United States, where a psychology of Cold War paranoia existed for so many years. The United States is probably the only Western democracy without a socialist political party at the national level. Canada does have a federal socialist party, the New Democratic Party, but it has never placed higher than third in any national election. There have, however, been socialist governments in some of the provinces.[1]

In spite of the vagueness and the negative picture painted of it in North America, socialism has strong appeal to many people all over the world, with socialist governments having been democratically elected in all continents except North America. And even in North America socialist ideas have been popular with many groups, including progressive social workers. As a political theory socialism is a relative newcomer compared to conservatism and liberalism, but it has emerged in the twentieth century as a set of ambitious philosophical and political doctrines with a vision of human nature that connects the two.[2] One writer has defined socialism as:

> ... an alternative to a society still based largely on private ownership and private profit. Generations of reformers and revolutionaries envisaged a world in which there would be no great inequalities of income and wealth, where common ownership would prevail, where economic (and political) power would be more evenly distributed, where ordinary people would have greater control over their lives and over the conditions of their work, in which deliberate planning for the common good of society would replace (at least in part) the elemental forces of the marketplace.[3]

There are certain characteristics that all schools of socialist thought accept, although in varying degrees. Four of particular importance are: (1) a planned economy geared toward the fulfilment of human need of all rather than a free market geared to profits for a few; (2) public ownership of productive property for the benefit of all rather than private ownership for the benefit of a restricted circle of private owners; (3) equality of condition, or at least to reduce, as much as possible, major inequalities of wealth, income, social status, and political influence; and (4) a belief that selfishness is the result of living in our present flawed social institutions and that social change can produce less selfish people who are concerned with the welfare of others.[4] These four characteristics or objectives will result from and, at the same time, support each other. Flowing from these four characteristics are certain socialist policy objectives such as an elimination of privilege in all its forms, an opposition to inheritance, a defence of the welfare state, and a strong affiliation with the labour movement.[5]

While these characteristics represent the major areas of consensus among all schools of socialism there is a fundamental source of disagreement among socialists – how to obtain and maintain the political power necessary to realize their common objectives. Disagreement among socialists tends to occur mainly over the means to achieve certain ends and not on the ends or goals themselves. A few historical events of modern socialism are highlighted below to distinguish for the reader some of the differences among the major socialist camps.[6]

Although socialism has a long history dating back to an early association with Christianity, it was given its classic formulation by Karl Marx and Friedrich Engels in their *Communist Manifesto* (1848). They departed from their utopian socialist predecessors by rejecting the belief that social change for the betterment of humanity could occur by appealing to reason. Marx and Engels believed that socialism could only come about by the political victory of the working class (i.e., the proletariat). Marx's attitude toward capitalism was one of total rejection rather than reform and he devoted most of his intellectual efforts to proving how it was both inhuman and unworkable.

Marx believed that the contradictions of capitalism – its association with imperialism and wars, overproduction, cyclical and deepening recessions, worsening conditions of workers – and the alienation of the working class would eventually become so intolerable that the working class, led by socialist intellectuals such as Marx himself, would eventually take over the state and use it to abolish capitalism. A system of social and economic collectivism termed *communism* would then be instituted by the proletariat. This system would involve communal ownership of all property and a classless social structure, and work would be directed by and performed willingly in the interests of the community as a whole – "from each according to his/her ability, to each according to his/her needs."[7] At this advanced stage of development, the state would wither away as "people would learn to conduct their affairs without a centralized apparatus of coercion."[8] According to Marx, all forms of domination and hierarchy would disappear.

Marx did not believe that the transformation from capitalism to socialism was automatic – it would require a deliberate political struggle on the part of the proletariat. Marx's view of the nature of this political struggle has been a source of major disagreement among Marxist scholars. One group makes the case that based on the number of times Marx (and Engels) advocated forcible measures (i.e., violent revolution) as the means for workers to assume political power and based on the number of times that Marx denounced reform as the means to transcend capitalism, there can be little doubt that his real convictions lay in *revolutionary socialism.*[9] Another group of Marxist scholars points out the occasions when Marx and Engels suggest or admit that a peaceful overturn of the social order might be possible and conclude that Marx actually had a dual approach to gaining power: (1) *revolutionary socialism* (use of forcible measures) in those countries where constitutionalism and rule of law did not exist; and (2) *evolutionary socialism* (election of an organized workers' political party) in constitutional countries with a parliamentary system.[10] The revolutionary socialist writers explain Marx's comments on peaceful means as tactical concessions he made to the reformist wing of the socialist party so that it would not split from the major party.

Whether or not Marx's revolutionary theory excluded peaceful means, his emphasis on forcible revolution caused a group of English socialists to repudiate revolutionary socialism and to advocate evolutionary socialism instead. This group formed the Fabian Society in England (1884), which developed social democracy in Britain and eventually created the country's official social democratic political party, the Labour Party (1906). The Fabian Society represents one of the earliest divisions among socialists and was based on disagreement, not with the goals of socialism, but with the means of achieving them. Evolutionary socialism in the form of social democracy spread to Germany in the latter part of the nineteenth century and soon after became the dominant form of socialism in Europe. Only in Russia did the revolutionary socialists remain in the majority.[11]

Social democratic parties have been elected in most Western European countries and have actually been the governing parties for most of the post-war era in the Scandinavian countries. Socialism, in the form of social democracy, is a familiar part of contemporary politics, but it has been considerably diluted since its original Marxian version. The modern-day social democratic paradigm is presented in the next section of this chapter.

Although social democracy has become the major school of socialist thought in Western Europe, revolutionary socialism held sway in Russia. The absence of a parliament and a constitution in Russia during the early years of the twentieth century made evolutionary socialism irrelevant. There were no democratic institutions or legal working-class organizations that could be used as the base of operations to transform Russian society from within. In February, 1917, Czar Nicholas II was dethroned, a constitutional democracy established, and in October of the same year Vladimir Lenin led the Bolshevik Revolution and seized control of the state. Lenin deviated from Marx's theory of revolutionary socialism because the conditions in Russia were so different from those of Western Europe. Faced with an economically and industrially backward country with a small working class and with a large peasant class, Lenin believed the socialist party had to be controlled from the top and that revolutionary consciousness had to be transmitted by intellectuals to the working class.[12] This, of course, was inconsistent with Marx's belief that the revolution was to grow from the spontaneous class consciousness of the proletariat or working class.

To solidify his control over the country and the socialist party, Lenin centralized political power, calling it "democratic centralism." Lenin rationalized this action as being consistent with Marx's revolutionary theory. Marx believed that there had to be a transition period between the end of capitalism and the beginning of advanced communism. Marx did not believe that people could throw off the yoke of capitalism one day and live as adjusted, productive communists the next day. A period of adjustment and transition was needed for the technological and social foundations to be put in place that were necessary for the achievement of an advanced communist state. The old state machinery must be destroyed and a new state constructed to serve as the means to the attainment of the final communist commonwealth where there is neither oppressor nor oppressed.[13] Marx's strategy for this transition period was for a government comprising workers to be set up that would actually function as a "dictatorship of the proletariat." This government/dictatorship would ignore the rules of law until the revolutionary fervour and violence subsided, and would gradually phase itself out as the transition to communism was made (i.e., the state would wither away).[14] Marx called this transition period socialism. During this transitional stage between capitalism and advanced communism the means of production would be taken into public ownership and the provisional government would oversee a new order of legality and a new system of rights that would allow the emergence of true common ownership and the eventual abolition of the state.[15]

Lenin exercised Marx's notion of dictatorship of the proletariat and outlawed all political opposition, even socialist opposition. His extensive use of dictatorship and his constant postponement of the withering away of the state appalled socialists of Western Europe. As a result an irreparable split in the world socialist movement occurred. Those who approved of Lenin and his methods organized themselves in communist parties in every country and adopted Marxism modified by Leninism as the official party ideology. Those who opposed Lenin regrouped under the social democratic banner and became the most prominent school of socialism in the Western world. Russian communism, with an extended dictatorship of the proletariat, was implemented by Lenin, developed by Stalin, and imposed by force on the less advanced nations of Eastern Europe using a distorted version of Marx's theory of revolutionary socialism as a rationale. Fourteen semi-autonomous regions and countries in Eastern Europe and western Asia were eventually annexed by Russia under the title of the Union of Soviet Socialist Republics.

Communist parties still exist in most Western European countries. The label applied to them today is "Euro-communism" and they differ from Russian communism in one very important area – political freedom. Although Soviet leaders did bring many reforms to the economic system in line with Marxist egalitarian ideology, they did not do the same in the political arena. Public ownership replaced private ownership and inequalities in wealth, income, and life chances were greatly reduced in the Soviet Union. However, the egalitarian and democratic elements of Marxism did not spread to the political life of the Soviet Union. Its political system may be described as totalitarian and monistic. No political parties except for the Communist Party were legally allowed, no other ideologies were permitted expression, and civil and political rights were denied. In effect, the Soviet Union had a socialist economy and a totalitarian political system so that any social security experienced by citizens was overshadowed by the existence of political insecurity.[16] This totalitarian nature of Soviet society violated Marxist socialism, and Euro-communist parties took exception to it. Euro-communism, unlike Soviet communism, subscribes to a pluralistic and parliamentary democracy where more than one ideology and one political party are allowed.

The fall of the Russian-led Soviet empire is now history. However, as this brief description of socialism suggests, the fall of Russian communism does not represent the fall of socialism or its ideas. Russian communism represented one school of socialist thought, albeit a prominent school. Many would argue it represented a distorted view of socialism because all that was achieved politically was the transfer of control from an old ruling class of aristocrats to a new elite of bureaucrats. Socialism originated as a doctrine concerned about the oppression of the working class. It would be difficult to find a true socialist today who would argue that the Russian experience contributed to an emancipation of the proletariat in the former Soviet Union. It was, in a word, an embarrassment to democratic socialists all over the world.

In sum, socialism does not represent a single unified ideology and it is not anti-democratic. Although the goals of socialism are essentially common to all schools, the major area of disagreement is the appropriate means to transcend capitalism. The fall of the Soviet bloc does not represent a failure of socialism. Its economic failures were due more to its centralized "command-administrative" socialism, which failed to generate stable growth and development, stifled workers' initiative, lagged behind in technological innovation, and misdirected new investment.[17] Its political failures were due more to its totalitarian practices. With the Soviet type of socialism gone, most socialists today hope that socialism will be able to learn from the mistakes of the Soviet experience, to reaffirm its claim to democracy, and to re-establish itself as the logical "political expression for collectivist and egalitarian impulses."[18]

Although there are several schools of socialist thought, the two major schools appear to be social democracy and Marxism. Many social welfare and social work writers divide socialists ideologically into two groups: (1) social democrats, who believe that social transformation of capitalism can occur by using the institutions within capitalism, such as the welfare state, trade unions, and the electoral process; and (2) Marxists, who believe that social transformation can occur only by using alternative organizations to state bureaucracies.[19] This division of socialists is adopted here and in the next chapter.

Social Democracy

Just as socialism consists of a range of theoretical and political divisions, social democracy occupies a wide area on the political spectrum, bordering on liberalism at one end and Marxism at the other. The divisions between social democracy and these other ideologies are not always clear.[20] For many people, social democracy is only a well-developed form of liberalism and it is a question whether or not social democracy is even a form of socialism. For others, social democracy is only a few steps away from Marxism. This chapter and the next will clarify these issues by presenting the similarities and the differences between social democracy and liberalism, and between social democracy and Marxism.

Most Canadian and British social policy writers, when writing about social democracy, use British Fabian social democracy as their reference point. This may be reasonable in terms of gaining an understanding of British social democratic values, beliefs, and principles. The danger, however, is that the British experience with social democracy may become the expectation for social democratic governments in all countries. Because the Labour government (Britain's social democratic party) did not fulfil the expectations that many socialists anticipated, the Marxists (and many social democrats) now believe that capitalism cannot be transformed into socialism with the election of a social democratic government. However, if one looks beyond Britain to Sweden, which has had a social democratic government for almost all the years since 1932, one might draw a different conclusion. This issue will be taken up later in this chapter.

Social Beliefs

Social democrats stress three central values – equality, freedom, and fellowship – and two derivative values – democratic participation (the derivative of equality and freedom) and humanitarianism (the derivative of equality and fellowship).[21]

Arguably, the primary social democratic value is equality, which rests on four interrelated grounds – social integration, economic efficiency, natural rights, and individual self-realization. With respect to social integration, social democrats believe that a reduction in inequalities reduces feelings of isolation or alienation and creates a greater sense of belonging or social cohesion.[22] With respect to economic efficiency, a society characterized by gross inequalities experiences little social mobility, which means that many talented people will not rise to a position where they can use their talents and abilities. With respect to natural rights, inequality means that some people have greater opportunity and/or greater power than others, not because of merit but because some are born into families of wealth and influence. Finally, inequality often denies the individual the opportunity to realize his or her full potential, which in effect diminishes people's basic humanity. In spite of a consensus that there must be greater equality in all areas of life, the social democrats do not agree on a definition of equality or on how much equality is desirable.[23]

Among the key social values social democrats hold, freedom ranks with equality. David Gil argues convincingly that freedom for all is the central socialist value but can only be achieved if greater social equality is attained first.[24] If some people have greater resources than others, they have greater freedom to control their conditions of life, which conversely means that others have less control or freedom to make choices with respect to their life conditions. Social democrats believe that genuine freedom for all can come about only through government action rather than, as neo-conservatives believe, through government inaction. Only government, according to the social democrat, can create the conditions of social equality vital for the attainment of freedom for all.

The third central social value of social democrats is fellowship or collectivism, which means "cooperation rather than competition, an emphasis on duties rather than rights, on the good of the community rather than on the rights of the individual, on altruism rather than selfishness."[25] A capitalist society does not subscribe to the value of solidarity. Rather, it encourages people to use their power and abilities for self-interest and to treat others not as people but as commodities to be bought, sold, or used to further one's own end. Social democrats reject such attitudes and behaviour.

Two other social values strongly held by social democrats – democratic participation and humanitarianism – were noted earlier. Democratic participation should extend to all areas of life, not just to the political and economic areas. For example, in the workplace employees should have a voice in the conditions of their work and employers should not be able to exercise arbitrary power or control over workers. In the areas of health and social services, lay people should have a say in formulating policies about the delivery of these services since they are the actual and potential beneficiaries. Social democrats believe also that people should be able to enjoy certain minimum standards of living and that social distress should be eliminated. Therefore, they would like to see a higher proportion of the nation's wealth spent on these goals, with proportionately more spent on deprived groups.[26]

Economic Beliefs

The central economic beliefs of social democrats are government intervention, public control of the means of production and distribution, and a more equitable distribution of income and opportunities. Just as social democrats do not agree on how much equality is desirable, neither do they agree on how much government intervention should occur or on the extent of public control of the means of production and distribution or on how equitable the distribution of income should be. Opinions vary from the Marxist belief that total public ownership is necessary to achieve socialist goals to the liberal belief that regulated capitalism is all that is necessary.

George and Wilding present five criticisms that social democrats have of a free market economy. (1) There is no social purpose or collective goal as individuals pursue their own interests, which result in social misery for many. (2) The free market is fundamentally unjust as it has no clear principles for distributing rewards other than a moral right to extract what one can without breaking the law. (3) The free market is undemocratic as decisions important to many, if made at all, are made by an elite few in privacy. (4) The free market is inefficient because without government regulation it leads to environmental devastation, regional economic disparities, periodic economic recessions, an oversupply of fundamentally useless products, and an undersupply of socially necessary goods and services. (5) The distribution of goods and services in a free market economy does not include goods and services needed by those who are disadvantaged by illness, age, or life circumstances such as widowhood.[27]

To overcome these inherent deficiencies of a free market economy the social democrats would attempt to replace the anarchy of capitalism and the motives of private gain by rational economic and social planning for the common good. In other words, economic mechanisms would be put in place to control the means of production and distribution. These mechanisms could include the Marxist notion of state ownership (i.e., nationalization of private ownership) as well as government regulation of private ownership and the development of workers' co-operatives, consumers' associations, and credit unions. The question of nationalization has caused a division in social democratic camps, with fundamentalists believing that nationalization is the only way to achieve socialist goals and reformists claiming that separation between ownership and control can achieve the same goals.

Both fundamentalist and reformist social democrats condemn gross inequalities of income, opportunities, and living conditions. Pay equity, progressive taxation policies, the elimination of inheritance of large fortunes, an emphasis on human rights, and affirmative action programs are mechanisms favoured by social democrats to reduce inequality. Again, the question of how much redistribution of resources is equitable or how far the wealth of the rich should be reduced is not answered unanimously by the social democrats.

Political Beliefs

The fundamental political beliefs of social democrats are: (1) the state has a positive role to play in society; (2) capitalism can be transformed into socialism by a social democratic government; and (3) the state should encourage broad participatory decision-making in all areas of life.

Social democrats view the state as an agent for redistributing benefits and resources. It is seen as acting independently of, and often in opposition to, market mechanisms.[28] Only the state, through legislation and government action, can protect the freedoms of the less powerful citizen from the ravages of the more powerful, and only the state can bring about certain changes and promote an ethic of collective preference over that of individual interest. Through the state the political process governs the economic process rather than the reverse – of economics determining politics. The rationality of planning, under a social democratic regime, guides society, not the magic forces of laissez faire.

Government planning, social democrats believe, can transform capitalism into socialism without endangering individual freedom, contrary to the belief of neo-conservatives.[29] Social democrats believe it is just as possible to plan for freedom as it is to plan for tyranny. Many social democrats claim that a social democratic government could use the state machinery (the government, the civil service, and the judiciary) to implement radical changes in capitalist society[30] and that over time, with proper public education about the benefits of its radical program, the citizenry would accept these changes and true democracy would flourish more than it does under capitalism. Social democrats, on the whole, believe that these changes must come through peaceful means and that violence would only contaminate socialism. Social democrats also believe that one of the major ways of transforming capitalism into socialism is to develop the social welfare state, which emphasizes distribution according to need and not according to one's social position.

Social democrats subscribe to the principle and practice of participatory decision-making. It is believed that this form of decision-making would spread responsibility, reduce power concentration, and increase productivity.[31] Social democrats would promote more worker control in industry and work organizations, more service-user involvement in the delivery of public services, such as health and social services, and more community development directed at boosting the power of people with respect to local, regional, and national governments. Of course, these involvements would essentially be of a decision-making nature and not merely of a cosmetic consultative nature.

View of Social Problems

Basically, two competing sets of theories in the sociological literature attempt to explain the nature of society and the nature and cause of social problems. These are *order* and *conflict* perspectives of society, which are rooted in nineteenth-century history and social thought. Essentially, order theories are of a social system characterized by equilibrium, stability, continuity, consensus, integration, and social control. Order theories perceive social problems to be caused when members of a society do not learn to revere its institutions or respect its rules.[32] As will be discussed in Chapter 8, neo-conservativism and liberalism adhere to order interpretations of society and social problems, whereas social democracy and Marxism adhere to conflict interpretations.

Conflict theories view the nature of society as a contested struggle among groups with opposed aims and perspectives.[33] In pursuing their own interests they are often in conflict with one another. Reasons and Perdue set out some of the major tenets of the conflict perspective. In the contested struggle among groups the state is an important agent because it is used as an instrument of oppression by the dominant class for its own benefit. Social inequality is a consequence of coercive institutions that favour the dominant groups, and this social inequality is a primary source of conflict.[34] In sum, conflict theorists see society as conflict-ridden rather than as stable, orderly, and integrated, and they question a social order marked by differences of race, class, gender, age, and so on.

Although there are several schools of conflict thought the two main theories, according to George and Wilding, are social conflict and class conflict.[35] The social conflict school believes that the sources of conflict are diverse and numerous and include such elements as race, religion, profession, region, gender, and economic status. Social democrats tend to subscribe to the social conflict analysis. The class conflict school sees the conflict between the two major economic classes – the owners of production and those who must work for them – as the most important conflict in society. And because class conflict originates from the production system of capitalism, the only way it can be resolved is to abolish the capitalist system itself. Class conflict theory is, of course, synonymous with Marxist theory.

Racism, poverty, pollution, and other social problems, from the social conflict view, are actually contests among various groups over the acquisition or control of desirable resources such as wealth, privilege, and political power. Because these issues are actually clashes of interest they represent political conflicts.[36] Conflict theorists would prefer to call these problems "political conflicts" or "social conflicts" because the term "social problems" implies some kind of social sickness that can be treated more successfully by the "dispassionate intervention of experts" than by political action.[37]

In short, social problems, according to social democrats, are not the result of deviance, as the neo-conservatives believe, or of industrialization, as the liberals believe, but are normal consequences of the way society is organized. Thus, they cannot be dealt with by technical means or administrative reforms. They can only be resolved by a reorganization of the society that caused the problems (conflicts) in the first place.

View of Social Welfare

When talking about socialist views of the welfare state we need to distinguish between a welfare state within a socialist society and a welfare state within a capitalist society. For all socialists (Marxists and social democrats) the ideal welfare system, which would be consistent with socialist values and an integral part of a socialist society, is what Mishra calls a "structural model" of welfare.[38] Although both social democrats and Marxists would subscribe to this ideal socialist model of welfare, they would differ in their views on the nature and functions of our present capitalist welfare state. Mishra outlines the socialist conception of a welfare state:

> Central to the socialist view of welfare is the notion that "to each according to his needs" should be the guiding principle of distribution. In other words collective consumption – that is, typically universal, comprehensive and free social services such as health and education – constitutes the basic model of distribution under socialism.[39]

Social democrats believe that the above form of equal distribution of societal resources is possible only after the production and distribution of all resources have come under state control (either by nationalization or by regulation). Only then will the market, the family, and private property cease to be the basic means of distribution of income and opportunities. The main feature of the structural model of welfare is that it considers welfare to be a central social value. The users of social services are not merely citizens entitled to a basic minimum of civilized life (as liberals believe) but members of a socialist community whose needs are to be met to the fullest extent possible.[40]

Consistent with the socialist principle of participation of people in all areas of life, the structural model of welfare includes citizen participation in social services decision-making rather than strict control by administrators and experts. This emphasis on lay power or deprofessionalization of the social services would necessitate a demystification of professional knowledge (e.g., medical knowledge) and a decrease in the power, status, and authority of professionals in the social welfare field. This does not mean that lay people would be delivering health, education, and other social services, but they would have a much greater say in how these services are to be delivered and how they are to be administered.

Another vital principle of the structural welfare state is prevention. Many socialists (particularly Marxists) do not believe that preventive services can be established in a capitalist system because: (1) social services are viewed by socialists as institutions that tend to problems created by a system that neglects human needs; and (2) where the social welfare state is controlled by professionals, primary consideration is given to professional interests rather than service-user interests. (For example, Mishra contends that the Soviet Union placed much greater emphasis on preventive medicine because lay people had more say than professionals concerning health policies.)

Although it is instructive to become informed about the social democratic ideal or preferred model of welfare, progressive social workers need to know the social democratic view of welfare capitalism. How does the welfare state in capitalist societies relate to the structural welfare model and to social democratic beliefs, principles, and values? If a social democratic party were elected to national office in Canada, for example, what would have to be done to its present welfare state to achieve social democratic goals?

Social democrats believe that the welfare state in capitalist societies has followed a course of historical pragmatism.[41] In other words, social problems accompanied industrialization, urbanization, and technological change and had to be attended to by the state. In the course of dealing with these problems the state has had to reconcile various group conflicts by compromise or by siding with one group and ultimately instituting a social policy to deal with the problem. Over time, this method of piecemeal social engineering has produced an accumulation of social policies that constitutes the welfare state.[42]

Social democrats value the welfare state for what it can and does achieve within a capitalist state. However, they believe that the welfare state should do more. For example: social welfare should help further justice and the prevention of problems rather than deal only with situations of injustice and the treatment of problems; social welfare should promote greater equality of opportunity; social welfare should focus on reduction of all inequalities, not just the elimination of poverty; and social welfare should promote greater control of social services by lay people rather than by bureaucratic administrators and experts.[43]

Perhaps the major belief of social democrats with respect to the social welfare state in a capitalist society is that it can be used as a stepping stone toward a socialist society. Because social welfare programs and services represent a break with the free market doctrine of distribution, social democrats believe that the advantages of such a system would be seen by the general public as preferable to that of the free market, thus aiding in the transformation from a capitalist to a socialist society. Social democrats are aware that a welfare state, by itself, will not provide a just society. This can only occur if the means of production and distribution come under public control – either by ownership or by regulation. However, the failure of the Labour government in Britain to live up to the expectations placed on it by social democrats has been interpreted by some to indicate that the welfare state only supports and strengthens capitalism, while others now see the road from capitalism to socialism as longer and more perilous than originally perceived.

Social Work Practice within the Social Democratic Paradigm

The nature of social work practice within our present capitalist society will be determined by the view of social democracy that one holds. In other words, if one views social democracy as a well-developed extension of liberalism (as many writers contend was the view of British Fabians), then that person's practice of social work will be quite different than if he or she believed that capitalism must be transformed into socialism in order to deal effectively with many of our modern social problems. The former would concentrate on a social work practice of individual and humanitarian care while the latter, in addition to performing tasks of individual and humanitarian care, would seek to create forces that would contribute to the transformation of capitalism to socialism.

Fabian social democracy, as will be argued below, violates too many principles of socialism even to be considered as socialism. Therefore, social work practice according to this view will not be discussed here as it would not differ significantly from liberal social work practice. An overview of social work practice based on the social democratic belief that the welfare state can be used as a stepping stone toward socialism is presented here.

Social democratic social work practice has a dual function: (1) to tend to the immediate and legitimate needs of people or groups of people who lose out in the ongoing group conflicts which occur in capitalist society over the acquisition of material resources and power; and (2) to work toward the transformation of capitalist society to one that adheres to the social, economic, and political beliefs and values of social democracy. That is, social work must aim toward the creation of a socialist state. Underpinning this view of social work practice is the belief that our present set of social arrangements can be transformed by working through the existing political and social institutions, which, according to the social democrats, "*are* relatively accessible, *are* democratic, and *are* therefore capable of radical reform."[44]

The above belief is different from that of Marxists, who believe that alternative organizations and institutions must be established outside the existing system to challenge the power of the capitalist state. In other words, social democrats believe that social work can contribute to radical changes of society by working within the existing system, but Marxists tend to believe that social work must work outside the existing system or it will become incorporated into the present social order and end up protecting it rather than changing it.

The dual function of social democratic social work – to provide practical, humanitarian care and to further the democratization and restructuring of society along socialist lines – means a politicized and radical social work profession. This does not mean, however, that the two functions are mutually exclusive – that you cannot carry out both at the same time. Indeed, as a reforming profession, social work must help simultaneously both the individual and society to evolve along more socially concerned lines. For example, a social democratic social worker may work with someone who is considered deviant or disruptive. The task would be to help this non-conformist to cope with his or her non-conforming but not necessarily to abandon it – an important qualification, as Pritchard and Taylor point out.[45] The non-conforming behaviour may not be at fault, but rather society's rules, norms, or expectations. More will be said about this in Chapter 8.

Much of social democratic social work practice at the micro level would be to normalize and depersonalize the problematic situations in which many people find themselves. In other words, the social worker would explore the social context of the situation with the service user and analyse it along social democratic lines to see if a relationship exists between the problem and capitalism. For example, if the problem is unemployment and over one million Canadians are unemployed, this does not mean that we have over one million unique personal problems. Rather, we have one social problem affecting over one million workers and their families. In other words, "the personal is political." As well as the incidence of unemployment, the reasons why capitalism needs and produces unemployment would be discussed with the service user. Subsequently, a plan of action would be jointly determined and would include helping the person deal with his or her individual situation of unemployment, at the same time exploring ways that can contribute to a transformation of the existing capitalist system.

At the macro level social democratic social workers, through their professional organization or association, would act:

> as a legitimate pressure-group operating within the present socio-political structure and campaigning for both specific policies and a general reorientation of strategy and/or philosophy (i.e., for policies based upon a more egalitarian, redistributive system which would also be far more concerned than at present with the achievements of social justice, the extension of welfare services and the protection of the rights of the underprivileged in society generally).[46]

The macro or political task, then, is to mobilize as much support as possible for social democracy, in general, and for social progress among and for social services users, in particular. Social democrats believe it is important to educate "both the 'advantaged' and the 'disadvantaged' in an acceptance of the interdependency of different sections of society."[47] The social work profession therefore must join forces with other socialistic organizations and institutions, such as the labour movement and social democratic political parties, to gain an ever-increasing control of the various institutions of the state and move eventually to a position where the attainment of a fully socialist system becomes possible. If the welfare state is to become a radical force for progressive social and political change, it is absolutely imperative that social work become radicalized. This is so because social work is a key sector within the welfare state structure and has an important influence on welfare state ideology.

Critique of the Social Democratic Paradigm

Some of the major criticisms levelled at social democracy are: it does not move capitalist society closer to a socialist society but only changes the face of capitalism; its anti-nationalization stance is inconsistent with one of the basic tenets of socialism; it leads to a centralized and elitist control of planning and decision-making; and the welfare state has not produced the desired reduction of inequalities. An overview of these criticisms and a response to each of them follows.

A common criticism of British social democracy is that although the social democratic Labour Party was the dominant political force in Britain for most of the sixties and seventies, it did not use this power to create an alternative to capitalism but adapted the labour movement to an acceptance of the existing system. Legitimation and public acceptance of social democracy in Britain seem to have been gained at the expense of socialism.[48] However, as mentioned previously, it does not logically follow that the course of social democracy in Britain must be the course of social democracy everywhere.[49] Writing from Sweden on that country's experience with a social democratic government for all the years between 1932 and the present (except for 1976-82), Himmelstrand *et al.* state that there are good theoretical and empirical reasons for "rejecting the simplistic notion of social democracy simply as a tool of capitalist development."[50] The authors present some recent Swedish social democratic reforms concerning the work environment and the relative power of labour and capital that would seem to change significantly the relations of production in a socialistic direction. Based on the Swedish experience, it would seem that social democracy may be used as a path to a socialist state, though this path is longer and more complex than originally conceived by social democrats.

A second criticism of social democracy, that its anti-nationalization stance is antithetical to socialism, is also rebutted by the Swedish example. Swedish social democratic policy has been to separate ownership of the means of production from its control. Rather than risking a huge backlash as a result of nationalizing industry, the Swedish Social Democratic government has gained control of industry through legislation and regulation. In other words, by regulating industry the Swedes can practically achieve the same economic and social goals as if they owned industry. In fact, the Swedes would point to the British experience of nationalization as contributing to capitalist development in that the compensation paid to the capitalists for nationalizing their firms was profitably reinvested elsewhere. One of the effects, then, was to see public industry subsidize private capitalism.[51] All this is not to say that Swedish social democrats are not interested in the labour force gaining capital ownership. Some of the recent Swedish workplace reforms move in this direction, but without use of the draconian action of nationalization.[52]

The criticism that social democracy leads to a centralized and elitist control of planning and decision-making is also based on the British experience. The trade union section of the Labour Party emphasized the democratic role of the working class within the transition to socialism, but the Fabians, who gained political control, actually opposed the idea of working-class control and mass participatory democracy.[53] The Fabians believed that the working class was an alien mass incapable of understanding the complexities of modern society. British social democracy thus consisted of substituting for the capitalist class an elite of disinterested experts to control the new socialist society, subject to control by the people through the parliamentary system.[54] Again, this elitist form of social democracy can be contrasted with the massive participation that goes into the decision-making process in Sweden. At any one time 200 to 300 parliamentary-sanctioned commissions of study[55] are looking at various public policy issues. All relevant individuals, organizations, and interest groups are consulted before a preliminary report is drafted. They are consulted again on the contents of the preliminary report, after which a final report is drafted and presented to Parliament for debate and policy formulation. The point to be made is that one of the fundamental social-political values of social democracy is participation in decision-making. It seems illogical to dismiss social democracy as elitist and undemocratic on the basis of what happened with one country's experience.

The final criticism of social democracy that will be looked at here is that it has not produced a significant reduction of inequalities. It was originally thought by social democrats that many socialist objectives, including greater equality, could be achieved through the welfare state. But as Ramesh Mishra points out, the British welfare state has failed to achieve a significant redistribution of income and opportunity.[56] Market forces have counteracted the effects of egalitarian policies (for example, fringe benefits have reduced the levelling effects of a progressive income tax system). Inequalities of income and wealth stubbornly persist in Britain and other social democratic countries. The universality of social services has meant that both the rich and poor alike have benefited from them. And social welfare has not resulted in an inter-class transfer of resources. "Those who use the social services by and large pay for them."[57] The response of the social democrats to this criticism is to acknowledge that there are deficiencies in the present welfare state. But they would argue that the welfare state is the creation of the Labour Party; without it many people would be much worse off than they are today; and with more time and the proper political will the welfare state can be further developed to the point where its socialistic aims can be achieved. Other social democratic writers, such as Furniss and Tilton, would argue that social democracy can achieve socialistic goals by pointing to Sweden as their model social welfare state because it has achieved much greater equality of income and opportunity than Britain and most other Western democracies.[58]

Table 5.1 shows that, unlike neo-conservatism and liberalism, there is a high degree of compatibility between the social democratic and social work paradigms. They share many of the same social, economic, and political beliefs and there are no contradictions between the two

Table 5.1
Overview of Social Democratic and Social Work Ideals

	Social Democracy	*Social Work*
Social Beliefs	Humanitarianism Collectivism Equality Freedom Democratic participation	Humanitarianism (humanism) Community Equality
Economic Beliefs	Government intervention Public control of the means of production and distribution Equitable distribution of income and opportunities	Government intervention Social priorities dominate economic decisions Equitable distribution of society's resources
Political Beliefs	Participatory decision-making in all areas of life Capitalism can be transformed by a social democracy The state has a positive role to play in society	Participatory democracy in both governmental and non-governmental areas
View of Social Welfare	Welfare capitalism can be used as a stepping stone to a socialist state Ideal = social welfare state or structural model	An instrument to promote equality, solidarity, and community Ideal = structural model
Nature of Social Work Practice	Provide practical humanitarian care to casualties of capitalism Further the democratization and restructuring of society along socialist lines	Treat people with respect Enhance dignity and integrity Facilitate self-determination and self-realization Accept differences Advocate and promote social justice

ideologies. Both have the same attitude toward the nature and some of the functions of the social welfare state. It would appear that social democracy (and eventually socialism) is one possibility as the kind of society that best meets and actualizes social work's values, principles, and ideals. If this is so, then a heavy emphasis would be placed on the structural components (restructuring society along socialist lines) of social work practice. In other words, social work practice would become much more like that described in this chapter than it is presently.

6

The Marxist Paradigm

Marxism

As mentioned in the previous chapter, the two most important schools of socialist thought are social democracy and Marxism. Marxism includes Karl Marx's own writings as well as the writings of others whose ideas and analyses are close to those of Marx. Marx's basic philosophy was humanistic, as he was deeply concerned about the well-being and life chances of the working class in Victorian England. With the rise of capitalism he saw the increasing degradation of industrial workers who had no control over their work process or product and who had to live in squalor, insecurity, and poverty. At the same time as workers' lives were reduced to a subsistence level, the industrial landowners (i.e., the capitalists) became enormously wealthy and their lives were greatly enriched materially and politically.[1] Marx's attitude toward this system was one of total rejection rather than reform, and he devoted most of his life seeking to prove that capitalism was both unworkable and inhuman.

Marx's view of welfare is that it is a social norm based on the values of solidarity and co-operation. "In concrete terms, welfare manifests itself in the social recognition of human need and in the organization of production and distribution in accordance with the criterion of need."[2] In a Marxist society production would be governed by social criteria and the distribution of the fruits of labour, produced through co-operation, would be distributed according to the needs of people. Thus, a welfare society in the Marxist sense is one where the well-being of people is of primary consideration and where the mode of production is set up to meet human need rather to make profits. To Marx, capitalism represented the very antithesis of a welfare society.[3]

For Marx, the central feature of any society is its mode of production – the way its system of productivity is organized. The mode of production determines the structure of society and its processes. In other words, the way society earns its living accounts for its political system, its educational system, the nature of its art and music, its ideology, its riches, its poverty, and how people relate to each other. The capitalist mode of production consists of the following structural (inherent) elements through which wealth, poverty, and inequality are generated and reproduced: private ownership of the means of production; production for profit; private property and inheritance; and the distribution of income and resources through the market mechanism.[4]

Marx did not believe that a welfare society could exist under capitalism. The dominance of the market as a distributive mechanism of income and life chances denies human need and social solidarity altogether. Coercion and competition rather than co-operation and solidarity are the bases of capitalist social organization. Welfare, as a central value, cannot make much headway in such a society. If welfare were to be institutionalized as a central value (i.e., production governed by social criteria and distribution determined by human need) private ownership of the means of production would have to transfer to public ownership. There are different interpretations of how Marx saw this transformation occurring: by reform or by revolution. This has been the source of much debate by contemporary Marxists.

In sum, Marxism is relevant to social welfare and social work on two counts. First, it provides a comprehensive theory of society that explains directly the nature and development of the welfare state and, indirectly, the nature and functions of social work practice in capitalist society. Second, it offers a normative theory about the transcendence of capitalism and the establishment of a welfare society whose central feature is to meet human need.[5]

Social Beliefs

Marxists adhere to the three central social values of socialism – liberty, equality, and fraternity or collectivism. Liberty, to the Marxists, can only exist if certain other conditions are present in society.[6] Without a substantial degree of economic security and equality, freedom is an illusory concept. Without these conditions some people will have more resources than others and, therefore, will have more privileges, more influence, and more liberties. Whereas neo-conservatives and liberals believe that civil rights are synonymous with liberty or freedom, Marxists believe that these rights or liberties can only be exercised fairly if they are complemented by social freedom – freedom from want, freedom from unemployment, and so on – and by opportunities to work, to earn, to develop oneself, to enjoy. The Marxists do not believe that true liberty for all can occur in a capitalist society based on inequality. Thus, while neo-conservatives equate liberty with inequality and liberals equate liberty with equal opportunity, Marxists equate liberty with equality of economic circumstances or human emancipation, which can only be achieved under socialism.

George and Wilding present the Marxist concept of equality[7] based on the writings of two Marxist writers – Harold Laski[8] and John Strachey.[9] Equality does not mean sameness to Marxists; rather, it means the absence of special privilege and the availability of opportunities to all. Differences in wealth or status are consistent with Marxism as long as they can be reasonably explained, that all can attain them, and that they are necessary for the common good. Economic equality does not mean equal incomes, for it would not be fair to reward equally unequal efforts and it would not be fair to reward equally unequal needs. Also, a strict interpretation of "distribution according to individual need" is recognized as problematic because individual need is difficult to define. Rather than "absolute equality" some Marxists view equality as "relative," with every need related to the social or civic minimum that, when not met, prevents one from attaining effective citizenship. These needs must be satisfied before dealing with needs above the social minimum, and, after the satisfaction of basic needs, differences in reward must be built into the system to acknowledge varying contributions of individuals in different occupations.

The third central social value, fraternity or collectivism, is antithetical to individualism. It views the individual as a social being in the sense that his or her thoughts and actions are influenced by those of others and vice versa. Collectivism recognizes people's need for each other and suggests that a good society is one where there is an absence of barriers to people living harmoniously and co-operatively with one another. Government intervention is legitimate, necessary, and beneficial according to this view of people.

Economic Beliefs

The major economic beliefs of Marxists are public ownership of the means of production (brought about by nationalization of private enterprises), distribution of resources according to need, industrial democracy, and a planned economy.

Unlike the social democrats, the Marxists do not believe that the means of production can be controlled by regulation in a capitalist society. Private ownership creates two main classes – the capitalist class and the working class – locked in a structurally antagonistic relationship because their basic interests (profits versus wages) conflict with each other. Class conflict, then, is an inherent part of capitalism and can only be abolished by the abolition of the private ownership of the means of production.

The means of attaining public ownership advocated by the Marxists is nationalization, which they justify on both political and economic grounds.[10] The private ownership of the means of production has resulted in a concentration of economic power in the hands of the capitalist class in Britain, the U.S., and Canada, and this inevitably has meant a concentration of political power in the same hands. Also, it is considered immoral by Marxists that profits are produced through the labour of the workers but are reaped by shareholders who do not have to work. In this way, workers feel alienated from the work process and suffer psychologically, which in turn reduces economic production. To deal effectively with these political and economic problems the Marxists would nationalize private enterprise.

A second Marxist economic belief is that each person should contribute to society according to his or her abilities and be rewarded by society according to his or her needs. Although this principle is problematic in workable terms, most Marxists would adhere to it in some form. For example, some Marxists[11] would establish minimal standards of living necessary to retain full citizenship in society and would ensure that everyone in society was living up to these standards before dealing with needs above the social or civic minimum. Other Marxists[12] would follow Marx's theory of revolutionary socialism by distinguishing between distribution according to the quality of work done under socialism (i.e., the transformation stage of socialism) and distribution according to individual need under communism (i.e., the final stage of socialism when capitalism has been abolished). This latter group of Marxists point out, however, that distribution according to need requires both economic affluence and a different value system.

Industrial democracy is a third Marxist economic belief. There is general acceptance among Marxists that nationalized industries in a socialist society must be democratically run with maximum participation on the part of workers. As George and Wilding point out, the benefits of industrial democracy are many and varied – it extends and gives real meaning to political democracy; it reduces industrial conflict and promotes industrial co-operation; it enhances individual work satisfaction; and it increases productivity, which in turn increases the overall standard of living of society.[13]

The final principal Marxist economic belief is that government planning with the widest form of participation must be a central feature of a socialist society.[14] Rather than a laissez-faire or free enterprise system, the Marxists aspire to a planned economy (as part of a planned society) where the market is subordinated to purposes upon which members of society have agreed. The Marxists believe that, contrary to neo-conservative argument, planning enhances democracy and efficiency and is less susceptible to government corruption.[15] The combination of nationalization and industrial democracy would obviously make it easier for governments to formulate and integrate economic and social policies.

Political Beliefs

The central political beliefs of the Marxists are government planning, a participatory democracy, a parliamentary system of government, and the view that capitalism can be transformed only by class conflict. The Marxist belief in government planning has been discussed above and the Marxist attitude toward participatory democracy is similar to that of the social democrats.

The suppression of parliamentary democracy in Eastern European countries, which are referred to as socialist by much of the media and by many commentators in capitalist countries, has caused many people to believe that Marxism is anti-democratic.[16] However, a belief in parliamentary democracy by most contemporary Marxists is unmistakable, as evidenced by its acceptance by Western Europe's Communist parties. The idea of a one-party socialist state is inconsistent with the concept of democratic socialism.

The Marxists believe that any significant social change can only come about through the vehicle of class conflict. This belief is different from that of the social democrats, who believe that capitalism can be transformed by social conflict between racial, religious, and other interest groups (including class) aided by a progressive social democratic government. Although the Marxists recognize other conflicts in society in addition to that which exists between exploited wage-earners and the owners of the means of production, they believe these other conflicts can be resolved within the legal postulates of capitalism. Marxists are united in their belief that class conflict will sooner or later lead to the downfall of capitalism. This change may come peacefully or violently, although most contemporary Marxist writers advocate peaceful means. Unlike social democrats, who believe that the welfare state can be used as a vehicle for socialist change, most Marxists view the welfare state as a social institution supporting capitalism. They would, instead, focus their efforts on labour as the vehicle for socialist change.

View of Social Problems

Marxists do not see so-called social problems as the result of individual fault as the neo-conservatives do, or as the result of industrialization as the liberals do, or as the result of social conflict among various groups as the social democrats do. Rather, social problems are "the result of the capitalist form of production and its accompanying forms of social relationships."[17] Marxists believe that the term "social problem" mystifies structural issues of inequality, oppression, and alienation by turning them into individualistic issues of deviance, inadequacy, or pathology.[18]

Marxists believe that by focusing on the victims of inequality, oppression, and alienation and calling them criminals, drug addicts, or poor people, we are actually labelling them as troublemakers. Consequently, we neglect the social conditions of inequality, powerlessness, and institutional violence that form the basis of our troubled society. Instead, the Marxists would trace these problems back to the social relationships determined by capitalism. Personal problems are rooted in capitalist politics. For some problems, such as poverty, this explanation is direct and simple; for others, such as crime, it is less direct and more complex. In sum, Marxists believe that social problems are caused by the capitalist system. Therefore, they cannot be abolished by social policy in a capitalist society but only by the abolition of capitalism.

View of Social Welfare

The ideal social welfare system in the Marxist view is the same as that espoused by social democrats or by any socialist group. Its major attributes are that social services should be distributed according to need; they should be universal, comprehensive, adequate, and free; prevention is a primary social welfare principle; and there should be participation on the part of lay people in determining policy.

Marxists, as noted previously, do not agree with the social democrats that the welfare state under capitalism provides a stepping stone to a socialist society. Instead, Marxists believe that although the welfare state does provide minimal help to some people, its main function is to support and strengthen the liberal-capitalist system. The welfare state represents one of the contradictions of capitalism. On the one hand, it works toward greater degrees of human well-being by tending to the immediate needs of some people. On the other hand, it denies and frustrates the pursuit of a just society as it supports and reinforces conformity to the very institutions and values that generate the problems the welfare state was established to deal with in the first place.

Two obvious questions arise from the Marxist contention that the welfare state does not move capitalist society any closer to a socialist society but, instead, supports and strengthens capitalism. Why does the welfare state prop up capitalism? How does it do this? The simple explanation of why the welfare state supports capitalism is that the major reason for the welfare state in a capitalist society is to protect capitalism. The welfare state is established within a certain political and economic context. Because of that liberal-capitalist context, the welfare state is part of a symbiotic relationship with all other major (liberal-capitalist) institutions in society. All activities and reform efforts of the welfare state are governed by the logic and requirements of capitalism. Marxists perceive all capitalist social institutions as functioning in such a way that they promote conformity to capitalism. This perception is part of the fundamental Marxist belief that the government in a capitalist state represents the interests of the capitalist class. How the welfare state promotes conformity is described below.

According to Marxists the welfare state in a capitalist society operates (1) to reduce working-class antagonism to the existing social order, (2) to increase efficiency of the economic system, and (3) to underwrite many of the costs that the owners of capital incur. Marxists believe that many of our social welfare measures are actually tactical concessions made to labour to avert social disruption or other threats to the social order. The classical example is the social insurance reforms introduced by Bismarck in Germany at the turn of the last century. These reforms were initiated to crush revolutionary socialism – a growing political force in Germany – and to win over German workers. Some Marxists view social welfare reforms as ransom for social harmony that the working class has squeezed out of the government, while others believe they are given freely by government but with an ulterior motive – co-optation of the working class. In either case, the effect is to cool out any drastic social reform efforts that would challenge capitalism.

Marxist analysis argues that the capitalist welfare state acts as a corrective for the inherent inefficiency of capitalism. Left on its own the capitalist system of production tends toward regular cycles of depressions and recessions, overproduction, underconsumption, falling profits, and stagflation. The state has been forced to intervene to enable the capitalist system to overcome these recurrent tendencies of economic crisis. The more advanced the economy the more government intervention seems to be needed. Thus, the welfare state, in this analysis, is largely the result of the functional needs of capitalism.

The welfare state also enhances the profitability of capitalist businesses by underwriting many of the costs associated with the capitalist system of production. Through public spending in the areas of education and health, the private sector has available to it an educated and healthy work force without any direct costs to it. As well, social insurance and other public financial assistance programs put money directly into the hands of consumers of the goods and services produced by the private sector, which keeps consumption at a higher level than it would be without social welfare programs. The welfare state also reduces costs to the private sector associated with accidents on the job (workers' compensation) and unsafe working conditions. (A Canadian Labour Congress study found that between 20 and 30 per cent of fatalities from cancer can be traced to the effects of chemicals and other products used on the job. Of course, publicly financed health care picks up the tab for the medical costs associated with these fatalities.)[19]

Many social programs certainly subsidize private enterprise indirectly. James O'Connor offers a more complete explanation of how the welfare state props up capitalism. He argues that the capitalist state tries to carry out two basic but apparently contradictory functions – accumulation and legitimation.

> The state must try to maintain or create the conditions in which profitable capital accumulation is possible. However, the state also must try to maintain or create the conditions for social harmony. A capitalist state that openly uses its coercive forces to help one class accumulate capital at the expense of other classes loses its legitimacy and hence undermines the basis of loyalty and support. But a state that ignores the necessity of assisting the process of capital accumulation risks drying up the source of its own power, the economy's surplus production capacity and the taxes drawn from this surplus . . . the state must involve itself in the accumulation process, *but it must either mystify its policies by calling them something that they are not, or it must try to conceal them.*[20]

O'Connor separates the economic functions of the state from the social welfare functions.[21] The former aim at serving the needs of capital by helping to increase profit, by offering tax incentives, by encouraging labour mobility, and the like. However, a government that is seen to attend only to the interests of the minority but powerful capitalist class will not be accepted by the working class. To legitimize itself to the working class, therefore, the government must also appear to represent their interests. It does this, in part, by developing a welfare state that the government claims strives toward fairness, equity, and justice. Marxists, however, believe that the welfare state does not live up to these claims because, in fact, much of the government's social welfare activities actually enhance capital accumulation. Thus, the functions of capital accumulation and legitimation may appear to be contradictory, but Marxists would argue that experience has shown they are mutually reinforcing and favour the capitalists.

Marxist critics have no difficulty citing evidence to substantiate their claim that the welfare state is the same as any other liberal-capitalist social institution in that it functions in such a manner to protect dominant class interests. In *The Politics of Social Services,* Jeffry Galper provides an insightful analysis of how social welfare programs support and nurture liberal capitalism.[22] Most public financial assistance programs support the labour market by making people's eligibility for assistance dependent on their past experience and present relationship to the job market. Even programs such as day care depend on the needs of the dominant class for labour, as day-care spaces tend to increase during periods of low unemployment and are cut back during recessions. Eligibility for many social welfare programs also relies on conforming to society's prevailing values. For example, public assistance regulations are often used to control the behaviour of recipients in such areas as parenting, sexual conduct, and market purchases. The fact that social welfare programs are often underfunded and provide minimal assistance gives the message to those who depend on such programs that people who cannot make it in the private market cannot really count on a public support system for much help. Also, they had better behave in a socially acceptable manner or they could easily lose the minimal benefits they do receive.

Even those government actions that have no obvious effect on increasing profits or ensuring a ready work force for private enterprise are viewed sceptically by Marxists. For example, the factory legislation enacted during Karl Marx's time in England was often not enforced. A contemporary example of governments appearing to act in the best interests of all citizens but not interfering with the capital accumulation of private enterprise is found in the fact that some very good anti-pollution legislation exists, but it is often not enforced when it is violated by large industries.

Mishra sums up the main features of the Marxist view of welfare.

(1) True welfare (i.e., a social norm based on solidarity, co-operation, and human need) involves the regulation of working and living conditions and the distribution of society's resources based on human need.
(2) As a socio-economic-political system, capitalism is the antithesis of true welfare.
(3) True welfare can begin to be partially established in a capitalist society through the collective efforts of workers. Given the nature of capitalism, however, the chances for meaningful and lasting reform are slight.
(4) In a class-divided society, the government and society largely attend to the interests of the dominant class. However, the universality of the state requires it to act (or appear to act) on behalf of all classes. Thus, the capitalist state is two-faced with respect to welfare. Social programs may be accepted in form but not realized in substance.
(5) True welfare can be established fully as a social norm only after

the means of production have been nationalized and the free market/private property system abolished.

(6) Social welfare in a capitalist society contributes to the efficiency and smooth working of the capitalist economy.

(7) Social welfare in a capitalist society has an important social control function – to moderate class conflict and stabilize the social order.

(8) Not surprisingly, the initiative for social welfare programs often comes from sectors of the dominant class.

(9) Attempts to reform the capitalist system only lead to new economic and social contradictions. The welfare state has stabilizing as well as destabilizing effects on the capitalist social structure.

(10) To avoid wrongful ideological conclusions, welfare activities in a capitalist state must be seen in conjunction with other state interventions and activities.[23]

In light of these beliefs about welfare, orthodox Marxists reject the notion that the welfare state in a capitalist society holds any potential for socialism. They differ, therefore, from social democrats, who believe that the welfare state, the trade union movement, and social democratic parties all have potential for socialist transformation and should be used in this fashion. However, not all Marxists reject the welfare state out of hand as a vehicle for socialism. It depends on whether one has adopted a revolutionary or an evolutionary Marxist perspective.

Social Work Practice within the Marxist Paradigm

The crucial question for the Marxist social worker is whether or not radical social and political change can come about through the social welfare institution in a capitalist society. The answer depends on whether one is a revolutionary or an evolutionary Marxist.[24] Although both types of Marxists favour the attainment of a socialist state, they differ on the means of such attainment. The evolutionary Marxist believes that a socialist state can be created by working within existing social institutions and organizations that have potential for socialism, such as the trade union movement and the welfare state. The revolutionary Marxist does not believe that any socialist potential is inherent in any capitalist social institution (except the trade union movement, which is a working-class organization) and, therefore, seeks to create and develop counter-institutions and organizations to challenge the power of the state.

It is difficult to see how a revolutionary Marxist could even practice social work in a capitalist society. Since social work occurs within the welfare state, which is rejected as a base of operations by revolutionary Marxists, what or where would be the basis of attempts to stimulate, create, and develop socialist institutions and organizations? Revolutionary Marxists maintain that social work has political potential for socialism only if it would dispose of its social reform illusions and join in the "revolutionary movement." However, they do not say how this could be done or who would employ revolutionary social workers. Unless one is self-supporting or employed by a radical union, there do not appear to be many opportunities for revolutionary Marxists to practise social work in a capitalist state. Social work practice within the social welfare institution is seen by orthodox Marxists as perpetuating an unworkable and undesirable system of capitalism because it is used as "a mechanism for identifying and absorbing potential social revolt against the status quo."[25]

Evolutionary Marxists do not reject the capitalist state as a vehicle for socialist change.

> There is, indeed, a significant number of evolutionary Marxian socialists arguing . . . for the creation of a socialist system . . . through the relatively untainted and indigenous institutions of the working class; most notably the trade unions and the welfare state.[26]

In other words, evolutionary Marxists believe that the welfare state can be used as a stepping stone toward socialism. In this regard they appear to have much in common with those social democratic social workers who attempt to create forces in their social work practices that would contribute to the transformation of capitalism.

The differences between social democratic social work practice and evolutionary Marxist social work practice would be more of degree and emphasis than of kind. Both would attend to the needs of people who have been hurt by capitalism and both would attempt to restructure society along socialist lines. However, the evolutionary Marxist social workers would undoubtedly emphasize the latter task more than would their social democratic counterparts.

> The ultimate function of [Marxist] social work must be to raise community, and thus ultimately political, consciousness by exposing the assumed class nature of existing society . . . the greater the 'awareness' the greater the potential for conflict between working-class activists and 'authority'.[27]

To reiterate the Marxist position on social work practice, both revolutionary and evolutionary Marxists would attempt to raise socialist political consciousness. However, the revolutionary Marxist social worker as part of this process would attempt to undermine the acceptance of, and support for, the very institution of which his or her profession is a part – as Pritchard and Taylor point out, "a dangerous but not altogether ignoble role!"[28] Evolutionary Marxist social workers, on the other hand, would join their radical social democratic counterparts and attempt to radicalize the power structure within the welfare state by means of increased participation, decentralization, and democratization and "to extend and fortify the working-class and socialist incursions into capitalism"[29] and move eventually to a position where the attainment of a fully socialist state becomes possible.

Critique of the Marxist Paradigm

As a social theory Marxism is "probably the best single theory available for a critical understanding of capitalist society. That is its major strength."[30] Part of this critical understanding is the way in which the Marxist view locates the welfare state within capitalism rather than seeing it in isolation. The view of the welfare state as a necessity for capitalism because it makes capitalism more efficient and productive while controlling the work force and legitimizing capitalism is a major contribution of Marxism. However, as a theory of building a socialist state it "remains sadly inadequate."[31] It has not come to terms with the entire historical experience of existing socialism. In fact, as Mishra points out, the actually existing socialism (i.e., Soviet socialism) is an embarrassment to western Marxists. There is no working model of socialism that Marxists can point to.[32]

The traditional Marxist view that capitalist societies comprise two monolithic classes and that all conflict in society runs along class lines has been criticized on the basis of being incompatible with the realities of contemporary societies.[33] The working class is divided along white collar and blue collar; private and public sector; rural and urban workers; skilled and unskilled workers; managerial and professional status; and so on. And it is very questionable whether all conflicts in society are based on class or capitalist oppression. For example, is the enemy of oppressed women capitalism or patriarchy? Are all racial conflicts or religious conflicts actually class conflicts?

The traditional Marxist claim that the state is the representative of the capitalist class and that all issues dealt with by the state are directly or indirectly relevant to the stability and reproduction of the capitalist system is doubtful. As George and Wilding point out, a group of government policies, including those on abortion, adoption, divorce, capital punishment, and drug addiction, are mainly moral issues and have nothing to do with the survival of capitalism.[34] These authors present

Table 6.1
Overview of Marxist and Social Work Ideals

	Marxism	*Social Work*
Social Beliefs	Liberty Collectivism Equality	Humanitarianism (humanism) Community Equality
Economic Beliefs	Public ownership of means of production Industrial democracy Distribution of resources according to need Planned economy	Government intervention Social priorities dominate economic decisions Equitable distribution of society's resources
Political Beliefs	Government planning Participatory democracy Parliamentary system of government Transformation of capitalism by class conflict	Participatory democracy in both governmental and non-governmental areas
View of Social Welfare	Welfare capitalism props up capitalism but also represents the fruits of working-class efforts Ideal = social welfare state or structural model	An instrument to promote equality, solidarity, and community Ideal = structural model
Nature of Social Work Practice	Revolutionary Marxists see no social change role for social workers in capitalist society Evolutionary Marxists' practice of social work is similar to that of Social Democrats, but emphasizes "class conflict" more	Treat people with respect Enhance dignity and integrity Facilitate self-determination and self-realization Accept differences Advocate and promote social justice

other considerations that have to be accounted for when assessing the autonomy of the state to act against the interests of the capitalist class. These are: the political ideology of the government (a social democratic government is more likely to pursue anti-capitalist policies than a conservative government); the nature of public opinion (public opinion, such as the public's wish for anti-pollution legislation, will often set limits on pro-capitalist policies); and the power of the working class (when the working class is well organized governments have to take notice of the demands of trade unions).

With respect to its view of the welfare state, Marxism is in the unenviable position of trying to balance both sides of a contradiction. "Social welfare may help shore up capitalism, materially and ideologically, but it also represents a gain for the working class in its struggle against exploitation."[35] This is the classical dilemma for Marxists. During good times Marxists have tended to focus on the broader political implications of the welfare state, often neglecting or denigrating its benefits to individuals and families. However, during periods of attack on the welfare state from the right, Marxists become its staunchest champions.

Table 6.1 shows that Marxism and social work ideology share many of the same values and ideals. It will be recalled from the previous chapter that there was also a high degree of compatibility between social democratic and social work ideologies. Because the social democrats and the Marxists both want the same thing – a socialist state – they naturally share many of the same primary values. There is much consistency among social democracy, Marxism, and social work in terms of their primary values. Each has egalitarianism as a central value and both social democracy and social work have humanitarianism as an explicit central value while Marxism has it as an implicit central value (i.e., Marxism seeks to abolish capitalism for humanitarian reasons). The major difference among the three sets of belief systems is that whereas social democracy and social work perceive the welfare state to be a stepping stone toward a better society, Marxism tends to view it as a mechanism that props up capitalism. Before dismissing Marxism as a possible course of action for social work, however, the theory and practice of the evolutionary Marxists should be looked at in more detail.

Part II

Conceptualization and Theory

7

Structural Social Work: Ideological Basis and Conceptual Overview

Social Work and the Paradigms Compared

Having reviewed the four societal paradigms in the previous four chapters, we are now in a better position to answer the question posed at the end of Chapter 2, "Which of the societal paradigms is most congruent with social work?" That is, which paradigm is most congruent with the fundamental values of humanism and egalitarianism; with the instrumental values of respect, self-determination, and acceptance; with a social belief in the individual as a social being; with an economic belief whereby societal decisions dominate economic decisions; with a political belief in participatory democracy; and with a social welfare system that emphasizes equality, solidarity, and community?

To help answer the above question an outline of the four paradigms and of social work ideology is presented in Table 7.1. Both neo-conservatism and liberalism adhere to the basic values of capitalism, with the former advocating a purer form (less government intervention) than the latter. Conversely, both social democracy and Marxism adhere to the basic values of socialism although they differ on the means to achieve a socialist state. While a major goal of the capitalist paradigms is to maintain basic capitalist structures, the socialists would have as their major goal the transformation of these capitalist structures to socialist structures. The implication for the social work profession is that by deciding which societal paradigm is most congruent with its ideology, it is also deciding its position with respect to preserving or changing the society within which it is located.

As has been discussed in the preceding chapters and as Table 7.1 indicates, social work ideology has much more in common with the socialist paradigms than it does with the capitalist paradigms.[1] If social work truly believes in the values and ideals it espouses, then it cannot subscribe to and try to maintain a social order that contradicts and violates many of these same values and ideals. If the social work

Table 7.1
Overview of Four Paradigms

	Neo-Conservatism	*Liberalism*
Social Beliefs	Freedom (or liberty) Individualism Inequality	Freedom Individualism Inequality (all the above modified by humanitarianism and pragmatism)
Economic Beliefs	Laissez-faire Competitive capitalism Private ownership	Mixed economy or welfare captalism
Political Beliefs	Elite rule Dominance of economic system Law, order, and stability Paternalism	Representative democracy Pluralism
View of Social Problems	Caused by individual weakness, deviance, or heredity	Caused by social disorganization, which is inherent in a capitalist system
View of Social Welfare	Hostile toward a well-developed welfare state Goal is to relieve destitution Ideal welfare model = residual system	Used to modify negative effects of capitalism Goal is to provide a social minimum Ideal welfare model = institutional system
Nature of Social Work Practice	Coerce people to look after themselves Social control Poor Law treatment Emphasize investigations to prevent abuse	Personal reform Limited social reform Advocacy

Table 7.1 continued

	Social Democracy	*Marxism*
Social Beliefs	*Primary values* Freedom Collectivism Equality *Derivative Values* Humanitarianism Democratic participation	 Freedom Collectivism Equality
Economic Beliefs	Government intervention Public control of economy Equitable distribution of income and opportunities	Public ownership of economy Industrial democracy Distribution according to need Planned economy
Political Beliefs	Participatory democracy Capitalism can be transformed by a social democracy The state has a positive role to play in society	Participatory democracy Government planning enhances democracy Transformation of capitalism by class conflict
View of Social Problems	Caused by various social conflicts inherent in a capitalist society	Caused by social relationships (owners vs. workers) inherent in capitalism
View of Social Welfare	Welfare capitalism can be used as a stepping stone toward socialism Ideal welfare system = structural model (goal is to promote egalitarianism)	Welfare capitalism props up capitalism but also represents efforts of the working class Ideal welfare system = structural model
Nature of Social Work Practice	Provide practical, humanitarian care to casualties of capitalism Restructure society along socialist lines	Revolutionary: no social change role possible in a capitalist society Evolutionary: essentially the same as social democracy

profession is to be true to itself it must, first of all, realize that in North America, at least, it embodies one of the contradictions of capitalism. The profession is based on humanitarian and egalitarian ideals but operates within a social order based on inequality in that a minority dominates (controls and exploits) the majority. Second, in light of this awareness, social work must do something about it. It must try to change the present social order to one that is more compatible with its own world view. To bring about this transformation social work must go beyond critical analysis of our liberal-capitalist social system and develop transformational theory or what is termed here structural social work theory.

Radical Social Work

Clark and Asquith have noted that social workers who are committed to some type of socialist vision, ranging from "mild social reformism to revolutionary Marxism," are attracted to the *radical social work perspective.*[2] This perspective chastises conventional social work for failing to develop a critical self-awareness and for pathologizing oppressed people by offering individualistic explanations of social problems.[3] The radical perspective also "urges social workers to get involved in socialist political action as much in their own interests as in the interests of those who depend upon their services."[4] The progressive view of social work discussed in Chapter 2 corresponds to the radical perspective. Davis summarizes the radical argument:

> . . . social workers need to understand the nature of state power and the role of social work as an element of state control and oppression, and to construct an approach to practice which is underpinned by this understanding. Such practice must be directed at challenging and changing structures which oppress.[5]

Social work has always had a radical element. Bertha Reynolds, an American Marxist social work academic and activist during the 1930s and 1940s, argued that to be a good social worker, one had to be a radical.[6] "Like many other radical social workers, Bertha Reynolds . . . viewed the rise of radical social work as *consistent* with the ethics and values of the profession."[7] In spite of its long history, however, radical social work has only developed a substantial literature and following since 1975 with the publications of Bailey and Brake's *Radical Social Work* in Britain and Jeffry Galper's *The Politics of Social Services* in the United States.[8] That these publications corresponded with the emergence of the world economic crisis and the fiscal crisis of the state should not be surprising. It is completely consistent with one of the features of the concept of a paradigm – when the dominant paradigm is no longer able to evade anomalies or to explain crises, competing paradigms will begin to emerge or re-emerge.

Because of radical social work's association with socialism, which is an extremely broad tendency, there is a wide range of opinion among radical social workers.[9] Different shades of socialism co-exist under the radical social work label.[10] Evidence of these differences is found in the following list of names that have been applied to radical social work: critical social work,[11] Marxist social work,[12] political social work,[13] progressive social work,[14] radical social work,[15] socialist social work,[16] socialist welfare work,[17] and structural social work.[18] These nominal differences suggest there is less homogeneity among radical social workers than is often believed by both enthusiasts and critics. Mullaly and Keating contend that the above schools of radical thought tend to fall into one of three traditional schools of socialist thought – social democracy, revolutionary Marxism, and evolutionary Marxism – and that these three perspectives differ on: (1) the place of radical social workers in the capitalist welfare system and whether they should work within or outside it; (2) the fundamental source of oppression in a capitalist society; and (3) the priority given to the personal versus the political in a strategy of social transformation.[19] These differences reflect disagreement on the means for transcending capitalism rather than any disagreement on the goal of social transformation itself.

There are also several areas of agreement. Mullaly and Keating have identified nine common themes found in the radical social work literature, with expected differences in emphasis:

(i) rejection of capitalism in favour of socialism;
(ii) rejection of liberal reformism as a way of dealing with social problems;
(iii) the capitalist welfare system carries out interrelated political and economic functions that prop up capitalism;
(iv) social welfare as a societal norm is antithetical to capitalism;
(v) conventional social work perpetuates social problems;
(vi) the "individual vs. society" is a false dichotomy because private troubles cannot be understood or treated apart from their social or political causes;
(vii) the feminist perspective is an epistemological imperative for radical social work; it not only decodes sexism and patriarchy but links the personal and the political better than any other theory and emphasizes transformational politics;
(viii) classism and patriarchy are not the only oppressions concerning radical social workers; racism, ageism, heterosexism, imperialism, and handicapism are increasingly viewed as structurally oppressive forces;

(ix) professionalism distances professionals from service users and serves the former at the expense of the latter; unionization is the preferred mode of organization for radical social workers.[20]

These major areas of agreement among radical social workers are not static. As radical social work theory continues to develop, other areas of agreement will emerge.

Structural Social Work: Historical Overview

Structural social work adheres to the above themes of radical social work and is part of the radical social work movement. Structural social work is the term adopted here for a number of reasons. First, the term "structural" is descriptive of the problems that confront social work in that they are an inherent, built-in part of our present social order. Our social institutions function in such a way that they discriminate against people along lines of class, gender, race, sexual orientation, disability, and so on. Second, the term "structural" is prescriptive for social work practice as it indicates that the focus for change is mainly on the structures of society and not solely on the individual. Third, structural social work appears to be more flexible and, in many cases, more realistic than most other radical approaches. For example, it is not only concerned with one group of oppressed people, such as the poor, but with all groups who are victims of the present social order. Also, it does not restrict social work practice to either inside or outside the existing social welfare system. And, finally, much of the developmental work of structural social work has been carried out in Canada, where it is now assuming increasing importance as a major social work perspective.

"Structural social work" is a term first used by Middleman and Goldberg in 1974. However, although these authors identified the social environment as the source of social problems, they attributed them to the liberal notion of social disorganization. Nowhere in their book do they call for wholesale social change, nor do they present a social or ideological analysis of capitalism. Instead, their prescription for social problems falls within the ecological approach. They state: "the assumption that inadequate social arrangements are predominantly responsible for the plight of many clients of social agencies suggests the need for social workers who can help people to *modify the social situations that limit their functioning*."[21] Although Middleman and Goldberg point out much that is wrong with capitalism (without mentioning capitalism, using instead the term "social environment"), nowhere do they call for its overthrow.[22] There are many radical social work writers in the United States, but none, other than Middleman and

Goldberg, have used the term "structural social work" to describe their particular radical approach.

Arguably, most radical social work literature has originated in Britain. As with the American literature, however, very few radical writers use the term "structural social work." Ann Davis is one exception. In "A Structural Approach to Social Work" she presents two contrasting approaches of structural social work that are offered in the literature:

> These two broad approaches which offer a contrasting analysis of, and ways of working with structural issues, provide different starting points for social workers in training and practice. The first, in arguing for maintenance within given conditions, promotes a consensual view of practice in which recognition of the discrimination suffered by vulnerable groups is dealt with through advocacy within organizational and political givens. The second, in arguing for change of existing structures which perpetuate inequality, promotes an adversarial view of practice which simultaneously seeks to alleviate and transform the conditions in which oppressed clients find themselves.[23]

The latter approach corresponds to the view of structural social work presented in this book.

Most of the developmental work on the structural approach to social work has been carried out in Canada. It was pioneered by Maurice Moreau[24] at the School of Social Work at Carleton University in the mid-1970s with the help of many of his colleagues at Carleton,[25] at the Université de Montréal,[26] and at the Université du Québec à Montréal.[27] This approach was presented by Moreau as an umbrella that spanned and included the major radical themes of Marxism, feminism, radical humanism, and radical structuralism.[28] One of the unique features of this structural approach was that it did not attempt to prioritize different forms of oppression – classism, racism, patriarchy, heterosexism, and so on – into some kind of hierarchical listing of most to least fundamental or most to least debilitating.[29] Rather, the structural approach views various forms of oppression as intersecting with each other at numerous points, creating a total system of oppression.[30] Another notable feature of the structural approach is that it does not restrict itself to working only with social institutions. Instead, it is a generalist model of practice[31] requiring knowledge and skills for working with individuals, families, groups, and communities, always making the connection between the personal and the political.

The structural social work approach has continued to develop in Canada since the mid-seventies. Moreau continued researching and writing on the subject until his death in 1990. The structural approach continues to be an integral part of the Carleton School of Social Work program, although it does not appear to be the rallying framework it was in the late seventies and during most of the eighties.[32] At least two other Canadian schools of social work publicize their programs as being structural or structural/feminist in orientation.[33] In addition to its analytical and theoretical appeal, the experience of many graduates from structural schools with respect to the practical relevance of structural social work is very promising.[34]

Structural Social Work: Conceptual Overview

Based on socialist ideology and located within the radical social work camp, structural social work views social problems as arising from a specific societal context – liberal/neo-conservative capitalism – rather than from the failings of individuals. The essence of socialist ideology and of the radical social work perspective is that inequality: (1) is a natural, inherent (i.e., structural) part of capitalism; (2) falls along lines of class, gender, race, sexual orientation, age, disability, and geographical region; (3) excludes these groups from opportunities, meaningful participation in society, and a satisfactory quality of life; and (4) is self-perpetuating. Writing from Britain, Pond presents some reasons why social workers should attend to inequality as a major part of the structural context in which they practice:

> The distribution of economic rewards between different groups in the population and different parts of the country, is an important determinant of the nation's economic and social structure. Economic and social inequality are inextricably intertwined, and the distribution of income and wealth, the extent of poverty and privilege, have their effects on living standards, life chances and opportunities. Individuals' health and well-being are influenced by their position in the labour market, income and access to economic resources. Thus, class differences in health (for example) have persisted, despite an overall improvement in national standards.
>
> Moreover, inequalities in wealth have political implications, providing the wealthiest individuals with access to economic, social and sometimes political power. For this reason, inequalities can become self-perpetuating, having an influence on the institutions that reinforce the class structure.[35]

Given this view of social problems, structural social workers seek to change the social system and not the individuals who receive, through no fault of their own, the negative results of defective social arrangements.[36] Thus, the goal of structural social work is twofold: (1) to alleviate the negative effects on people of an exploitative and alienating social order; and (2) to transform the conditions and social structures that cause these negative effects. This goal involves a two-tiered process: immediate relief or tension-reduction on one level accompanied by longer-term institutional and structural change.

As mentioned previously, the term "structural" in structural social work is both descriptive and prescriptive. It is descriptive in the sense that the major source of social problems is described as being located in the way our society is *structured.* It is prescriptive in the sense that because social problems are rooted in our social structures, then the *structures* must be changed and not the individual, the family, or the subculture adversely affected by social problems. Even if it were possible to change everyone presently harmed by our social structures, the source of these problems – our social structures – would still be there to harm, oppress, and alienate more people along lines of class, gender, race, and so on. Figure 7.1 illustrates the general structural arrangement of any society.

The substructure or foundation of society consists of a dominant ideology, which is transmitted to all members of society through the process of socialization and determines the nature of a society's institutions and the relations among its people. If the foundation of society is comprised of liberalism, for example, the social institutions of that society and its social relations will rest on and reflect liberal beliefs, values, and ideals. In other words, the social institutions and social relations of a particular society will be determined by the dominant ideology and, in turn, will operate in a manner consistent with and supportive of that ideology.

Fundamental social change presents a difficult challenge. Each level of the social structure is interdependent and mutually reinforcing of the other levels, which suggests that a serious approach to social change must occur at all three levels. At the substructural level, the dominant ideology must be challenged by raising the consciousness of people with respect to the alienating and oppressive features of our present liberal-capitalist system.[37] At the level of social institutions not only must the social welfare institution be changed so that its control functions are minimized and its liberating features maximized, but all social institutions must change in a similar manner.[38] At the level of social relations we must not only attempt to break down the superordinate-subordinate relations around us, we must also attend to the way we live our own personal lives so that we do not contribute to the reproduction of our present social relations, which are often based on classism, sexism, racism, and so on.[39]

The ultimate goal of structural social work is to contribute to the

Figure 7.1 Structural View of Society

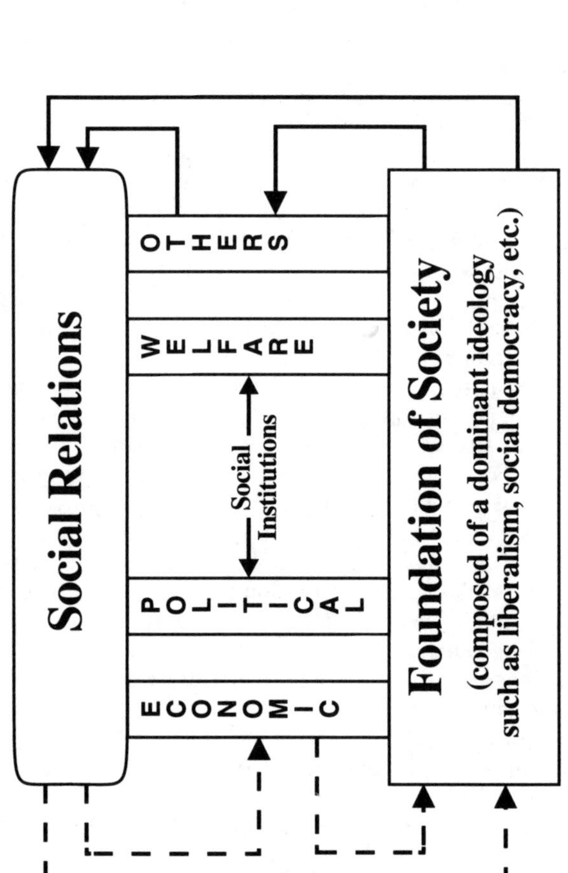

Superstructure

Consisting of:
i) social institutions that carry out society's functions; and
ii) social relations among all social groupings

Substructure

an ideology that underpins all social institutions and determines the nature of social relations

Figure 7.2 Transformational Goal of Structural Social Work

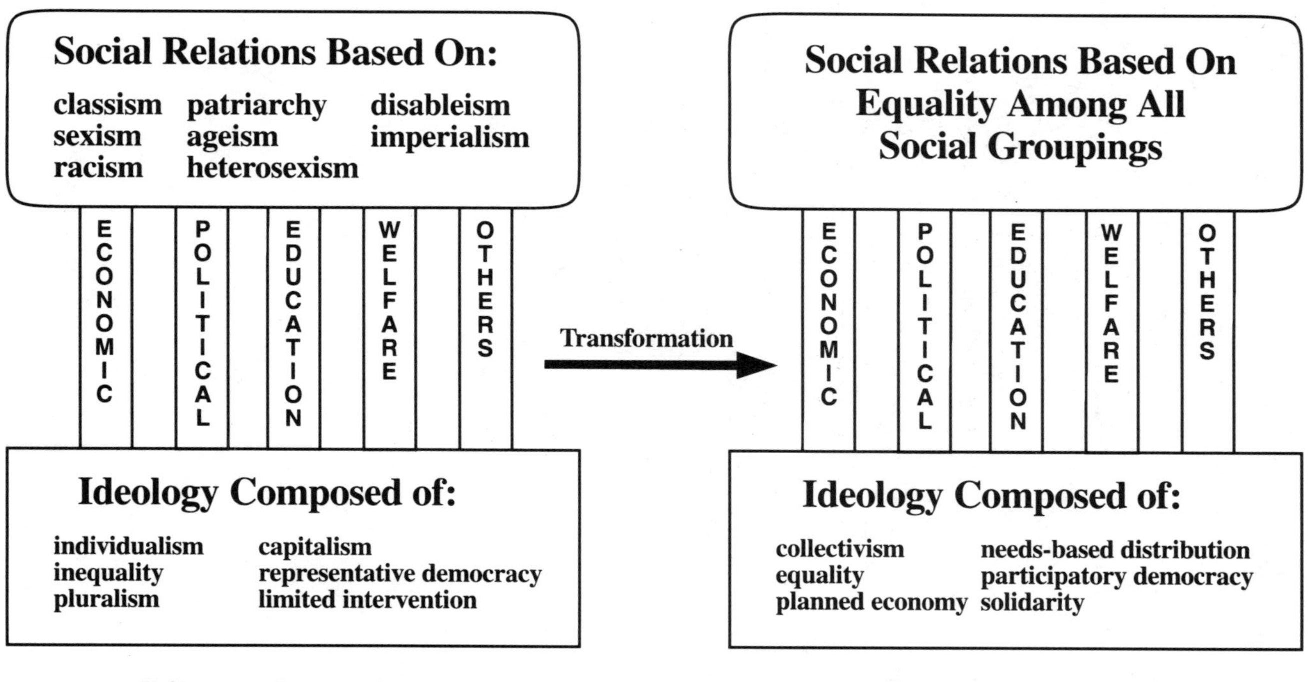

transformation of liberal-capitalist society to one that is more congruent with socialist principles. Carniol says of this transformation:

> A new form of intervention would call for a restructuring of our major institutions, so that they become answerable to the public rather than being strictly controlled by a relatively small class of people composed primarily of white wealthy males. Without such transformation those social problems now experienced will be perpetuated endlessly into the future, with bandaids being busily applied by a profession that should know better.[40]

This goal of social transformation is illustrated in Figure 7.2.

Langan and Lee articulate the challenge for radical social work:

> It is possible to be simultaneously committed to a set of socialist principles and to helping people as a social worker. What is much less clear is *how* it is possible to connect the two in a manner that allows them to merge into forms of feasible practice in the here and now.[41]

We now turn to this dual task of helping people while simultaneously working toward the transformation of the liberal paradigm. Given the inroads that neo-conservatism has made in the past two decades with respect to replacing liberalism as the dominant paradigm, it is imperative that structural social work develop theory and practical application that reflect its commitment to socialist principles.

8

Structural Social Work Theory

The Imperative of Theory for Social Work

Most social workers either turn cold or rebel at the mere mention of theory. Theory is often viewed as esoteric, abstract, and something people discuss in universities. Practice, on the other hand, is seen as common sense, concrete, and occurring in the real world. Social work is viewed by many as essentially a pragmatic profession that carries out practical tasks. Theory has little direct relevance and actually obscures the true (i.e., practical) nature of social work. Spontaneity and personal qualities of the social worker are more important than theory.[1]

Reinforcing this anti-theoretical orientation of many social workers is the way the social work curriculum is ordered and presented in social work educational programs. Students leave the university and their theory-based classroom courses to go out into community agencies to learn field practice. This theory/practice dilemma is a constant problem for social work educators concerned with the integration of theory and practice.[2] Exacerbating the tension between classroom and field settings is the fact that social work students in their field placements come into contact with practising social workers who are sceptical of the theory being taught in social work courses and who emphasize instead the value of experience.[3] Students are often described as (or accused of) being naive, idealistic, and in need of "seasoning" (i.e., practical experience).

This tendency on the part of many social workers to elevate theoretical ignorance to a level of professional virtue is wrong for two main reasons: (1) theory is part of everyday life – we all use theory; and (2) theoretical ignorance is not a professional virtue but an excuse for sloppy and dishonest practice.[4] We often use theories in our everyday life without even being aware that we are doing so. When we see dark clouds in the sky and tell ourselves it is going to rain, we have expressed a theory about the relationship between dark clouds and water falling from the sky. Imagine if we could not make generalizations about things and every time we saw a dark cloud we had to get wet in order to conclude that it was going to rain.[5]

Just as we use theories in everyday life, often without realizing it, social workers, too, often use theories in their everyday professional lives without realizing it. David Howe takes to task those "practical-folk" social workers who declare that their practice is not related to theory by showing that all practice is theory-based.[6] Social workers who appeal to common sense or declare themselves to be pragmatists or announce they are eclectics see people and their situations in one way or another. Perceptions are never theory-free because they are based on certain fundamental assumptions about the nature of people, society, and the relationship between the two. These assumptions enable social workers to make sense of any situation, and making sense is what Howe calls a "theory-saturated activity." And just because a social worker cannot imagine how else to view a particular situation does not mean that it is not related to theory. It just means that this one taken-for-granted reality (theory) is the social worker's entire world of sense. In other words, those persons who call themselves common-sense, pragmatic, or eclectic social workers base their practice on personally constructed theory rather than on scientifically constructed theory.[7]

A review of the literature by Howe[8] on what service users want in social workers and a review of the professional literature by Fischer[9] on what makes social workers effective converge on two aspects of practice: (1) social workers must create the conditions conducive to a trusting, caring, and accepting relationship; and (2) social workers must make deliberate use of well-articulated theories and methods that organize and direct practice in a way that is systematic and recognized by both worker and service user.

Without going into a discussion of them, theory carries out four basic functions: description; explanation; prediction; and control and management of events or changes. Social work is a practice-based profession that pursues all four of these functions: it describes phenomena; it attempts to explain what causes them; it predicts future events, including what will happen if certain interventions occur; and it attempts to control and manage events or changes at all levels of human and social activity.[10] "If drift and purposelessness are to be avoided, practice needs to be set within a clear framework of explanation, the nature of which leads to a well articulated practice."[11]

Classification of Theory

There is no shortage of social work knowledge. Many students, in fact, often believe there is an overabundance of knowledge. Social work textbooks and professional journals contain a plethora of theories and theoretical positions. As if the problem of reading and understanding the various theories were not difficult enough, many writers have attempted to group or classify them according to some simple differences. But because any classification scheme is always arbitrary to a degree, our social work theories are classified in different ways. This has tended to muddy the theoretical waters for social workers. However, since these classifications do exist they must be mentioned. Some of the more common classification schemes in social work are outlined here.

(1) *Objective vs. subjective theories.* Either theories seek to discover the real objective nature of things (e.g., behavioural theories) or they reflect the subjectively generated explanations of what things mean for people (e.g., client-centred theories).
(2) *Individual change vs. social change theories.* This classification is based on the dual-function notion of social work. Theories seek to explain how personal change can be brought about or they seek to explain how social change can be realized.
(3) *Macro (policy and planning), mezzo (community and organizations), and micro (individual, family, and small groups) theories.* These are based on the level of social unit that social workers focus on.
(4) *Grand, mid-range, and practice theories.* These theories are based on different levels of abstraction. Grand theories are highly abstract and provide comprehensive conceptual schemes (e.g., Marxism). Mid-range theories offer an explanation for a particular phenomenon or group of phenomena (e.g., labelling theory) or model of intervention (e.g., family therapy). Practice theories are located at a more specific level of action and comprise practice principles (e.g., establishing a trusting relationship with service users).

Other common classification schemes of theory include: "normative vs. non-normative" and "theory of practice vs. theory for practice."

The scheme used here to classify theories consists of two competing perspectives of society and of social problems – the order perspective and the conflict perspective.[12] These are both all-inclusive and mutually exclusive in that all social theories fall within one perspective or the other, but not in both. Other reasons for selecting this classification scheme are: (1) it is used by many social science writers when discussing social theory; (2) it not only accommodates the notion of paradigm as used in this book but recognizes that it is the core of social science (i.e., research is carried out within a paradigm once its boundaries have been established); and (3) it makes the connections among ideological

Table 8.1
Assumptions of Order and Conflict Perspectives

	Order	*Conflict*
Nature of Human Existence	competitive, contentious, individualistic, and acquisitive	co-operative, collective, and social
Nature of Social Institutions	must endure and regulate human interactions (political, economic, educational, religious, family) to avoid disorder	dynamic with no sacred standing; facilitate co-operation, sharing, and common interests
Nature of Society	consists of interdependent and integrated institutions and a supportive ideological base; viewed as an organism or system with each part contributing to the maintenance of the whole	in a society of structural inequality the social nature of human existence is denied with social institutions serving private rather than public interests
Continuity of Social Institutions	prevail because of agreement (consensus) among society's members	prevail in a class-divided society because of control and coercion
Nature of Relationship between People and Society	members are expected to conform and adapt to consensus-based social arrangements	acceptance, conformity, and adaptation to a coercive social order is questioned

Table 8.1 continued

	Order	*Conflict*
Nature of Social Problems	socialization will occasionally fail whereby reverence for institutions and respect for rules will not be learned; such occurrence on a large scale is a social problem	faulty socialization is more a matter of defective rules than defective control; rules are problematic
Approach to Social Problems	a) behaviour must be changed through resocialization (rehabilitation, counselling, etc.) or neutralized through formal systems of state control (criminal law, prisons, asylums, etc.)	institutions and ideology must be changed to protect social nature of human existence
	b) social change can only involve minor adjustments that are consistent with the nature of the existing system	behavioural change can only involve minor adjustments consistent with co-operative and collective nature of society; massive commitment to behavioural change is a form of blaming the victim
Paradigms	neo-conservatism liberalism	social democracy Marxism

preferences, mid-range social work theories, and actual social work practice.

Order and Conflict Perspectives

Order and conflict perspectives represent two competing views on the nature of people, society, and social problems. The former views society as orderly, stable, and persistent, unified by shared culture, values, and a consensus on its form and institutions. The latter views society as a continually contested struggle among groups with opposing views and interests. From a conflict perspective, society is held together not by consensus but by differential control of resources and political power. The neo-conservative and liberal paradigms, as well as conventional social work, are based on the order view (i.e., maintenance of the capitalist system). The social democratic and Marxist paradigms, as well as radical social work, are based on the conflict view (i.e., transformation of the capitalist system): "As a generalization, groups or individuals committed to the maintenance of the status quo employ order models of society. . . . Dissident groups, striving to institutionalize new claims, favour a conflict analysis of society."[13]

Reasons and Perdue have set forth two sets of logically interrelated and essential assumptions, one underpinning the order view of society and one the conflict view.[14] Table 8.1 contains a modified version of these assumptions, which concern: (1) the nature of human existence, (2) the nature of society, (3) the nature of the relationship between the two, and (4) the nature of social problems.

Order Perspective

The order perspective, which presently dominates North American social thought, is associated with Durkheim and Weber and more recently with Talcott Parsons. Parsons is usually regarded as the founder of an explicitly functionalist theory of society,[15] which is synonymous with a systems analysis (i.e., structural-functional analysis) of society and social problems.[16]

Society. Any society is comprised of people who are by nature competitive, acquisitive, self-absorbed, individualistic, and therefore predisposed toward disorder. To establish and maintain order, enduring social institutions are created and rules (laws) established so that human interaction can be regulated. In this way all parts of society can be co-ordinated so that members of society and society's organizations and institutions all contribute to the support, maintenance, and stability of the social system. The basic assumption is that there is agreement on the values and rules of society so that they, along with the social institutions regulating the system, must be learned, respected, and revered by everyone. "We learn what is expected of us in the family, at school, in the workplace and through the media."[17]

Social problems. If a person does not behave in ways expected of, say, a parent, a wage-earner, or a law-abiding citizen, it is assumed that something went wrong in that person's socialization process. To ensure itself against disequilibrium, society will attempt to return the person to normal functioning through its social institutions. If society's official agents, such as teachers, social workers, or police, fail to correct or control the malfunctioning or out-of-step person, then he or she may have to be removed from society and the individual's behaviour neutralized by institutionalization. This removes a threat to social stability and also serves as an example to other would-be non-conformists and deviants.

Because it is assumed that there is essential agreement among members of society on the nature of the prevailing institutions and supporting ideology, their existence is taken for granted and the existing order legitimated.[18] And because these institutions and their supporting ideology fend off disequilibrium, discontinuity, and disorder of the system, their preservation becomes a social imperative. These assumptions about social institutions being good, necessary, and agreed to, as well as the belief that people are contentious and must be controlled, lead order theorists to conclude that social problems are best described and understood by focusing on lower levels of society than on the societal or structural level. In other words, order theorists look at three levels of society for describing, analysing, and explaining social problems: (1) the individual level, (2) the family level, and (3) the subcultural level.[19]

At the individual level it is believed that the source of social problems lies within the person him or herself: a person is not conforming to the rules, norms, and expectations of society because of some individual trait. Poverty, mental illness, drug addiction, and criminal activity are blamed on supposed personal defects. As Reasons and Perdue point out, at the individual level social problems are personalized. Poverty and crime, for example, are blamed on some defect of the person and what emerges is "a biographical portrait that separates the individual from society."[20] Individuals are carefully scrutinized (diagnosed, assessed) to discover the source of the problem.

Examples of this level would include early criminologist Cesare Lombroso's explanation of criminal activity being caused by persons who are physically distinct from non-criminals. Freud's psychoanalytic theory where intra-psychic phenomena were hypothesized as the determinants of maladjusted behaviour is another example. Much of social work's earlier casework and psycho-dynamic practices were based on individual explanations of social problems. Socio-biology is a contemporary development of a theory that holds that genetic information explains social behaviour. As recently as 1988 a psychology professor from the University of Western Ontario created international controversy when he published an article alleging that race was connected to intelligence, sexual restraint, and personality, among other personal characteristics.[21]

Most order theorists (and most social workers), because they operate from a systems perspective or employ an ecological model when dealing with social problems, are not satisfied with individual levels of explanations of social problems. From this, mentioned in Chapter 4, comes the liberal concept of social disorganization. This concept is based on the notion that the present liberal-capitalist social order contains some defects that create disorganization and bring harm to some people, and it is the job of social work (and other occupations) to rectify these defects (i.e., to fix the parts of society not working properly so that society works better and persists). Systems theory and an ecological approach to social work, however, do not try to change the essential nature of the system but deal with individuals and/or environmental influences *within* the system. The types of environmental influences most frequently dealt with by order social workers are the family and the subculture.

The family as an important social unit has received enormous attention from social workers and others since the early sixties. Family disorganization has been cited as an explanation for most social problems that social workers deal with. The family is routinely analysed in an attempt to find its contribution to situations of poverty, juvenile delinquency, mental illness, alcoholism, family violence, poor school performance, and so on. Family therapy was viewed as almost a panacea to society's problems and "family dysfunction" replaced "individual pathology" as the popular explanation for social problems (but did not eliminate individualistic explanations). Rather than blaming social problems on some defect of the person, at the family level problems are attributed to poor parenting, undeveloped communication skills, and the like. Rather than a "sick" individual being blamed for social problems, as neo-conservatives contend, problems are blamed on "maladaptive" or "dysfunctional" families. Social problems are really family problems.

Explanations of social problems at the subcultural level of society focus on various categories of people who are distinct from the majority population by reason of such features as race, ethnicity, and class. Subculture theorists believe these distinctive groups have distinctive subcultural values that put them at a disadvantage or in conflict with the larger or dominant culture.[22] Social problems are not blamed on the individual or the family but are attributed to one's culture.

An example of a subcultural theory is the "culture of poverty" or what is often termed "the cycle of poverty theory," which attempts to explain poverty. The culture of poverty theory assumes there are common traits among poor people (feelings of inferiority, apathy, dependence, fatalism, no sense of deferred gratification). These traits are passed on to subsequent generations through the process of socialization so that by the time poor children are of school age they have internalized the basic traits of poverty and are not psychologically prepared to take advantage of the opportunities available to them. No thought is given to the possibility that many of these so-called traits of poor people are actually adaptations and adjustments on the part of the poor to cope with poverty rather than actual causes of poverty.

Another subcultural theory is the "cultural deprivation theory," which attempts to explain the situation of North American aboriginals and other minority groups. This theory attributes the second-class status of Native people and other minority groups to an inferior culture. In other words, Native culture is inadequate to prepare Native persons to function properly (successfully) in the larger society. Examples include: Native people do not read to their children; they do not take vacations abroad to expand their children's horizons; there is low motivation for school achievement or for work; there is no concept of the importance of time; welfare and alcoholism are part of this inferior culture. The end result is that children of Native ancestry are culturally deprived. Once so labelled, of course, they are expected to fail in school and often do so.

Both of the above subcultural explanations of social problems are part of a larger process of "blaming the victim."[23] William Ryan outlines this process:

1. Identify the problem.
2. Study those affected by the problem and discover how they are different from the rest of society.
3. Define the differences (which are in fact the effects of injustice and discrimination) as the causes of the social problem.
4. Assign a government bureaucrat to invent a humanitarian action program to correct the differences by *changing the people* affected by the problem.

Thus, the solution to social problems originating at the subcultural level is to try and untangle, correct, and make up for the deficiencies of these inferior cultures by changing the people from them. This strategy involves counselling, resocialization, cultural enhancement services, upgrading, rehabilitation, and community education programs. In effect, people are worked on so they can better fit into the mainstream, into the culture of the majority. This process of acculturation leaves society's social institutions unchanged. It is better to change a minority culture than to change social institutions so that they could accommodate the minority culture.

Social work and the order perspective. Within the order perspective social work operates at the three levels where social problems are seen to occur – the individual, family, and subcultural levels. Because the social order is assumed to be accepted by members of society, then the primary function of the social worker is to preserve it. Both the neo-conservative and the liberal paradigms subscribe to the goal of preserving the capitalist system. In the case of neo-conservatism, social work preserves the capitalist society by coercing and controlling persons who stray from the capitalist way of life. From a liberal perspective, social work preserves the capitalist system by helping people to adjust and cope, by modifying the immediate environments of persons, or by advocating on behalf of certain groups that have been disadvantaged by capitalism.

Most current social work theories and practices are based on the order perspective. Major activities are personal reform, limited social reform, and advocacy, all of which are carried out in an effort to humanize capitalism, not to change it. The major theories – psychoanalytic, family therapies, general systems theory, and the ecological approach – all emanate from the order perspective. In the case of psychoanalytic theory the major task is clearly personal reform. In the case of family therapy and general systems theory the major task is to repair the harm or disruption that has upset the healthy functioning of the family or the equilibrium of the system. The ecological approach aims to find the best fit between the person and the system. In none of these theories or approaches is any thought given to the possibility that the source of the problem lies not *within* the system but *is* the system itself. This critical omission is the Achilles' heel of conventional, mainstream social work carried out in the order tradition.

Conflict Perspective

The harmony and consensus extolled in the order perspective as characterizing society are not recognized in the conflict perspective. Or, if they are, it is because of an illusion created by the dominant group in society to lead the less powerful into accepting an unequal social order in which the dominant group is the main beneficiary.[24] The conflict perspective is strongly identified with Karl Marx (and therefore with socialism) and a variety of later writers.

Society. Conflict theorists accept the view of society as a system of interrelated parts but do not believe the parts are held together by consensus and shared interests and values. Rather, they see society comprising inherently opposing groups with respect to interests, values, and expectations. These groups compete for resources and power and those who win exercise their control and power by imposing an ideological world view that holds capitalism as the best of all economic systems.[25] Part of the ideological climate or hegemony established by the dominant group is the formulation of laws, the creation of social institutions, and the distribution of ideas favouring the dominant group. This results in structured inequality marked by vast differences in wealth, status, and power, and the social nature of human existence is denied.[26]

Conflict theorists do not accept the present social order. They want radical change. True order can only come about through the radical reorganization of society, not through the extension of social control.[27] Conflict theorists' vision of society is one where a new economic order of production would bring with it new social relations, with no one group dominating another.[28]

Social problems. Horton tells us that conflict analysis is synonymous with historical analysis, an interpretation of intersystem processes that bring about the transformation of social relations.[29] A key concept in this analysis is alienation, which means both separation from the social system and that people are alienated from each other in a society that reduces them to commodities. To the order theorist this situation is known as "anomie," which occurs when people lose their sense of collective consciousness. The role of the state, from the order perspective, is to promote this collective consciousness in order to protect and preserve the status quo. To the conflict theorist this situation is known as "alienation" and the progressive response would be change. In sum, the order theorist perceives anomie as synonymous with deviance and disorganization and the task is to bring people back into society. The conflict theorist views the same situation as alienation and the task is to change the society that creates and perpetuates inequality and alienation.

Conflict theorists do not believe that social problems normally originate with the individual, the family, or the subculture, as do order theorists, but "arise from the exploitive and alienating practices of dominant groups."[30] Given the nature of a society marked by inequality and structured along lines of class, gender, race, age, and so on, the explanation for social problems must lie at a higher societal plane than those perceived by order theorists. For conflict theorists the societal plane where social problems are more realistically described, analysed, and explained is at the structural level.[31] This level includes society's institutions and its supportive ideology. At this level a social problem is defined as:

> . . . a condition that involves the social injury of people on a broad scale. The injury may be physical in manifestation (as with disease stemming from a health service geared to income), social-psychological (as with alienation), economic (as with poverty), political (as with the oppression of dissident groups), or intellectual (as with nonexistent or inadequate education). Social problems ensue from institutional defects and are not to be best interpreted or understood through individuals, families, or subcultures. Thus, the social problem as such is not an aberration but rather a normal consequence of the way in which a society is organized.[32]

Reasons and Perdue point out that the above definition of social problems does not mean that conflict theorists ignore individuals, families, and subcultures as areas for study.[33] The difference is that conflict theorists will always connect these societal planes with the broader structural order of society. In other words, the conflict theorist will always look to public issues (i.e., social institutions and their supportive ideology) as the source of private troubles. And because social problems are rooted in the social order they cannot be resolved by technical or administrative reforms. They can only be resolved by a massive reorganization or transformation of the social system. In sum, the major postulates of the conflict perspective are:

1. Society is the setting within which various struggles occur among different groups whose interests, values, and behaviours conflict with one another.
2. The state is an important agent participating in the struggle on the side of the powerful groups.
3. Social inequality is a result of coercive institutions that legitimate force, fraud, and inheritance as the major means of obtaining rights and privileges.
4. Social inequality is a chief source of conflict.
5. The state and the law are instruments of oppression controlled and used by the dominant groups for their own benefit.
6. Classes are social groups with distinctive interests that inevitably bring them into conflict with other groups with opposed interests.[34]

Social work and the conflict perspective. The conflict social worker must fight for change at all social, economic, and political levels. A conflict analysis of society reveals who is benefiting from established social arrangements; it shows how domination is maintained; and it suggests what must be done to bring about changes in power and resources. To assist the victims of an oppressive social order the social worker needs to know who holds the power, whose interests are being served by maintaining the status quo, and what devices are being used to keep things as they are.[35]

Because social democracy and socialism are based on conflict thought, then social work from a conflict perspective would be very similar to the nature and type of social work practice outlined in Chapters 5 and 6. Social work would have a dual function: (1) to provide practical humanitarian care to the casualties of a capitalist social order; and (2) at the same time, to further the democratization and restructuring of society along socialist lines.

The conflict-based dual function of social work does not preclude intervention at the individual, family, and subcultural levels. The difference is that instead of dealing with each of these levels by itself, the connection between people's private troubles and the structural source of these troubles would be made in every case. Rather than looking within the individual or within one's family or within one's subculture for the source of distress, the way in which the larger social order perpetrates and perpetuates people's problems would be identified and communicated to the person or group experiencing the distress. Although conflict social workers would do many of the same things that order social workers would do, many differences emanate from the different explanations each holds about the nature of society and of social problems. These differences will be discussed in the next two chapters.

Critical Theory

The conflict perspective underpins a school of social theory known as *critical theory*. Critical theory concerns itself with social transformation – moving from a society characterized by exploitation, inequality, and oppression to one that is emancipatory and free from domination. Karl Marx is arguably the founder of critical theory. His ideas and emancipatory intentions have been extended and developed by the Frankfurt School (most notably Theodore Adorno, Max Horkheimer, and Herbert Marcuse) and by its heir apparent, Jürgen Habermas.[36] The vision of critical theory held by these thinkers is referred to as "modernist." A more recent version of critical theory, known as "post-modernism," has been developed with Michel Foucault as its most prominent proponent. Although the two versions share a commitment to a conception of social theory as politically engaged, post-modernism indicts the idea that modernism contains within itself the potential for human emancipation.[37]

In *Critical Theory in Political Practice*, Stephen Leonard defines critical theory:

> A critical theory of society is defined as a theory having practical intent. As its name suggests, it is critical of existing social and political institutions and practices, but the criticisms it levels are not intended simply to show how present society is unjust, only to leave everything as it is. A critical theory of society is understood by its advocates as playing a crucial role in changing society. In this, the link between social theory and political practice is perhaps the defining characteristic of critical theory, for a critical theory without a practical dimension would be bankrupt on its own terms.[38]

Critical theory, then, is different from most social science theory constructed according to the canons of scientific inquiry. Social theory may describe and explain social processes, but is quite independent of political practice.

Leonard contends that there are three requirements or undertakings of a critical theory: (1) it must locate the sources of domination in actual social practices; (2) it must present an alternative vision (or at least an outline) of a life free from such domination; and (3) it must translate these tasks in a form that is intelligible to those who are oppressed in society.[39] Current examples of theory that satisfy these requirements and, therefore, are critical theories (by definition) in practice are Paulo Freire's "pedagogy of the oppressed," "liberation theology," and some forms (i.e., transformative forms) of feminist theory.[40]

In accordance with the above requirements of a critical theory, structural social work theory is a critical theory. It is critical of existing social, economic, and political institutions and practices and seeks to change them. It has articulated an alternative social vision (or at least an outline) consistent with progressive social work values in which life is free from domination. And, as will be seen in the following two chapters, a major thrust is to involve people in its social analysis and its political practice.

The Dialectic in Structural Social Work

The most prominent aspect of structural social work is its dialectical analysis and approach to practice. The concept of dialectic is an essential component of structural social work theory. It sensitizes practice to the opposing and contradictory forces within capitalism,[41] the welfare state, and social work, and it helps social work avoid the construction of false dichotomies or dualisms that have been part of the social work tradition. This tradition is actually two traditions – an idealist tradition that persuades individuals they can effect great changes through self-determination, and a structural determinist tradition that sees individuals as the victims of a deterministic social environment that cannot be changed. Neither tradition comprehends the dialectic between the individual and the social world – the individual is both the creator of the social world and is created by the social world.

Dialectical analysis is based on a view of society and social processes as containing contradictory opposites that must be unravelled and understood. A dialectical social work theory recognizes the false dualisms of orthodox social work theory and attempts to replace them with a recognition of the symbiotic relationship between contradictory elements with all their attendant mutuality. For example, the welfare state has both social care and social control functions, it contains both liberating and oppressive features, and it represents both the fruits of the struggles of oppressed people and a mechanism used by the dominant group to "cool out" the powerless.[42] Without a dialectical understanding of social process, false dichotomies or dualisms are constructed and incorporated into social work theory and practice. The social welfare state and social work may be viewed by one group as solely part of the state apparatus that controls and oppresses people (e.g., orthodox Marxists). Another group may view them as instruments of human liberation representing only humanitarian concern (e.g., conventional social workers). A dialectic perspective recognizes that social welfare and social work contain both of these contradictory forces. Given this dialectical perspective the strategy for structural social work is to maximize the emancipatory potential of social welfare and social work and to neutralize or minimize their repressive elements.

A question addressed by a dialectical perspective is whether or not individuals are subjects (creators of their social structures) or objects (created by their social structures). Wardell and Benson argue that they are both:

> Fundamental to the dialectical view is the conception that human beings actively produce their social and material world. In doing so they objectify themselves in the form of social relations and material objects. This productive dimension of social life exists because human beings are able to imagine future social arrangements and then engage in purposeful activity to create those arrangements. . . . The instability of societies stems from this reflexive process since human beings may set out to intentionally reconstruct their world. This production process undermines established arrangements,

> edging them toward fundamental change. And, at critical junctures, people may act jointly to construct alternatives . . . . But because of the form of the present social structure, human beings may be only partly conscious of themselves, others, and the alternative possibilities when producing their social world . . . the production of social life is [not] random or extremely relative. The social structure of any society sets limitations upon what can be produced and by whom. . . . *Any social structure will limit and restrain the production of future alternatives, but the same structure contains openings through which human beings can construct innovative alternatives to the present limitations.*[43]

Mullaly and Keating contend that many of the philosophical, theoretical, and practical disagreements that exist among radical social workers are actually due to the inadvertent acceptance on the part of many of certain false dichotomies. They further argue that a dialectical approach would lead to greater integration of theory and better informed radical practice.[44] In the chapters on social democracy and Marxism three schools of socialist thought were identified – social democracy, evolutionary Marxism, and revolutionary Marxism. These three schools differ with respect to their individual prescriptions for social transformation. Three questions that are fundamental to structural social work and that would elicit disagreement among the socialist schools are: (1) Should structural social workers work inside or outside the social welfare system? (2) What is the primary or fundamental source of oppression in a capitalist society? (3) Do structural social workers concentrate on changing people's consciousness (i.e., radical humanism) as a prerequisite to social change or do they concentrate on changing material conditions and structural patterns as a prerequisite to changing people's consciousness (i.e., radical structuralism)? The following responses to these questions should help to explain and clarify the dialectical nature of structural social work.

(1) Where should structural social workers work – inside or outside of the social welfare system? Social democrats appreciate the welfare state within a capitalist society for providing people with a minimum standard of living, but they believe it should also promote greater equality and social justice. They view the capitalist welfare state as a stepping stone toward a socialist society and, therefore, advocate working within the system. Revolutionary Marxists believe that the capitalist welfare state promotes the survival, not the transformation, of capitalism. Therefore, they maintain that structural social workers should work outside the welfare system and support welfare rights groups, co-operatives, self-help groups, and other alternative services

and organizations that challenge capitalism. The evolutionary Marxists join with the social democrats in their belief that the welfare state can be used to transform capitalism, but agree with the revolutionary Marxists that many welfare state activities support and preserve capitalism. Thus they would work within the system but would separate the forces for socialist change from the forces that preserve capitalism.

A dialectical analysis recognizes the place of human consciousness in the creation and re-creation of human circumstances, but also recognizes that circumstances affect people and shape their consciousness. The state is shaped both by the logic of capitalism, patriarchy, and racism and by the conscious struggles of people along lines of class, gender, and race. Modern states contain both emancipatory and repressive forces.[45] This requires structural social workers to work both inside and outside the welfare state.

(2) What is the primary or fundamental source of oppression in a capitalist society? Subscribing to a social conflict rather than a class conflict perspective, social democrats believe that conflict in a capitalist society derives from various sources, including gender, race, economic status, and religion. These diverse conflicts result in a system of winners and losers, with power and privilege going to the winners and alienation and oppression going to the losers. Social democratic social workers consider all social conflicts when developing strategies for social transformation. Revolutionary Marxists believe that class conflict is the primary and fundamental source of oppression in a capitalist society. They recognize other conflicts as well, but believe that they can be resolved within capitalism whereas the resolution of class conflict requires the abolition of capitalism. Revolutionary Marxists differ about the relative importance of other conflicts and their relationship to class conflict. (The emphasis on class conflict has been moderated somewhat by Marxist feminism, which stresses a class analysis but also sees patriarchy as rooted in capitalism.) Evolutionary Marxists regard class conflict as the primary source of oppression in a capitalist society, but include gender, race, age, and other conflicts as secondary sources of oppression. These secondary conflicts are also sources of alienation and oppression and must be included in any strategy for social transformation.

Frankel, a dialectical theorist, states the dialectical view on oppression in a capitalist society:

> Only the full recognition of the decisive and contradictory role of the state apparatuses can help create political organizations adequate to holistic struggle needed to defeat capitalism. Because the state is involved in everything from wage fixing, to sexual, racial,

> urban, and ecological policies, any political organization which claims to be revolutionary must abandon the notion that certain struggles are primary and others secondary.[46]

Structural social work theory is all-inclusive with respect to sources of oppression in capitalist society and does not attempt to prioritize them.[47] Initially, radical social work focused only on the oppression of white, male members of the working class. Today, structural social work includes in its analysis the role and functions of patriarchy, racism, ageism, ability/disability, colonialism of North American Native people,[48] imperialism of Third World countries by developed countries,[49] and heterosexism.[50]

Although the inclusion of non-classist forms of oppression has made structural social work more relevant for more oppressed groups, it also divides the progressive ranks. The segmentation and fragmentation of oppression is one of the major obstacles to social transformation. Treating the various forms of oppression as distinct fails to recognize that they are also related to one another, that they are mutually reinforcing, that they intersect and interact in people's everyday lives, and that they are part of a total system of oppression. Without a dialectical analysis there is a danger of identifying only a single fundamental source of oppression, which, according to Wineman,

> . . . fails to create a basis for unity which respects the dignity and felt experience of all the oppressed individuals and groups who are supposed to become unified, and it fails to generate a practical strategy and process which can . . . challenge all forms of oppression even if it is true that historically one or another of the various "fundamental" factors was actually the "root cause" of all other forms of oppression, the plain fact is that effects are capable of outliving their original causes. . . . Thus, even if it were true that capitalism was the original cause of sexism (which in itself is highly dubious . . .), it is a matter of record that sexism has persisted following the overthrow of capitalist systems. It seems equally plain that the overthrow of male domination would not inevitably eradicate racism . . . and so on.[51]

(3) Radical humanism vs. radical structuralism: which comes first, the personal or the political? Although radical social workers recognize the connection between private troubles and public issues, there is disagreement on which should come first in a strategy of political transformation, the personal or the political. Should changing people (by consciousness-raising) be a prerequisite to changing society or is the redistribution of wealth and power necessary to change people's

consciousness? The former approach is known as "radical humanism" and the latter as "radical structuralism."[52] Each reflects a different set of ontological (the nature of being) and epistemological (the nature of knowledge) assumptions.[53]

Radical humanism is a subjectivist orientation to social change and radical structuralism is an objectivist orientation. Each would provide a different answer to the question, "Are we creators of or created by our social reality?" Subjectivist radical humanism holds that knowledge and social reality are created in people's minds through personal experience,[54] and that no social facts exist because we create our own social reality. Conversely, objectivist radical structuralism holds that knowledge and social reality are external to the individual, that social reality is composed of concrete structures, and that this external social reality has a deterministic impact on an individual's development and circumstances.[55]

Obviously, radical humanists and radical structuralists favour different means (i.e., social work practices) to achieve a society free from inequality. The former, who believe that personal consciousness-raising precedes political change, would focus their efforts on raising people's consciousness about how inequalities shape, limit, oppress, and dominate their experiences.[56] By understanding how capitalist hegemony operates to make people accept their subjugation they can free themselves to regain control over their present experiences and their destiny.[57] Paulo Freire's work is relevant to the subjectivist approach of radical humanists. Radical structuralists, who believe that reality resides in the social world rather than in the person, would focus their efforts on changing material conditions and structural patterns along socialist lines. With enough changes a socialist society would become the new reality. Radical structuralists would organize and mobilize social service users, trade unions, and other social activist groups to achieve this transformation. This approach involves consciousness-raising focused on the reality of unfair social structures and how they are perpetuated rather than on constrained individual reality. Each of these approaches to social transformation contains limitations.

> Radical humanism naively and optimistically assumes that raising people's consciousness will effectively address social problems and expose an exploitative social system. It ignores the fact that power and privilege, whether rooted in class, gender, or race, is [*sic*] not likely to be relinquished without a struggle and that part of this struggle would involve supporting the ideological hegemony required to continue to control people's consciousness. Radical structuralism is overly simplistic and deterministic in its

understanding of the complexity of human need and the depth of oppression. It is difficult to understand how describing external power empowers people to change it.[58]

A dialectical analysis would view these two different approaches to radical practice as a false dichotomy. Although both link private troubles and public issues, they dichotomize praxis (political practice) along personal-political lines. Subjective reality and objective reality are irrevocably locked into a dialectical relationship. We are conscious creators of our surroundings, using thought, information, and emotion to act and to choose. At the same time, we are created by our surroundings. A dialectical approach to structural social work avoids the simplistic linear cause-effect notion of historical materialism and the naive romanticism associated with the notion of totally free human will.[59] Dialectical analysis helps to illuminate the complex interplay between people and the world around them and to indicate the role of social work within society. "We are not only objects of the prevailing social order, we must also be subjects who are able to move beyond it."[60] In short, structural social work incorporates both these radical traditions into its theory base, recognizing that they constitute a dialectical whole rather than distinct and contradictory approaches. It is not a question of which comes first, the personal or the political. Neither is a prerequisite to the other; both must occur conjointly.

Feminism, Anti-Racism, and Structural Social Work Theory

Feminist theory and analysis are enormous sources of information and inspiration for structural social work theory and practice. Although early radical social work theory neglected patriarchy and racism as sources of oppression, recent feminist insights of the ways patriarchy structures virtually all social institutions, such as families, the market, and the welfare state, have been incorporated into structural social work analyses.[61] Given its increasing importance as a major social work perspective,[62] along with the predominance of women among users and providers of social work services, the feminist perspective is an epistemological imperative for structural social work.

Feminist analysis not only decodes patriarchy and stresses the links between the personal and political better than any other theory, it, like structural social work, emphasizes transformational politics.[63] Some feminist theories do not limit this transformation to a constituency of women but seek the end of domination and oppression of all people.

It (feminism) is a vision born of women, but it addresses the future of the planet with implications accruing for males as well as

> females, for all ethnic groups, for the impoverished, for the disadvantaged, the handicapped, the aged and so on.[64]

Although feminists share the basic view that patriarchal society is oppressive, different feminist analyses exist with respect to the fundamental source of oppression in society. In their frequently cited *Feminist Frameworks,* Jagger and Struhl identify four feminist approaches.[65] Liberal feminism accepts liberal capitalism and seeks to reform it by removing gender-based discrimination from all social institutions. As such, because it accepts liberal capitalism, it is largely incompatible with structural social work. Socialist feminists believe capitalism and patriarchy are co-determinants of oppression. Marxist feminists believe that capitalism is the fundamental form of oppression, but that patriarchy is the fundamental source of oppression. Both socialist and Marxist feminists see the solution to ending sexism as transforming capitalism into socialism. Radical feminism places gender ahead of class, asserting that patriarchy is responsible for women's oppression. Control over women's reproductive capacity is often favoured as a social change strategy. Socialist, Marxist, and radical feminists have much to offer structural social work theory and practice in their understanding of the nature and dynamics of patriarchy.[66]

Just as early radical social work neglected patriarchy as a source of oppression, it also largely ignored racism as a major source of oppression.[67] And just as black women criticized the early feminist movement for ignoring the special and more complex situation of women of colour, so, too, have black social workers criticized the early radical social work movement for overlooking anti-racist social work practice.[68]

> Racism institutionalizes the myth of white superiority by creating social structures and processes that support this pattern of domination. The political, social, and economic marginalization experienced by people of colour reinforces racist beliefs within white society and helps to maintain the oppression of non-whites.[69]

While feminist writers have shown that a radical social work practice that ignores gender reproduces sexist practices, so black activists have shown that a colourblind social work practice reproduces racist practices. An anti-racist structural social work practice would raise the consciousness of practitioners and service users about the oppressive effects of racism and its interplay with capitalism and patriarchy.

As other oppressed groups such as Native persons, gays and lesbians, and the disabled develop and make known structural analyses of their subordinate positions in society with their attendant exploitation and oppression, these perspectives will be incorporated into structural social work theory, as were the feminist and anti-racist analyses. Obviously, the theory base of structural social work is not static. It will continue to grow and to change as more information on current and new sources of oppression is gained and as information on the application of structural social work theory is received.

Part III

Structural Social Work: Practice Elements

9

Working Within (and Against) the System

Introduction

The ultimate goal of structural social work is to contribute to the transformation of society. To accomplish this goal social work must operationalize an ideology within a society where another ideology dominates. And to carry out this task the social worker should possess the following attributes:

- an awareness of the limits of patriarchal, liberal capitalism as a satisfactory social system;
- an awareness of an alternative vision of society where human need is the central value;
- an awareness that social work is a political activity that either reinforces or opposes the status quo;
- an awareness that social problems are not amenable to individual, family, or subcultural solutions;
- an awareness that critical social analysis by itself is an important social work skill;
- an awareness that structural social work is much more than an approach to practice; it is a way of life.

The guiding principle for structural social work practice is that everything we do must in some way contribute to the goal of social transformation. This does not mean that the legitimate, here-and-now immediate needs of people are ignored. Rather, structural social work practice comprises a simultaneous two-pronged approach: (1) to provide practical, humanitarian care to the victims and casualties of our patriarchal, liberal-capitalist society; and (2) to restructure society along socialist lines. This two-pronged approach to practice is consistent with the concept of dialectic discussed in the previous chapter.

The purpose of this chapter is to present certain practice elements that characterize structural social work practice and that therefore distinguish it from conventional social work practice. Although these practice elements are presented and analysed separately here, in reality they cannot be separated so easily, for they are all interrelated, functionally intertwined, and mutually reinforcing. These elements of practice help to operationalize structural social work theory. Through the practice of this structural social work theory, social workers will contribute to the long-term transformation of society by tending to the short-term needs of people within the social welfare institution – the very system that oppresses those who depend on it and those who work within it.

The theory of structural social work does not consider any level of social work practice as inherently conservative or oppressive. Nor does it consider that one level of practice is inherently more progressive and liberating than another. For example, Galper has shown how community organization, as it has traditionally been practised, is just as conservative as traditional casework.[1] And a substantial literature now shows how casework or clinical work can be emancipatory as opposed to oppressive.[2] The major distinction between liberal mainstream social work practice and structural social work practice is that the former reflects and perpetuates the present social order whereas the latter attempts to transform it.

The approach to structural practice within the social welfare system emanates from the radical humanist school of thought. This approach is based on the belief that changing people by personal consciousness-raising on a massive scale is a prerequisite for changing society. This consciousness-raising, which is carried out by structural social workers with service users and with co-workers, focuses on raising people's awareness of how capitalist society shapes, limits, and dominates their experiences, thus alienating them from social structures, from each other, and from their true selves. Only by becoming aware of how others define us to suit their own interests and by understanding how ideological hegemony makes our subjugation appear acceptable can we become free to regain control over our lives and our destiny.[3]

Working with Service Users

The Personal Is Political

Although social work has always espoused an awareness of the connection between the personal and the political,[4] the emphasis for the most part has been on personal change, adjustment, and/or coping. This emphasis, of course, is consistent with the order view of society discussed earlier. In fact, a dichotomy emerged in social work practice in that most social workers chose and worked within the areas of casework, group work, and family therapy (i.e., intervention on a personal level), leaving the larger socio-political issues to the numerical minority of community organization and social policy social workers. Social workers who subscribe to a conflict analysis of society view this split as a false dichotomy[5] and would point to what C. Wright Mills said about the relationship between the individual and society, "Neither the life of an individual nor the history of a society can be understood without understanding both."[6]

"The personal is political" is a slogan associated with the feminist movement. It is a method of analysis developed and refined by feminists for "gleaning political insights from an analysis of personal experience – in particular, female experience."[7] Most writers today use the statement when analysing or discussing how the socio-economic political context of a society is critical in shaping who we are in terms of our personality formation and what we are in terms of our personal situation.[8] Social work deals with many personal issues, troubles, and situations. If the personal is political, then social work is political also.

The premise that the personal is political has two major implications for social work practice. First, it signals that a social worker's individual practice has certain political ends. This applies to the practice of all social workers. Our personal practices contain political ends. For conventional social work the political end is to maintain the status quo. This is done by personalizing social problems. For structural social work the political end is to change the status quo and leave oppression behind. This does not preclude intervention at the individual or family level, but instead of dealing with each of these levels by itself the connection between private troubles and the structural source of these troubles is made in every case. Each structural social worker must see her or his individual work as an integral element of the larger movement of social transformation.

The second major implication that "the personal is political" has for social work practice is that it forces the worker beyond carrying out mere psycho-social manipulations, which in effect pathologize those people who are forced to use social work services. Understanding the political (structural) reasons for private troubles enables the worker to communicate this information (i.e., consciousness-raising) to the persons experiencing difficulties and to put their situation into its proper perspective (i.e., normalization), thus reducing some of the internalized guilt and blame (i.e., internal oppression) that many people experience as part of their troubled situations. These processes, along with some of the techniques that facilitate them, are discussed below.

Structural social work owes a great deal to feminist analysis. It has shown us the nature and extent of patriarchy in our society and it has given us ways of dealing with women's oppression that do not further contribute to it. Too much of conventional social work practice locates the source of many problems women face within the person herself. This psychologizing of what are essentially social problems contributes to women's oppression by not looking at women in the context of a patriarchal social context and by placing the blame for personal troubles squarely on the shoulders of women experiencing them. Because of the many social workers who have been actively involved in and/or influenced by the feminist movement, there is now a major social work perspective and practice based on feminist theory and analysis.[9] In addition, feminist social work writers have shown us that sexism exists within our own profession.[10] And, of course, the identification, awareness, and analysis of sexism in social work is a prerequisite to purging us of it.

The personal is political as a method of analysis has relevance and utility for dealing with all sources of oppression in our society. It can be used to understand better the nature and extent of racism in our society and how it contributes to the oppression of visible minority groups. It can be used to understand better the nature of colonialism and how it contributes to the oppression of Native persons in our society and to the oppression of Third World countries by the developed societies. It can be used, as well, to understand better oppression based on classism, ageism, physical disability, mental disability, heterosexism, and so on. What conventional social workers treat as private problems belonging to isolated individuals, structural social workers would treat as public problems belonging to a society where classsism, sexism, ageism, heterosexism, and racism exist.

Oppression

Much of structural social work practice involves working with oppressed people. Therefore, it is crucial to have an understanding of the nature of oppression, its causes and sources, its dynamics, its effects on the oppressed, and the social functions it carries out in the interests of the dominant groups (i.e., the oppressors) in society.

To understand what oppression is, it is necessary to know what oppression is not. Since people are social beings and live in societies, no one is free from social structures. Such structures consist of boundaries, barriers, expectations, regulations, and so on. One could make a loose argument that everyone in society is oppressed because one's choices or freedoms are restricted by the facts of social structures. For example, when a person drives an automobile she/he is obliged to buckle up her or his seat belt, to drive on the right-hand side of the road, and to obey all traffic laws and regulations. These restrictions on our freedom cannot be regarded as oppressive. Not everything that frustrates or limits or hurts a person is oppressive. So, if one wishes to distinguish between what oppression is and is not, one has to look at the social context of a particular restriction, limit, or injury.[11]

Everyone suffers frustrations, restrictions, and hurt. What determines oppression is when these happen to a person not because of individual talent, merit, or failure, but because of his or her membership in a particular group or category of people, for example, blacks, women, poor people, and gay persons. "If an individual is oppressed, it is by virtue of being a member of a group or category of people that is systematically reduced, molded, immobilized. Thus, to recognize a person as oppressed, one has to see that individual as belonging to a group of a certain sort."[12] Of course, not all groups in society are oppressed. Those in the dominant mainstream of society are less likely to be oppressed and more likely to be among the oppressors. Women are oppressed (by men) as women. Men are not oppressed as men. Non-whites are oppressed (by whites) as non-whites. Whites are not oppressed as whites. Gay persons are oppressed (by heterosexuals) as gay persons. Heterosexuals are not oppressed as heterosexuals.

It was pointed out earlier that there are two schools of thought regarding the causes or sources of oppression, the monist view and the pluralist view. The former targets different "domination relations" as the primary source of oppression (such as sexism or classism) whereas the latter believes that there is no single class of determining relations but more than one that operate simultaneously. The monist approach is too simplistic, as it reduces complex social phenomena to a single set of causal factors that compete with other sets (e.g., sexism vs. classism) for theoretical explanation. The pluralist approach is used here, with the recognition, however, that it also is inadequate as a theory of oppression because it does not attend to the more subtle ways that, for example, gender relations redefine class definitions.[13] Until such a theory is developed the pluralist approach will have to suffice.

In addition to the fact that oppression is group-based (i.e., mainstream groups tend to be the oppressors of groups outside the mainstream), another feature of oppression is that it is not accidental.

> The experience of oppressed people is that the living of one's life is confined and shaped by forces and barriers which are *not accidental or occasional* and hence avoidable, but are systematically related to each other in such a way as to catch one between and among them and restrict or penalize motion in any direction.[14]

Given that oppression is perpetrated and perpetuated by dominant groups and is systematic and continuous in its application, a logical question is why does it occur? The simple and correct answer to this question is that oppression occurs because it benefits the dominant group. Oppression protects a kind of citizenship that is superior to that of the oppressed. It protects the oppressors' access to a wider range of better-paying and higher-status work. It protects the oppressors' preferential access to and preferential treatment from our social institutions. The oppressed serve as a ready supply of labour to carry out the menial and dangerous jobs in society, and they also serve as scapegoats during difficult times for the dominant group, often being blamed for inflation, government deficits, recessions, social disruptions, and so on. In short, oppression carries out a social purpose for the dominant group, ensuring that society reproduces itself and maintains the same determining relationships.

The dominant class in society probably does not really subscribe to oppressive behaviour as a means of protecting its favourable position. Most people do not consider themselves as oppressors. In fact, most people would probably believe that oppressive behaviour should not be a part of a democratic society. Why, then, do they engage in oppressive acts? Paulo Freire eloquently answers this question:

> The oppressors do not perceive their monopoly on *having more* as a privilege which dehumanizes others and themselves. . . . For them, *having more* is an inalienable right, a right they acquired through their own "effort," with their "courage to take risks." If others do not have more, it is because they are incompetent and lazy, and worst of all is their unjustifiable ingratitude towards the "generous gestures" of the dominant class. Precisely because they are "ungrateful" and "envious," the oppressed are regarded as potential enemies who must be watched.[15]

Thus, the view that the oppressors hold of the oppressed is that they constitute a dangerous class that must be controlled for the good of the whole society.

Social control of the oppressed is carried out in two ways. First, society is structured in such a way by the dominant class that it primarily meets its own needs. All the state's institutions – the law, the army, the political system, the economic system, the social welfare institution, education, the media – are controlled by the dominant group. Inequality is built into the social structures and relationships to protect and further the interests of the dominant group. In essence, we have structural oppression.

Second, social control is carried out through a process of legitimization of oppression known as *ideological hegemony.* This is the capacity of the dominant group to rule by control not only over social institutions but over ideas as well. This control is exercised through such institutions as education, religion, and the mass media. The dominant class deliberately manipulates and distorts the knowledge, ideas, and values of oppressed people to generate the acceptance or legitimation of liberal-patriarchal capitalism. Marcuse, writing in the 1960s in the United States, argued that this hegemonic ruling process is so successful that most people cannot even conceive of any alternative to capitalism. Through its control of our social institutions and its ideological dominance the ruling class alliance has managed to secure through the state such a total social authority over the subordinate classes that it shapes the whole direction of social life in its own interests.[16] When this happens a consensus seems to exist in society – the general population appears to consent to the direction imposed on society by the dominant group.[17]

The liberal ideology, with a resurgence of some conservative values, constitutes the present ideology in North America. Through the process of ideological hegemony many people believe that if they cannot make it in our society, that if they are experiencing problems, then it is their own fault because they were unable to take advantage of opportunities available to everyone. In other words, one of the consequences of ideological hegemony is that people will often internalize their own oppression and blame themselves for their difficult situations and problems. It is, as Paulo Freire said, as if the oppressor gets in the head of the oppressed.[18] People understand their interests in ways that reflect the interests of the dominant group.

When people internalize their oppression, blaming themselves for their troubled circumstances, they will often contribute to their own oppression by considering it as unique, unchangeable, deserved, or temporary,[19] or else blame other significant people in their lives, such as parents or family. Oppressed persons often contribute to their own oppression also by psychologically or socially withdrawing or engaging in other self-destructive behaviour, thereby causing them to be rejected by others, which in turn confirms the low image they have of themselves.[20] The radical psychiatric movement considers all alienation to be the result of oppression about which the oppressed have been mystified or deceived. That is, the oppressed person is led to believe he or she is not oppressed or that there are good reasons for his or her oppression.[21]

Freire discusses several positions oppressed people may adopt that either reinforce or contribute to their own oppression.[22] Fatalism may be expressed by the oppressed about their situation: "There is nothing I can do about it" and "It is God's will" are common expressions of fatalism. However, this fatalistic attitude is often interpreted as docility or apathy by the oppressors, which reinforces their view of the oppressed as lazy, inferior, and getting all that they deserve. Horizontal violence often occurs among oppressed people whereby an aboriginal, for example, may strike out at another Native for petty reasons, which again reinforces the negative images held by the dominant class of the subordinate groups. Self-depreciation also occurs when a group hears so often that they are good for nothing that in the end they become convinced of their own unfitness. Moreau and Leonard call this process inferiorization.[23] Another characteristic of some oppressed persons is that they feel an irresistible attraction toward the oppressor and his or her way of life. This affirms, of course, the belief that oppression is legitimate and that it is more desirable to oppress than to be oppressed.

In sum, oppression is a complex social phenomenon based on social groupings that results in negative living conditions for many so that a few might benefit. It is essential that structural social workers understand the nature, dynamics, and social functions of oppression. It is also necessary to understand how oppression is internalized and how people might contribute to their own oppression. We must now look at ways to overcome the oppression of people with whom social workers work.

Empowerment

From the preceding discussion it is obvious that oppression leads to alienation and powerlessness of the subordinate classes. Most definitions of power or powerlessness refer to the control or lack of control persons have over their environment and their destiny. Oppressed people, as individuals, have limited choices over most aspects of their lives and are ruled by forces of which they are not even aware. A tenet of mental health is that "Throughout life, the feeling of controlling one's destiny to some reasonable extent is the essential psychological component of all aspects of life."[24]

The lack of control that oppressed people experience over their life situation and their destiny robs them of their essential human dignity, for without any real control life becomes meaningless. We drift through it, controlled by others, used by others, and devalued by others for the interests of others. Oppression, then, violates, contradicts, and nullifies several important social work values and beliefs: self-determination, personal growth and development, the inherent dignity and worth of people, social equality, and even democracy itself.

Empowerment, as a goal and a process, has been a recurrent theme in social work history.[25] However, since the 1980s it has been receiving increasing attention in social work theory and practice.[26] One writer identifies empowerment as the major goal of social work intervention,[27] while another "calls for a revision of social work practice theory in a way that defines the major function of social work as empowering people to be able to make choices and gain control over their environment."[28] Empowerment is typically understood as a process through which people reduce their powerlessness and alienation and gain greater control over all aspects of their lives and their social environment. Simon points out that empowerment (1) has its basis in the self-help or mutual aid traditions and in the civil and human rights activities of the 1960s; and (2) because of the many groups, organizations, and professions involved with empowerment in all its dimensions, it should be considered as a social movement. "Empowerment, in short, is a series of attacks on subordination of every description – psychic, physical, cultural, sexual, legal, political, economic, and technological."[29]

As a dialectical process empowerment occurs in two ways. Consistent with radical structuralism, empowerment for some disciplines and groups is essentially a political and economic process whereby these structurally oriented groups will actively attempt to gain more power and influence over those organizations and institutions, such as schools, hospitals, and the workplace, that affect their lives. This area of empowerment will be examined in more detail in the next chapter. Consistent with radical humanism, the empowerment process involves the psychological, educational, cultural, and spiritual dimensions involved when individuals are helped to understand their oppression and to take steps to overcome it. This latter humanistic empowerment process is discussed here.

Simon points out that empowerment is a compelling topic for social work for three major reasons.[30] First, the people that social workers work with tend to be in marginal and disadvantaged positions and are among the most oppressed, alienated, and powerless. Second, social work is a profession disproportionately staffed by women, who themselves comprise a group that historically has been oppressed and powerless, even within the profession of social work.[31] And third, "Social workers of both genders are no strangers to the experiences of being discounted, scapegoated, dislodged, underpaid, and overlooked by legislatures, public administrators, executive directors of agencies, colleagues in other professions, academics, clients, and the public."[32] We know firsthand the meaning of occupational subordination.

This trinity of interests in empowerment should serve as a catalyst for social work to continue to devise theory and strategies for working with oppressed and disempowered groups, including the profession itself. Hasenfeld contends that empowerment must occur on at least three levels in social work: (1) at the worker/service-user level, where activities are carried out to increase the service user's power resources; (2) at the agency level, where organizational policies should be aimed at increasing people's power resources rather than conformity to prescribed behaviours; and (3) at the social policy level, where the formulation and enactment of policy decisions are influenced by those directly affected by them.[33]

Many inherent difficulties are involved in such work, but if three considerations are kept in mind at all times then the process of empowerment will be greatly facilitated. First, social workers cannot empower others but can only aid and abet in the empowerment process. Service users "who are empowered by their social workers have, de facto, lost ground . . . in their battle for autonomy and control over their own environment and existence." The role of social work is to provide "a climate, a relationship, resources and procedural means through which people can enhance their own lives."[34] The relationship between social worker and user is one of collaboration, with the latter retaining control of the purpose, pace, and direction of the collaborative effort.

A second important aspect of the empowerment process is that instead of being an expert problem-solver the social worker becomes engaged in a mutual learning situation with the service user.[35] The worker should not assume that a compatibility of interests exists between service user and worker.[36] What could be more presumptuous and more disrespectful on the part of a social worker than to think that she or he knew exactly what the problem is and what the solutions are? To avoid this elitist, expert, disempowering practice, social workers should: (1) continually update their knowledge of the history of race, gender, class, and other relations of subordinate groups (i.e., know as much as possible about the groups one is working with);[37] and (2) help the service user define and contextualize his or her situation and problems while always encouraging him or her to question and to express disagreement or reservations about particular interventions the social worker might suggest.[38]

A third aspect of empowerment for social workers is to avoid exploiting the helping encounter for their own benefit.[39] It was mentioned that social work experiences subordination as an occupation. Also, we are often stigmatized because of our association with marginalized groups. Thus, we may be vulnerable in terms of compensating for the powerlessness we experience at work and may use our professional role to gain a sense of power. Rather than empowering the people with whom we work we may actually reinforce their victim status by playing the role of benefactor and exploiting the power differential between ourselves and service users.

Empowerment is not a technique but a goal and a process. As a goal, it will not be reached overnight, just as the oppressive conditions within our current social order did not suddenly appear. As a process it is ongoing. The major premise underpinning empowerment is that people are not objects to be exploited, to be controlled, or to be oppressed. People are subjects with inherent dignity and worth that should not be conditional on race, gender, class, or any other inherent characteristic. All people should have reasonable opportunities and choices over their life situations and their social environments. Empowerment is a goal and a process for overcoming oppression.

Consciousness-Raising

Although the idea of revolutionary praxis involving both subjective and objective elements was formulated by Marx, the more recent versions have come from Paulo Freire and the contemporary women's movement.[40] Consistent with the precept that the personal is political, consciousness-raising is legitimized on the basis of the relationship between the social order and many people's human misery. "Thus, consciousness-raising involves the politicization of people."[41] Freire has developed a total pedagogy based on the "conscientization" of the peasant population living in Latin America. With a similar set of ideas and purposes the women's movement has used consciousness-raising as a powerful tool for combatting gender oppression and empowering women.

There are two elements of consciousness-raising:

> First, consciousness-raising is reflection in search of understanding dehumanizing social structures. Second, consciousness-raising is action aimed at altering societal conditions. The two must go hand in hand; action without reflection is as unjustifiable as reflection without action.[42]

The techniques used in consciousness-raising are similar to those used in conventional social work, with one significant difference. Conventional social work is introspective, often motivating people to change their behaviour and adjust to their circumstances. Consciousness-raising, on the other hand, encourages people to gain insights into their circumstances with a view to changing them.[43]

Obviously, consciousness-raising is part of the radical humanistic school as it is predicated on the belief that reflection must precede action. Although it sees practical action as an outcome, consciousness-raising places its initial emphasis on the understanding of oneself in the context of the social order. As Leonard points out, "The hegemony of the ruling class involves the domination of its world view, a view which drenches individual consciousness and which must therefore be actively struggled against *at the level of consciousness.*" Thus, changes of consciousness regarding societal relations are a precondition of the transformation of those relations.[44]

Much of consciousness-raising occurs in the form of political education whereby structural social workers, in the course of their daily service efforts, attempt to educate service users about their own oppression and how to combat it. This type of education is not a process of depositing knowledge (i.e., the banking concept of education) into the head of a service user,[45] nor is it a process of haranguing people about social injustice.[46] First and foremost it involves reflection based on the service user's experience and individual consciousness. This does not mean that the structural social worker will not introduce new ideas or challenge ideas held by the service user, however. Rather, the political education process takes the form of a dialogue where both the social worker and the service user assume roles of mutual sharing and learning.

The service user will present his or her world view and where he or she sees him/herself fitting into this view. The social worker, in turn, will ask questions that might expose any of the service user's stereotypical or socially conditioned assumptions. This type of questioning is called "critical questioning," which is different from "normal questioning"[47] because it focuses on any socially conditioned answer the service user may give. To facilitate this process of dialogue, mutual learning, and critical questioning, the social worker must express empathy at a very high level to signal to the service user that his or her world view and explanation of any difficulty are understood by the social worker. Empathy "is a large part of the substance of critical consciousness for a social worker."[48]

A major topic of dialogue between social worker and service user is how our present society works, including the social functions that poverty, sexism, racism, heterosexism, and so on accomplish. If members of various subordinate groups realize that their personal difficulties are related to their membership within a particular oppressed group and that their oppression is socially useful to the dominant groups, then this awareness should alleviate much of the internalized guilt and blame that exist. In turn, awareness of their oppression, coupled with the energy unleashed from not feeling guilty or responsible for their subordinate status anymore, should lead to some kind of social action against that oppression. For this consciousness-raising to be successful, however, it must be based on peoples' experiences and not on some foreign, academic critical analysis laid on people in sophisticated quasi-Marxist jargon. "Consciousness raising methods require the same sensitivities to self-determination and relationship building that traditional . . . [social work] requires."[49]

Often, service users will demonstrate what Marxists call "false consciousness" in that they understand their troubles in ways that promote the interests of the dominant groups in society.[50] At the same time, a part of all of us tells us that society is not working in a way that supports a satisfying and enriching life for large numbers of people. From a structural social work perspective we should look for and reinforce that part of the service user's perspective that is aware of social oppression.[51] In this way we are not imposing a brand of politics unrelated to the normal events of service users. Instead, we are focusing on their experiences in an empathic, respectful, and relevant manner.

Some examples may help clarify the discussion so far. People who are forced to apply for welfare benefits will often express humiliation, guilt, and shame because they have been socialized into believing that all people in society should be able to make it on their own. One of the ideological myths of capitalism is that equal opportunity exists and only the lazy, the inferior, and the weak do not take advantage of opportunities available to everyone. To be on social welfare is a sign of weakness, inferiority, and laziness. When people seek social welfare benefits or any other kind of social service, we must help them deal with their pressing immediate problems. Most people cannot develop a larger critical perspective of their distress until they experience some symptomatic relief. However, we have an obligation as structural social workers to move beyond symptomatic relief, since we know the symptoms will likely reappear.[52] We must help raise the consciousness of the welfare recipient about why poverty exists in a capitalist society (i.e., the social functions it carries out); why the receipt of social welfare is seen as a failure in our society; the social control functions of social welfare; and how it operates in the best interests of capitalism and the dominant groups in society. In other words, a structural analysis of the welfare recipient's situation and experiences is discussed in an empathic manner at a level and in a language that the recipient understands. As mentioned previously, although most people are victims of false consciousness, a part of everyone knows that society is not working in the interests of large numbers of people. Similarly, many social welfare recipients have some awareness that their situation is not necessarily or completely of their own doing. It is these thoughts that the structural social worker uses to begin the consciousness-raising process.

The consciousness-raising process should always be based on the service user's situation and experiences. Oppression, remember, is group-based, so consciousness-raising should focus on a structural analysis of the position the service user's group occupies in society. If we are working with senior citizens, then the structural social worker must know all about ageism. If this analysis is discussed in a meaningful way with senior citizens they will see how many of their problems –

limited housing options, inadequate or non-existent home care, high cost of drugs, meagre pensions, transportation difficulties – are not their own fault but stem from a society that treats people as commodities where, if you are a non-producer and have no market value, then you have no social value.

Longres and McLeod make two additional points about consciousness-raising as social work practice.[53] First, because consciousness-raising focuses on the negative features of society and politicizes people around these features, then structural social workers will not be favoured by politicians, administrators, and many conventional social workers. Consciousness-raising will not make life easier for the social worker. Second, although consciousness-raising should be a cornerstone of social work practice, it does not represent the totality of practice; giving support, dealing with crises, providing hard services, advocacy, making referrals, and helping to make people's immediate lives more bearable are also important activities. It should also be noted here that consciousness-raising is greatly enhanced when it occurs on a group basis. More will be said about this later. Four activities that are part of the consciousness-raising process are normalization, collectivization, dialogical relationships, and reframing or redefining situations.

Normalization

The purpose of normalization is to assist service users to see that their problems and/or situations are not unique. It is a way of learning that many others of the same social grouping, whatever it might be, also experience the same problems and that in their situation it is not unusual to have such problems. Normalization breaks with that part of conventional social work that does not look at an individual as part of a social group subject to all the vagaries involved in a dominant-subordinate relationship. Normalization is an activity consistent with Cloward and Piven's belief that:

> . . . we have to break with the professional doctrine that ascribes virtually all of the problems that clients experience to defects in personality development and family relationships. It must be understood that this doctrine is as much a political ideology as an explanation of human behaviour. It is an ideology that directs clients to blame themselves for their travails rather than the economic and social institutions that produce many of them. . . . This psychological reductionism – this pathologizing of poverty and inequality – is, in other words, an ideology of oppression for it systematically conceals from people the ways in which their lives are distorted by the realities of class structure.[54]

Structural social work is not anti-psychological. However, it does not automatically assume pathology or deviance on the part of someone who is experiencing problems. It understands that the political and economic context of liberal-capitalist society favours the dominant group at the expense of the subordinate groups. Unlike conventional social workers, structural social workers do not overlook class, gender, race, and the like as possible sources of personal problems.

One of the first normalization activities is to deal with the service user's notion that the problem or situation being experienced is something unique to that service user. This may be done in two ways: individually and collectively. First, giving some factual information to the service user may help him or her to see that other people are in the same situation. For example, people are socialized into believing that those who are not employed in the labour market are in some way defective and, therefore, are responsible for their unemployed status. However, if the unemployment rate for a community is 10 per cent, there obviously are more workers than there are jobs so that some people, through no fault of their own, will not be able to find work. And, if there are one million unemployed people within a labour force of eleven to twelve million (as there were in Canada during the recession of the early eighties), this does not mean there are one million unique problematic situations of the involved individuals' own doing. Rather, there is one social problem affecting one million workers and their families, and a problem of this magnitude is well beyond the control of any individual negatively affected by it. If persons experiencing unemployment are able to place their situation in the wider political and economic context and understand that there are many other people like themselves, much of the internalized guilt and blame should be alleviated. Unemployment is a structural problem that negatively affects lower socio-economic groups so that the dominant group will benefit by having an available work force to compete with each other for carrying out dangerous and menial jobs at subsistence wages, which of course contributes to larger profits for the dominant group.

Feminist social workers are able to provide female service users with all kinds of information on how our patriarchal society oppresses women, how it causes problems for them, and how it then convinces them that they are responsible for the emotional, financial, marital, and family problems they might encounter. Normalizing information helps to combat internalized oppression and to reject blaming-the-victim explanations. An example is that of an abused woman who believes she is one of a very tiny minority of women and, because this happens to so few, there must be something she is doing to cause her spouse to abuse her. Providing some basic statistical information, such as abuse rates of women, should help normalize this woman's situation and dampen her internalized belief that, somehow, she has brought this abuse on herself. Once the internalized guilt, shame, and blame are eliminated or alleviated, a certain amount of energy is freed up that can be used to take a deeper and broader look at the situation and deal with it in a more fundamental way.[55]

A second and more effective normalization activity is to link the service user with others experiencing similar situations and problems. One of the difficulties of trying to normalize a service user's situation on an individual basis is that "the weight is too strongly distributed in favor of individual uniqueness and private troubles."[56] The collective sharing and consciousness-raising that occur within these types of self-help groups show people that their situations and problems are not idiosyncratic but are part of a larger social dynamic. Other aspects of collectivization are discussed in the next section.

In sum, normalization puts situations and problems in their proper political, economic, and social context. The emphasis is not on the uniqueness or individuality of a service user's situation but on the sameness and common ground of the service users. It is a way of reducing guilt and raising self-esteem. A precondition for carrying out normalization activities is that the social worker is able to move beyond the traditional diagnostic mindset that ascribes all social problems to personality defects and family dysfunction. If this diagnostic mentality remains in place, chances are greatly reduced that the service user will be able to move beyond the traditional "personal inadequacy" perception of problems.

Collectivization

Collectivism is a primary social value of both of the socialist paradigms. This value is a recognition that people are social beings who depend on one another for the satisfaction of most of their primary and social needs. It is the antithesis of individualism and, therefore, should be reflected in structural social work practice. Galper points out that because we live and experience problems within a social context, analysis of the causes of problems, developing awareness of the extent to which problems are widely shared, and mobilizing collective activity toward the solutions of these problems must take place in conjunction with others. "[I]t is important for all of us to experience the power of a mutual, collective exploration of the dilemmas we face . . . the group context of practice goes further than the individual context in pointing toward solutions."[57] Leonard makes the same point when he says, "through the practice of collective consciousness-raising, the individual's experience is contextualized by an understanding of the social order which stands *against* the dominant messages contained in the ideological inculcation of subordinate people."[58] In other words, problems and solutions often are defined differently in consciousness-raising groups of service users than they are in the traditional "individual pathology" approach.

Longres and McLeod conclude that "The first step to consciousness-raising is forming groups based on common social statuses" and that "consciousness-raising in a *holistic way* is only possible within groups"[59] because such a medium is free of what Corrigan and Leonard call the "cult of individualism."[60] This does not deny the necessity for individual work with service users, for it is recognized that many people will feel overwhelmed in a group or that a group focus overshadows their immediate personal needs. Some individualizing is necessary to show care, respect, support, and encouragement to participate in a group process. Treating people as individuals with unique differences is very different from treating their problems as unique and idiosyncratic. It is useful, as Galper points out, to think in terms of stages.[61] Initially in the worker-service user relationship the situation will call for the relief of any pressing and immediate stress as well as a demonstration of personal empathy for the service user. Once the initial crisis is dealt with and a trusting relationship is established, the service user will be in a better position to look at his or her situation in a broader but more fundamental way with others.

Groups of service users may serve a number of different purposes: therapy, consciousness-raising, political action, or a combination of these. If such groups exist the structural social worker should refer all services users he or she comes into contact with to these groups. For example, a structural social worker should refer anyone in receipt of, or applying for, social welfare to any welfare rights or anti-poverty organizations that might exist in the community. As well, structural social workers should support such groups however they can, including alerting them to policy developments that have the probability of negatively affecting them.[62] Although structural social workers should support mutual aid groups of service users they should not violate the social work value of self-determination by attempting to lead them. Withorn underscores this point when she discusses the functions of mutual aid groups:

> Political practice means establishing groups of clients, not staff-led therapy groups, but "mutual aid" groups, in the best sense. Such groups can discuss common concerns and organize joint demands on workers. They can also provide support and assistance to each other. We do not live in a socialist society: we cannot organize real "mass organizations." Any efforts will be compromised and feel contrived. But the presence of such groups could help articulate

client demands: They may be a safe place for sharing "bootleg" information about the agency, and they may give clients a place to do their own "power analysis".[63]

To these functions of the collective process Leonard would add two psychological benefits: (1) positive changes in self-conception occur; and (2) people are able "to move away from the cult of individualism which dominates people's lives within capitalist societies."[64]

In working with groups organized on the basis of a common status, the social worker ideally is assigned to groups that share her/his gender, race, class of origin, and so on. Maurice Moreau cites research showing that if the social worker is of the same social group as that which he or she is working with (1) the worker is better able to empathize with the group members; and (2) the group members tend to explore themselves much more than when the social worker has a different background. The caution for the worker, however, is not to project his or her own life onto the service users.[65]

Eight practices that Moreau and Leonard use for the operational definition of collectivization are useful here:

i) Drawing a service user's attention to the links between her/his personal difficulties and the similar problem situations of other service users.
ii) Putting service users of the same agency who are living similar problem situations in touch with each other.
iii) Grouping service users for the purpose of mutual aid.
iv) Grouping service users for the purpose of creating necessary resources the agency itself should provide.
v) Grouping service users for the purpose of creating necessary resources other agencies should provide.
vi) Grouping service users for the purpose of changing aspects of the agency that are problematic to them.
vii) Grouping service users for the purpose of changing aspects of other agencies and organizations that are problematic to service users.
viii) Referring service users to larger social movements directly related to their situations.[66]

Redefining

Redefining is a consciousness-raising activity in which personal troubles are redefined in political terms, exposing the relationship between objective material conditions and subjective personal experiences. Society, as discussed earlier, is characterized either by order or by conflict, and each view defines social problems differently. According to the order view, social problems emanate from individual defects, family dysfunction, or subcultures outside the mainstream. The conflict view ascribes most social problems to the present set of social relations where the dominant group controls the subordinate groups. Because social agencies are established within the present liberal-patriarchal-capitalist system they tend to embody the ideology and thought structure of the larger system, that is, an order perspective. This includes the problem definition that underlies all services and social work-service user interactions. Rose and Black argue that the thought structure of operating assumptions that typically characterizes social agencies validates the American political economy and invalidates users of social services. They contend that the validation of American social reality and invalidation of service users are hidden (not stated or publicized or even recognized by many) and pervasive.[67] Rose and Black cite a study by Warren *et al.* of fifty-four agencies in nine cities:

> . . . people either needing service or failing to fit into already established service delivery patterns were defined as defective; their difficulties in living, rather than resulting from poverty, underemployment, discrimination or inadequate care were seen as results of their individual behaviors or values . . . whether the defect was located in individuals' intellect, personality, discipline or values or in family structure or neighbourhood, one or more of these factors were taken to be the determinants of the client's social position in society. Agency responses, in the form of programs and service designs, for example, were incapable of recognizing poverty as an inherent structural characteristic of our society; incapable of recognizing race, sex, age or handicap as structurally and historically determined aspects or characteristics of American society.[68]

Contributing to the entrenchment of this personalist definition of social problems within social agencies is the fact that this thought structure benefits these agencies in two ways. First, it allows them to attribute program failure either to client defects (i.e., they are not capable of receiving help) or to a form of quantitative management rationality. This latter factor permits the agency to make continuous demands for more funds and resources, which is the second way the agency benefits from adopting the prevailing problem definition.[69] There are several effects on service users of such problem definition. (1) It invalidates the service user by validating the larger system. (2) It decontextualizes the service user as it severs his or her subjectivity from the objective and materialist context that frames and shapes all social life.[70] (3) It shapes people's behaviour to correspond to the given social reality and the more one deviates from "proper and appropriate" behaviour, the more severe is society's treatment. (4) It saturates service users with a new language, a language of pathology and deviance that contains such concepts as diagnosis, treatment, symptoms, acting-out behaviour, resistance, and so on. (5) It forces service users to accept the problem definition imposed on them, in other words, to accept a false reality. If one were seeking an operational definition of oppression these five effects on service users of the prevailing definition of problems would be a good starting point.

Redefining represents an alternative social reality, an alternative definition of problems. "It [redefining] asserts the primacy of reconnection to objective circumstances as the central problem to be addressed, and an ever-present theme to be interwoven in every aspect of practice."[71] Validation is derived from reconnecting people to their objective social and historical context. The task, rather than working on personal change and accommodation to society, is to engage people as producers and participants in comprehending and acting on their contextual environment. As with consciousness-raising and normalization, priority is given to group rather than individual work because the former is consistent with collectivization and mutual sharing among persons with similar social statuses.

Moreau[72] outlines a number of redefining or "reframing" techniques. These include the following: critical questioning;[73] dialectical humour;[74] metaphors and storytelling;[75] cognitive dissonance;[76] the checking of inferences;[77] mental imagery;[78] persuasion;[79] and the use of silence.[80] Such techniques help to contextualize not only the service user's problem but often the service user's behaviour. Behaviour that may be labelled as inappropriate and self-destructive according to the personalist problem definition may be re-labelled as perfectly appropriate and normal with an alternative problem definition.

An example may help to make this discussion more concrete. Many graduates from the social work program (a structural program) where this writer is a faculty member are employed in departments of social services where one of the services is "child protection." They report that the problem definition of child abuse and neglect is that these occur because of inappropriate behaviours and attitudes on the part of parents. Case recordings of non-structural social workers highlight personal inadequacies, emotional immaturity, poor coping skills, and family dysfunction as the areas to focus on in working with child abuse and/or neglect situations. Large amounts of money are spent each year in providing family therapy training to the social workers so that they might work more effectively with child protection families. If there is any mention that maybe the service users' problems are largely material and institutional, it is dismissed as either incorrect or by stating that

"There is nothing we can do about that. Our job is to work with these families."

The problem definition of the social agency is that child abuse and neglect are problems of personal inadequacy, when, in fact, child abuse and neglect are in large part a class problem.[81] Contrary to the myth of classlessness, which is part of the current system's thought structure, both evidence and reason lead to the unmistakable conclusion that "child abuse and neglect are strongly related to poverty, in terms of prevalence and of severity of consequences. . . . adherence to the myth [of classlessness] diverts attention from the nature of the problems and diverts resources from their solution."[82] This is not to say that child abuse and neglect do not occur among other socio-economic classes; the evidence does say, however, that the great preponderance of abuse and neglect occurs among those who have the fewest resources to work with, who are struggling the most trying to secure the basic necessities of life, and who have the greatest number of and most sustained pressures on them – that is, the poor. This is not an excuse for child abuse or neglect, but it is an explanation. The job of the structural social worker, then, is to redefine the problem from one of personal pathology to one of class. This should be done not only with the service user but should be stated at case conferences, and the case recordings should be redressed to reflect the service users' problems as largely material and institutional.

Dialogical Relationships

Normalization, collectivization, and redefining are the means of carrying out consciousness-raising. The medium within which these activities are carried out is dialogue, between the social worker and the service user and among service users. Dialogue is the vehicle for uncovering peoples' subjective reality and opening it to critical reflection.

> Dialogue cannot be professional interviewing, application of therapeutic technology, instructions for improved functioning or casual conversation. It is purposive in both process and focus. It directs itself to validation of the oppressed as persons, attempting to demonstrate their capacity to inform you, and it struggles to direct the content towards depiction and analysis of the objective situation. . . . To unveil oppressive reality is to be willing to enter it more fully, to encourage the elaboration of expression, to support the expression of experiences, to initiate the early steps in critical reflection.[83]

To be able to engage in meaningful dialogue the structural social worker must develop a dialogical relationship[84] with service users – a relationship based on horizontal exchange rather than a vertical imposition. A dialogical relationship is one wherein all participants in the dialogue are equals, each learning from the other and each teaching the other. Of course, the social worker will have some skills and insights that the service user does not have, but the service user has experiences and insights that the worker does not. The structural social worker must make conscious efforts to dispel any myths of expert technical solutions to fundamental political problems. Consciousness-raising can only occur within the context of a non-authoritarian relationship. Criticism of conventional social work practice has often centred on an elitist, impersonal, and overly technical approach. "In essence, a dialogical relationship is exchanging, comparing and communicating, rather than indoctrinating, proselytizing and generally issuing a 'communique.'"[85]

As structural social workers we do not want to reproduce with service users the kinds of social relations that have oppressed them in the first place. One of the contradictions of social work practice is that on the one hand it attempts to provide practical humanitarian care for people in distress and on the other hand it often provides this care in a superordinate (helper-helpee), authoritarian (worker has the answers), and mystical (helping process is not explained) way. A dialogical relationship minimizes these aspects. Burghardt points out that "one of our pivotal, potentially 'insurrectionary' roles can be to produce relationships between client and worker that run counter to the dominant social relationships produced elsewhere."[86] Such relationships are not only conducive to structural social work practice but they challenge the ideological hegemony of the larger society.

To demystify any social work activity, technique, or practice, social workers must not be possessive of them but must make them broadly available to people at large as part of their job. For instance, the use of any technique, skill, or process is an opportunity to demystify it by discussing its origins, purpose, and other situations that might prove useful and by encouraging the service user to ask questions. The content of service users' files should be made available to them, and they should have the right to be present at all conferences that affect them. Hidden strategies and manipulative approaches are not used and the rationale behind all questions asked by the worker is explained.[87]

In discussing empowerment Moreau and Leonard present the following dialogical practices:

- sharing with the service user the content of case recordings;
- directly involving service users in the decisions that affect them;
- directly involving the service user in providing feedback on the kinds and quality of services provided;

- reducing the social distance between worker and service user by use of self-disclosure, casual dress, giving the rationale for techniques and questions, personal empathy, home visits, first names, direct clear speech, and use of body language;
- sharing with the service user one's personal biases and limits as part of the "helping" contract;
- providing information on the role of the agency and the rights of the service user, and letting him/her know the worker is there to serve the service user.[88]

Surviving and Changing the Workplace

This section presents and discusses a number of ways a structural social worker can survive within and change social agencies that hold the same oppressive thought and ideological structures as the larger society. Although social work by itself cannot eliminate oppression and injustice, it can help to erode oppressive structures and practices starting within its own arena for struggle – the social agency.

Contradictions of Agencies as a Basis for Radicalization

The basic contradiction of social agencies and services is well known: they "deny, frustrate and undermine the possibilities of human liberation and a just society, at the same time that they work toward and, in part, achieve greater degrees of human well-being."[89] Social agencies and services provide social care and social control at the same time.

Agencies and services are organized so that "they support and reinforce conformity, among both clients and workers, to the very institutions and values that generate the problems to which the services were addressed in the first place."[90] To receive services, people are often forced to accept roles and behaviours for themselves that reinforce and support the status quo.[91] And social workers are constrained in a variety of ways by various means, such as traditional individual supervision, a reward structure based on conformity to agency need rather than service user need, heavy caseloads that yield little opportunity to step back and consider the larger picture, and computerization with programmed problem definitions and solutions.

While structural social workers recognize that conventional social agencies do not offer real solutions to social problems, are too often inadequate within their own terms, frequently constrain workers to behave in ways that are deleterious to service users, and offer limited opportunities for a rewarding social work career, the vast majority of social workers find themselves working somewhere in "the system."

Structural social workers need to support themselves and, because there are limited opportunities for employment with alternative social agencies, with radical unions, or in other positions geared to undermine the system, most will continue to be employed by mainstream agencies. Thus, the challenge to the structural social worker is to remain true to one's structural mission while not alienating oneself from management and from other workers in the agency.

Most social workers enter their work because of a concern about people and an interest in responding to social problems. However, studies show that "it is adjustment to the bureaucratic reality of the job that causes the most discomfort among new workers and is the most responsible for the loss of 'idealism.'"[92] Understanding the contradictory functions of social agencies, of course, helps one to make sense out of the frustrations, limitations, and obstacles experienced by the worker. Many progressive social workers believe that their only option for structural social work practice is that of "protecting the poor, the sick, the criminal, and the deviant against the agencies."[93] Their belief is that they must become guerrillas in the bureaucracy and undermine the agency at every turn from their political underground position.[94] But not all agencies are alike and, as Withorn notes, not all the negative aspects of social service work can be attributed to the social control functions of capitalist social agencies.[95]

Given a structural understanding of the nature, operations, and political functions of social agencies, social workers should be able to operate above the political underground in combining social care with our structural social work goals.

> The overriding goal must always be to politicize the workplace so that activists, clients, and fellow workers understand the political dimensions of the work and take the greatest advantage of the contradictions of the system. This can only be done by a self-conscious strategy that is sensitive to specific workplaces with their particular personalities, structures, and political imperatives and is aware of broader bureaucratic, economic and social realities.[96]

The contradictions present in most social agencies and the fact that social workers always have some measure of autonomy permit us to undertake more intra-organizational change than is often believed possible. And, as Scurfield[97] and Patti and Resnick[98] point out, according to our own Code of Ethics our primary obligation is to the people we serve and not to the agency that employs us. The legitimation for radicalizing the agency is derived from our ethical obligation to place professional values above organizational allegiance. Some of the ways to radicalize social agencies by taking advantage of the positive potential created by their inherent contradictions are presented below.

Radicalizing the Agency

The purpose of politically radicalizing the agency is to emphasize its service function and de-emphasize its control function. To carry out this purpose it is necessary to engage in "anti-capitalist practice"[99] within the agency. This opposes those assumptions of professional social organizations that flow from the prevailing thought and ideological structures of our liberal-capitalist society. If one of the goals of structural social work is to transform society from capitalism to socialism, then a logical place to begin is with the social welfare institution of which we are a part and, more specifically, with the social agency within which we work. Thus, as we practise anti-capitalist social work we are also practising socialist or structural social work. We de-emphasize capitalist values and practices while emphasizing socialist values and practices. This means we must challenge the agency's traditional definitions of problems and their resultant oppressive policies, attempt to democratize the agency, strive for more egalitarian relationships within the agency, and defend the service user from the agency.

When agency policies and definitions of people's problems are based on assumptions of individual deficiencies or family dysfunction the structural social worker has an obligation to confront these oppressive assumptions. Workers can press for definitions of these problems that are grounded in people's social, economic, and political circumstances. When to press and how to press are two considerations when challenging personalist interpretations of structural problems. With respect to the first consideration Galper says, "Every staff meeting offers an opportunity to raise questions, to challenge conservative assumptions, and to encourage coworkers to do the same. Every supervisory session provides an opportunity for political encounter. . . ."[100] The most effective strategy for presenting these challenges is not based on confrontation but focuses on asking questions about current practices while presenting information that leads to a different definition of the problem. For example, at a staff meeting of a child protection unit of a provincial Department of Social Services that views child abuse/neglect problems as essentially family problems to be solved by family therapy, one could ask, "Why are we doing all this family therapy work when we know from our own experience that if most of the families we work with had a decent job with a decent income they wouldn't be having so many problems? Also, these articles that I have here [and which are then distributed] clearly show that most child abuse and neglect situations are problems related to poverty and not to bad parents."

Most social agencies are managed from top to bottom. The social work literature is replete with accounts of how this hierarchical management model works against the front-line worker's attempts to deliver an adequate and quality service to people.[101] Policies are formulated at the top of the organization with little or no input from workers, let alone service users, and are passed down the line for implementation. This type of management is anti-democratic as it excludes worker or service user participation, it promotes inequality in that a small elite makes the decisions and imposes them on workers, and it results in oppressive policies because the decision-making is based on capitalistic myths, assumptions, and stereotypes. Thus, part of the struggle for structural social workers is to democratize the workplace. This may take various forms, such as union activity to build in and increase service user participation in the decision-making process, more peer supervision, development of a consultative relationship with supervisors rather than that of boss-subordinate, and a struggle to implement more democratic means of sharing decisions, responsibilities, and information. Much more research and many more written accounts of democratic collective experiences of administering and delivering services are needed.[102]

In addition to challenging personal pathology definitions of social problems and attempting to democratize social agencies, structural social workers must also confront all agency policies and practices that oppress or negatively affect service users in other ways. Major areas of concern are to maximize the service user's use of resources, benefits, or services provided by the agency, to link service users together and to support service user advocacy groups, and to combat any behaviour that demeans or defames service users. It is preferable, of course, for the structural social worker to use overt means in performing these tasks, but it is a fact of life that in many work situations workers are forced to use covert strategies. This presents a dilemma for social workers, but, as mentioned previously, social work's Code of Ethics is clear in this regard. The social worker's primary responsibility is to the service user, and when the needs of the service user conflict with the needs of the agency the social worker has an ethical and professional responsibility, first and foremost, to the service user.

Moreau and Leonard call the maximizing of the service user's use of an agency's services or benefits "defense of the client."[103] The aim of this defence is to maximize the client's use of resources while minimizing their negative effect. Moreau and Leonard operationalize defence of the client by outlining five practices that defend the service user within the worker's own agency and two practices that defend the service user in relation to outside agencies.[104] The five practices within the worker's agency are:

(1) Provide service users with confidential inside information on how best to present a request for service from the agency.
(2) Alter or falsify statistics to satisfy organizational requirements, all the while giving more time to needy service users. (For example, an agency may require that each service user receive a monthly home visit, which is virtually impossible because of the heavy caseloads. A worker may report that he or she has fulfilled this requirement, but in fact has not because he or she has chosen to give more attention to those service users who are most in need. At the same time the worker has the obligation to protest the heavy caseload to the agency, to his or her union, and so on.)
(3) Deliberately avoid recording certain facts, for example, a welfare recipient receiving some money from an outside source that, if reported, would be deducted from his or her welfare.
(4) Turn a blind eye to a service user's violation of policies, rules, or procedures of the agency, for example, residency requirements for eligibility of a service.
(5) Become involved in making efforts to change organizational rules, regulations, or practices which work against the needs or interests of service users.

The two practices of defending the service user in relation to outside agencies are:

(1) Provide service users with confidential "inside" information on how to present a request for service from another agency.
(2) Turn a blind eye to a service user's violation of the rules, policies, or procedures of an outside organization, for example, violation of a probation order or illegally receiving a financial benefit.

Another way of enhancing the service user's power and influence within the agency is to link service users with one another and to outside advocacy groups. Just as groups enhance consciousness-raising, so, too, do they enhance the ability of service users to challenge destructive agency policies. Groups of service users should be supported in every way the social worker is able to do so, such as providing information (including so-called confidential information), referring other service users to the group, forewarning the group of destructive policy discussions being held within the bureaucracy so that they might prepare to counter them, and identifying workers within the agency the group can trust and those who should be avoided.

Finally, in carrying out "anti-capitalist" or radical work within the agency, structural social workers must confront any behaviour that demeans or defames service users. Derogatory remarks about service users by workers are far more common than they should be, with some groups such as inmates and welfare recipients being especially hard hit. Blair's classic study of welfare workers found that anti-client statements served as a way of affirming social solidarity among workers and were part of the normative culture of the workplace as these derogatory remarks showed that the worker was not "naive or sentimental about clients."[105] Just as racist or sexist remarks or jokes are unacceptable, so, too, are anti-client statements because all such statements perpetuate stereotypes and devalue people. Such behaviour can be initially dealt with in subtle ways, such as not laughing or responding to it, or by silence, or by disapproving looks, or by a general discussion at a staff meeting about such behaviour and what it represents. If, as Withorn notes, subtle tactics do not work, then structural workers may have to resort to overt disapproval.[106]

Protecting Ourselves

Social agencies are often repressive because they enforce service user conformity to capitalist values and relations. Also, they "enforce worker conformity through direct coercion, subtle pressures and ideological indoctrination."[107] Therefore, any attempts at democratizing or radicalizing the agency put the worker at risk. However, the risks to the worker are probably not as great as is often assumed. It was pointed out earlier in this chapter that the inherent contradictions of agencies give the worker some latitude for structural work. Although most agencies contain repressive elements, usually their goals are couched in terms of equality, democracy, social justice, human need, and optimal service. These stated goals, along with a certain degree of autonomy that the worker enjoys, give the worker a foothold for structural practice within the agency.

Galper offers guidelines for radical or structural practice in social agencies that, if followed, would minimize the risks of reprisal by the agency against the worker.[108] He says that the first step is to be competent in carrying out the agency's assigned tasks. If a worker is competent, he or she will be of value to the agency. In turn, the agency will be more tolerant of efforts at democratization and radicalization than it would be if the worker was not competent. If a structural worker is incompetent the agency has an easy reason for getting rid of her or him. Galper also cautions us to avoid "adventurism or isolation." The radical activities we carry out within the agency should not be overly militant, irrational, or destructive. What is the sense of making a public scene over a principle if your action gets you fired (unless this is your strategy)? People cannot continue to carry out structural practice in the agency after they are fired. Martyrs are of limited practical use for ongoing radical work within agencies. Another important guideline is to know your agency – its history, policies, points of vulnerability, and so on – and the people in it – who is likely to be supportive, who is not to be trusted.

There is consensus in the literature that the most important way of protecting ourselves, not just from agency reprisal but also from burnout, is to have peer support. Withorn contends that a "workplace caucus" of "politically compatible people" is essential to combat the bureaucracy's inherent tendency to divide workers through hierarchy and specialization. Such caucuses provide support to members, facilitate consciousness-raising of the workers' situation, enable planning to radicalize the agency to occur, and give members a sense of collective and individual efficacy to change their agency.[109] Galper echoes the need for a caucus of radical/structural workers and says that the process of establishing such a caucus does not have to start in a grandiose way but may begin with two or three like-minded workers meeting informally.[110] Sherman and Wenocur believe that a mutual support group of workers "weakens the impact of the disempowering socialization process in an organization by creating an alternative subculture governed by workers' values."[111] And, finally, a study of graduates from a structural social work program in Canada found that peer support either from within or from outside the agency was the most important factor in carrying out structural social work practice.[112]

There are risks in attempting to change the social agency from within, yet a number of ways exist for protecting ourselves and our jobs. We can do our work well, we can plan strategies that take into account the tolerance of the agency, and we can work collectively. The alternative to working within and *against* the agency is to work within and *for* the agency. The former entails risks of retaliation by the agency. The latter entails risks of cynicism, despair, and burnout because we deny much of the social, economic, and political reality around us.[113] Put in these terms it seems that working within and against the system/agency is the better choice.

10

Working Outside (and Against) the System

The previous chapter presented and discussed a number of structural social work practice elements that are carried out in the course of one's work. This chapter considers a number of modes and forms of structural practice outside the social welfare system. The reason for carrying out structural practice outside the system is that the system places institutional limits on much of our social work practice. Although much good work may be carried out within the system, it "must be linked to struggles for structural change outside agency walls. In practice, this means the worker should keep in touch with and support parallel social change movements going on outside of social agencies."[1]

Structural social work practice *within* the system is based mainly on the radical humanist school of changing people's consciousness on a massive scale as a prerequisite to changing society. Structural practice *outside* the system is based mainly on the radical structural school of changing material conditions and oppressive structural patterns such as patriarchy, racism, and ageism. These would be replaced by a socialist society that, once in place, would become the new social reality for people. By itself, each approach has limitations, which were discussed in Chapter 8. Both are necessary.

This chapter discusses each of the following as arenas for carrying out structural social work practice outside the social welfare system: alternative services and organizations, coalitions and social movements, unions, professional associations, electoral politics, and how we live our lives.

Alternative Services and Organizations

If we are to contribute to social transformation, a logical starting point is the workplace. However, structural social workers should not focus on the workplace to the exclusion of overall social change efforts outside their agency walls. Changing the social relations within agencies does not, by itself, change the basic elements of our patriarchal, liberal-capitalist social order, such as severe discrepancies of wealth and power, domination by giant corporations, a dependence on industrial production that pollutes our environment, and so on. And, as Carniol points out, we may help someone obtain better housing or the full entitlement of a welfare benefit or cut through red tape or overlook a few rules or regulations so that someone does not lose a needed benefit or service, but we know: (1) that most of the benefits or services we deliver are inadequate; and (2) that we have done nothing to change those structural causes of the person being in need in the first place.[2]

One of the ways for structural social workers to contribute to social transformation is to create, develop, and/or support alternative social service organizations.

> If a cohesive radical movement is to emerge, focus on an alternative human services policy and program could serve an important integrating function. Because the recipients of human services are overwhelmingly poor and/or female and/or people of colour and/or young or old, it is an issue which creates bridges between the "narrow" interests of pivotal oppressed groups. Because human services implicate economic and political and social issues, radical alternatives could create a "cutting edge" in efforts to achieve comprehensive change.[3]

In other words, alternative services and programs are counter-systems to mainstream social agencies and can be used ultimately to develop "a base from which larger social changes can be eventually effected."[4]

Alternative services and organizations are founded on different principles, values, and ideals than our traditional liberal services and organizations. Alternative services and organizations attempt to institutionalize new forms of social relationships[5] by incorporating community control, mutual social support, and shared decision-making as key features. These function to meet the needs of people in the community and are growth-producing for those working within them. "Alternative services usually spring from the work of a specific oppressed community or movement,"[6] such as people living in poverty, women, Native people, gays and lesbians, and social service users. Examples of alternative services are welfare rights groups, tenant associations, rape crisis centres, transition homes for battered women and their children, off-reserve Native friendship centres, gay and lesbian associations, ex-psychiatric groups, Alcoholics Anonymous, and prisoners' societies.

Structural social workers do not see alternative services and organizations as competitive or as disruptive to the operations of mainstream services and organizations. They understand that alternative services represent attempts by people associated with them to connect the personal with the political and to gain control over their own destiny. Structural social workers would support alternative services in a variety of ways: by becoming involved with them to the extent that they can without endangering their employment in mainstream agencies; by providing material resources since alternative organizations are usually strapped for funds (e.g., money, stationery, photocopying); by providing inside information from one's own organization; by referring users of a mainstream service to an alternative service; and by encouraging the formation of such services or organizations where none exist.

Structural social workers must be careful not to romanticize alternative organizations. Anyone who has ever been associated with such an organization will know how difficult it is to work collectively and co-operatively and to share all decision-making when we, as North Americans, have been socialized into working and living in social institutions where hierarchy, specialization, and an overreliance on rules prevail. Withorn cautions us that old habits die hard, our expectations for alternative services are often too grand, and we may not always be clear on what an anti-capitalist, anti-racist, feminist practice is.[7] In addition, Carniol warns those workers who have developed a critical awareness and are involved with alternative services against becoming arrogant and self-righteous and forgetting the importance of listening to and learning from the very groups we see as most oppressed.[8] Most writers on the subject of alternative services point out the problem of funding these services because of a strong push toward co-optation by establishment funding agencies such as United Way and government departments.

Alternative services and organizations, then, clearly have some limitations. By themselves they will not bring about the transformation of the welfare state (contrary to revolutionary Marxist thought), but they do make an essential contribution to this goal. They embody the values, beliefs, principles, and practices of structural social work. They provide building blocks by which we learn workplace democracy. And they become prototypes of social service organizations of the future, providing us with positive and hopeful glimpses of what might be.[9]

Social Movements and Coalition-Building

As has been emphasized, one of the major goals of structural social work is to transform our present patriarchal, liberal-capitalist society to one based on a different set of values and social arrangements. However, by itself, social work cannot transform society; it can only contribute to its transformation. The previous chapter focused on ways and means that structural change can be carried out on a daily basis within the social welfare system generally and within our agencies particularly. On a more macro scale, social work can contribute to social transformation by forming coalitions and alliances with other groups and organizations also committed to changing the destructive social relationships and operating principles of our present society. Social work must become part of a social movement. Galper warns us as structural social workers that if we do not strive "to build a revolutionary social movement, we can rightly be accused of failing to take seriously our own analysis of the need for fundamental change."[10]

The concept of social movements has been variously defined as "a wide variety of collective attempts to bring about change in certain social institutions or to create an entirely new order," as "socially shared demands for change in some aspect of the social order,"[11] and as "an organized effort, usually involving many people representing a wide spectrum of the population, to change a law, public policy or social norm."[12] From these definitions it is obvious that the goal of a social movement is to bring about some kind of social change. It is important, however, to distinguish between two different types of social change: social reform and structural change. The former refers to improving or altering existing laws, policies, and social conditions without changing the fundamental nature of society. The latter refers to fundamental changes in the very nature of the social, economic, and/or political order of society. The former is concerned with changes *within* the present social order and is usually associated with liberal social work based on the order view of society. The latter is concerned with changes *of* the present social order and is usually associated with social democratic or Marxist social work based on the conflict view of society. Obviously, given its goal of social transformation, structural social work is more concerned with movements for structural change than with social reform movements (though it does not ignore or necessarily refuse to work with reform groups). Many individuals and groups of individuals in society have gone through consciousness-raising processes similar to that of structural social workers and have concluded that social transformation of our present society is necessary. An integral part of social movement work is to build coalitions[13] with such groups and, together, to seek structural social change. The biggest obstacle to building coalitions is that many groups with potentially shared political interests will focus solely on their respective single issues. This tendency has some obvious problems, which Biklen[14] delineates in his discussion of self-help groups: (1) social issues are defined in a narrow parochial fashion; (2) single-issue groups often fail to make alliances with other groups whose interests they share because there is no awareness of the common causes of the oppression that each group experiences; (3) when single-issue groups focus on single issues they may even compete with each other for resources, attention, acceptance, and political dominance; and (4) even when a single-issue group effects change in a particular area it is not likely to bring about broad social change.

Wineman contends that the biggest obstacle to coalition-building is the ability of the American liberal-capitalist system "to create and sustain deep divisions among oppressed people."[15] This segmentation of oppression has historically been manifest in perceived conflicts of interest running along lines of class, gender, race, age, disability, sexual orientation, and so on. With this segmentation each group is prone to analysing society along parochial lines wherein a single but different basic source of oppression is identified by each group. For example, conventional Marxist analysis places economic organization and class oppression as the fundamental societal problem; blacks, Native people, and other people of colour may identify racism as the fundamental source of oppression; women's organizations may identify patriarchy as the fundamental source of oppression.

As Wineman points out, the problem with each oppressed group identifying a single source of oppression is "that it at once fails to create a basis for unity which respects the dignity and felt experience of all the oppressed . . . who are supposed to become unified, and it fails to generate a practical strategy . . . (to) challenge all forms of oppression."[16] Without unity a competition emerges among oppressed groups for resources and attention. And, with any competition, there are winners and losers. Thus, Social Darwinian principles of survival of the fittest dominate social change efforts, with a few oppressed groups making some gains while others fail to. In fact, the gains some oppressed groups may make are often at the expense of other oppressed groups. Meaningful social change is denied because nothing was done to change the basic nature and structures of society that caused the oppression in the first place.

The dominant group in society has become very proficient at using this situation to its advantage by playing one oppressed group against another and exacerbating tensions among them. For example, the dominant group will often categorize oppressed people in ways that cause tension and hostility among them: working vs. non-working poor, the troubled single-parent family, the Indian problem, the black ghetto, and so on. This "divide and conquer" behaviour on the part of the dominant group effectively obscures the commonalities that underpin the situation of these and other oppressed groups.

Overcoming the imposed divisiveness among oppressed groups and other barriers to coalition-building requires several actions and strategies. One essential element of successful coalition-building is to create a "mutual expression of *solidarity*."[17] This does not mean that one oppressed group must submerge its perceived interests in the name of unity. Rather, members of groups oppressed in one way will identify with members of groups who are oppressed in other ways, regardless of the severity (but not pretending that all oppressions are equally severe). This kind of mutual identification is necessary to overcome competing claims of who is more oppressed and to bring about the unity required for successful movement-building.

Mutual identification of one another's oppression, by itself, is insufficient to generate a strategy and process that effectively challenges all forms of oppression. Mutual identification may lead to various oppressed groups supporting each other in the struggles of each against the immediate source of their respective oppressions. For example, groups oppressed by classism may identify with the oppression experienced by groups oppressed by racism or sexism. But this identification with other oppressed groups may not go any further than sympathetic understanding unless it is recognized that all forms of oppression are related. "Different oppressions intersect at innumerable points in everyday life and are mutually reinforcing, creating a *total system* of oppression in which one [category of oppression] . . . cannot be addressed in isolation from all the others."[18] It may be true that sexism is at the base of gender inequality and that racism is at the base of racial inequality and that classism is at the base of economic inequality, but it is also true that inequality is a value and an established practice in our present patriarchal, liberal-capitalist society. It makes no political sense for workers to demand economic equality but ignore gender inequality as someone else's problem or for women to demand gender equality but ignore racial inequality. Although each oppressed group may fight oppression on its own front, the recognition that we live in a society that requires inequality for its very survival will cultivate coalitions among groups by providing them with a common goal – the transformation of our present society based on inequality to one based on true equality, not just equal opportunity.

A goal of social transformation necessitates a shared ideological position among various oppressed groups. This common base provides the cement for building and maintaining coalition structures. Without a common ideology there is no common cause, issues are viewed in a parochial fashion, and single-issue reform becomes the goal of each group. The net result is that if any change occurs it is only a minor change *within* the system and not a fundamental change *of* the system itself. System-tinkering is liberal-style social change.

Not unrelated to a goal of social transformation is a shared political analysis as a prerequisite for coalition-building. Whatever the original causes of various forms of oppression the fact is that they have become culturally ingrained in our patriarchal, liberal-capitalist society and have themselves become mutually reinforcing. Coalition-building for purposes of broad structural change becomes more crucial but more realistic when oppressed people understand that the same political and economic elite that allows the devastation of our environment for profits is also responsible for the immoral and gross inequalities of living conditions between rich and poor; that the same political and economic elite that promotes imperialist policies abroad for economic gain is also responsible for policies at home that discriminate against the poor, women, people of colour, gays and lesbians, and so on; and that the same political and economic elite that promotes militarism for political and economic domination is also responsible for consumerism whereby people measure their own and others' worth and social standing in terms of what they own. This kind of awareness makes it imperative for structural social workers to join with the women's movement, the peace movement, the environmental movement, the human rights movement, and any other movement seeking a transformation of society in order to end oppression of any kind.

An important dynamic of oppression that should facilitate coalition-building is that "no category of oppression, however distinct, creates an irreducible group which is only oppressed in one way."[19] Racism does affect people of colour, but people of colour include the working class, women, gays and lesbians, the young and old, and the disabled. In turn, classism affects the working class, but the working class consists of women, people of colour, gays and lesbians, the young and old, and the disabled. Most oppressed people are multiply oppressed both individually and in groups. This dynamic should help oppressed groups overcome any tendency toward single-constituency movements if there occurs within oppressed groups what Wineman calls "a flowering of internal caucuses based on sex, race, class, sexual orientation, age, disability, and various combinations of these characteristics."[20] An internal caucus is a recognition of the fact that people bring their gender, race, class, sexual orientation, and so on with them into various struggles. A caucus of women within an anti-poverty group's struggle against economic exploitation becomes a link between women's organizations and poor people's organizations. A Native women's caucus within an anti-poverty group becomes a link between Natives', women's, and anti-poverty organizations. These internal caucuses not only manifest overlapping oppressions among single-constituency organizations but become the points of contact between various oppressed organizations and spearhead common goals and joint actions.[21]

Progressive Unionism

An effective practice of structural social work must include the trade union movement as a major vehicle for carrying out its social transformation mandate. Unions provide social workers with opportunities for worker empowerment in the workplace, for better understanding of class issues, for contributing to the development of economic and social alternatives, and for participating in coalitions with other workers, consumer groups, and progressive social movements. To realize these potentialities, however, social workers must be familiar with the two opposing views of the nature and purpose of unionism that exist both within and outside the trade union movement.

Jeffry Galper uses the concepts "class-conflict" and "class-collaborationist" to differentiate radical and non-radical unionism.[22] The former, based on workers' awareness that they constitute a distinct class in society, views the role of unions as protecting and advancing the interests of the "total" working class and to do so necessitates the eventual abolition of capitalism. The latter, based on a lack of workers' awareness that they constitute a distinct class in society, views the role of unions as protecting and advancing the interests of the union membership only by fighting for a larger share of the wealth that workers produce within the context of capitalism. The trade union movement in Sweden would typify (although not exactly) the class-conflict view of unions, and that of the United States would be the closest case of a pure class-collaborationist union movement. Great Britain and Canada would fall in between these two types, with Britain closer to the class-conflict view. Canada, because of its proximity to the United States and because many unions in Canada were once (and some still are) controlled by American unions, would be closer to the class-collaborationist view than most trade union movements in other countries.

Obviously, if unions are to become an effective vehicle for promoting the welfare state and for socialist transformation, they must adopt a class-conflict view. A class-collaborationist view is based on the conservative-liberal belief that there is a harmony of interests between capital and labour. American unions often opposed social welfare schemes such as social insurance because they were seen as a rival to the protection unions had secured for their members through bargaining.[23] As a result an extensive but inequitable occupational welfare system has developed in the United States instead of an adequate public welfare system that would cover more people.[24] Piven and Cloward argue that the American trade union movement has not been a force for social welfare concessions in the post-war era.[25] And, in view of the fact that the proportion of the U.S. labour force that is unionized has been declining for over a decade, it is unlikely that the trade union movement will be a significant political force in the near future.

A class-conflict view is based on the belief that there is an inherent conflict of interests between capital and labour. Whatever one group gets is at the expense of the other group (i.e., profits vs. wages). This view also recognizes that the welfare state in capitalist societies has benefited the working class, but it has benefited the capitalists even more by subsidizing certain costs of production, such as maintaining an educated and healthy work force and guaranteeing a certain level of consumption of goods and services purchased with social welfare benefits. As long as capitalism exists there will never be a true welfare state based on the principle of distribution according to need.

The progressive class-conflict concept of unionism has much in common with structural social work. Both reject capitalism as a social and economic system and seek to replace it with a social order where human need is the central organizing principle. Both reject narrow, self-interested individualism in favour of collective association, rights, and responsibilities. Both reject elitist, hierarchical decision-making and advocate active participation in and control over all aspects of one's living and working conditions. And both reject exploitation and oppression based on such grounds as class, gender, and race, with the progressive union movement focusing on its elimination specifically in the workplace.

One other major reason for structural social workers to become involved with the trade union movement is that the growth of the welfare state is, in part, a product of the union movement.[26] International comparisons show that those countries with extensive and well-organized labour movements, such as Austria, Germany, and the Scandinavian countries, tend to have extensive and well-developed welfare states. And, conversely, those countries without a high percentage of the work force unionized tend to have primitive welfare states. For example, the United States, which has the lowest rate of organized workers in the Western industrialized world (less than 20 per cent), also has the least developed welfare state.

Mishra outlines four ways in which organized labour has contributed to the development of the welfare state.[27] First, the growth of labour movements is often perceived by the ruling classes as a threat to capitalism, and to reduce this threat the ruling classes have often conceded social programs to the working class. Bismarck's social legislation in Germany in the latter part of the nineteenth century is a good example. Second, ruling classes and liberal and conservative governments have often implemented social welfare programs that were being promoted by socialist parties and were very popular with the working class. An example would be Canada's public health care program, which was originally a socialist party idea but was legislated by bourgeois governments to dampen the rising popularity of the socialist (CCF/NDP) party. Third, labour movements have themselves demanded social legislation as a means of improving the life situation of working-class people. And fourth, social democratic governments, as in Sweden and Great Britain, have aligned themselves with labour movements as a means of transforming capitalist societies to socialism. As well as promoting the social welfare state, the labour movement organizes the strongest opposition to cutbacks during periods when social programs are under attack.[28]

In addition to its contributions to the development of the welfare state, unionism holds many benefits for social workers. Several writers have commented on these benefits. Galper views unions as fertile ground for radical social work. Besides being necessary for the protection of workers' jobs, wages, and benefits, unions are an important source of political education and growth because they help us understand that conflict is real in our society despite being socialized into an anti-conflict ethic. Unions can provide the experience of collective work, organizing, and engaging in political analysis. Union negotiating allows workers to have a say about service provisions and delivery, such as caseload sizes, and to have input into policy formulation and decisions. Galper believes also that unionism provides a counterbalance to the elitist, exclusionary, and self-serving tendencies that characterize the "ideology of professionalism."[29] Withorn shares this belief.[30]

Carniol suggests that unions have potential for social workers to empower themselves in the workplace by working toward greater industrial democracy; to link broader issues such as employment equity, better pension legislation, and day care to the more traditional "bread and butter" issues; and to form important links with other workers and other social movements.[31] Corrigan and Leonard emphasize that the union movement is the only powerful force defending the welfare state against cuts and that social workers must use the union to defend both themselves and the interests of service users.[32] Wineman thinks that unions enhance worker control, sensitize social workers to issues of class, contribute to the growth of economic and social alternatives, and facilitate social worker participation in coalitions.

Wagner and Cohen believe that unionization symbolically draws a line between social workers and their employing agency, and helps to crystallize the fact that the workplace is an arena of conflict, with administrators and workers often having different interests. They argue that social service settings raise political questions more readily than industrial settings in that social workers daily observe the lives of victims of capitalism and the failure of reformist solutions. To challenge the system, social workers can provide important leadership to the rest of the working class as they have done in Latin America and in parts of Europe.[33]

Although it is imperative that structural social workers recognize the strength of the union movement as the most economically well-organized working-class organization with potential for taking on capitalism, the weaknesses and the limitations of the current union movement must also be understood. Corrigan and Leonard note that the major limitation of the union movement is its apparent lack of political consciousness and activity.[34] They point out that, historically, trade unions were created to advance and defend the interests of the working class within capitalism and that we should not be surprised to find that many workers do not have an inherent belief in revolutionary change. Nor are workers free from the racism, sexism, and conservatism that are part of the larger societal consciousness. To realize the revolutionary potential of the union movement, union members must understand how social transformation is in their best interests and how it has a direct material importance. Galper also addresses this issue by suggesting that the union movement has to move away from a class-collaborationist mentality to one of class conflict if its revolutionary potential is to be tapped.[35] Without a class-conflict mentality, unions simply become one more socially reproducing bureaucracy with which to contend.

Professional Associations

Unlike unions, professional associations, as a form of organization, are not the products of an inherent conflict among particular groups in society. They are, in fact, created by society to carry out particular functions for society and *not* to oppose society. Given the fact that professional associations are part of the current social structure, the critical question for structural social workers is: Can professional associations of social workers be used as another means of social transformation?

Mullaly and Keating have summarized the main radical social work criticisms of professionalism.[36] First, professionalism emphasizes technical aspects of helping, such as impartiality, emotional neutrality, and apolitical service. Thus, it masks the political component of social work practice and perpetuates the notion that capitalist social relations are natural and normal functions of an industrialized society. As well, professionalism promotes technical solutions to problems, implying that these problems are individual rather than larger social and political problems.

Second, by organizing into an exclusive group based on academic credentials, professionalism divides social workers from other workers and from persons who use social work services. By requesting certification from the state, professional social workers implicitly align themselves with the state. In exchange for state recognition, social workers are required to deliver services that contain elements of oppression and control. In effect, professionalism blinds social workers to issues of class, particularly their own class position and class function.

Third, by organizing themselves into social and occupational hierarchies, professional social workers are practising inequality. By treating social problems as individual misfortunes, they promote individualism. And by accepting an ethic of "service to others," they disempower those they would serve. The messages conveyed are that intervention should focus on people and not on social structures, and that the best source of helping rests with the "expert" social worker and not within the service user.

Finally, the history of professionalism, such as in law and medicine, indicates that such hierarchical organization benefits the professionals, not the service users. Despite its "service to others" ethic, professionalism becomes self-serving as professionals tend to seek personal, social, economic, and political power for themselves.

The above criticisms of professionalism have led many radical social work writers[37] to reject professionalism and to opt for unions as the most appropriate means for social workers to organize to pursue social transformation. However, not all radical writers and certainly not all social workers believe that there is necessarily an incompatibility between unionism and professionalism as means of engaging in collective forms of organization. Three separate studies, one Canadian[38] and two American,[39] found that the majority of social workers do not believe that unionism and professionalism are incompatible. A recent study[40] looked at the correlations between professionalization and activism among rank-and-file social workers in 1968 and 1984. It found, contrary to the speculation of radical critics of professionalism, that professionalization is not associated with a neutralist political ideology and that participation in political activities was associated with greater institutionalized activism. The study also suggested that differences in activism among social workers are likely to be a product of factors independent of professionalization, such as different recruitment patterns, different background characteristics, and so on.

The position taken here is that structural social workers should join professional associations for the same reason they should join unions – to engage in collective action with the purpose of social transformation. Given the present class-collaborationist nature of most unions in North America and the evidence cited above, which suggests that professionalism by itself does not deter social activism, it is a false dichotomy to present unionism as the radical form of social work organization and professionalism as the conservative form. Most social workers will belong to both a union and a professional association. Just as structural social workers work within the social welfare institution to radicalize it and to use it as a means of social transformation, so, too, should they join professional associations for the very same purposes. To argue that "working within" only applies to one institution in our society and not to others is contradictory and illogical. Moreau and Leonard argue that to refuse to join professional associations means to abandon its membership to the right wing.[41]

One of the criticisms of professionalism is that it tends to be self-serving in that narrow interests to increase the well-being of its members are pursued. Leslie Bella has outlined some recent actions of the Canadian Association of Social Workers (CASW) that did not seek direct benefits to its members but instead were carried out for the broader purposes of public welfare.[42] The Association has fought for progressive tax reform to bring more equity and justice to the present system in Canada. It has also defended social programs and has sought changes to current legislation, such as the Canada Assistance Plan, that would bring more fairness and integrity to Canada's welfare state. The Association has campaigned against free trade with the United States and has become an active member of the peace movement. It opposed U.S. President Ronald Reagan's "Star Wars" defence plan, advocated compensation for victims of the internment of Japanese Canadians during World War Two, lobbied for sanctions against South Africa, and has made presentations to several commissions, committees, and task forces. One may quarrel with the success or effectiveness of these actions and whether or not they are radical or only reformist, but the CASW cannot be accused of being purely ethnocentric and self-serving.

To prevent professional associations from falling victim to the conservative forces of professionalization and becoming supporters of the status quo, some guidelines should be considered. Wilding, for example, has expressed concern about the lack of mechanisms for consumer groups to comment on those aspects of professionalism that ultimately impact on the users of social work services.[43] Just as frontline social workers should be able to participate in formulating policy, so should service users have some input into professional associations.

Lay representation on the boards of professional associations and the establishment of liaison committees are a couple of possibilities.

To ensure that professional bodies of social workers concern themselves with issues confronting traditional socially disadvantaged and oppressed groups in society, caucuses should be established consisting of association members who are also members of disadvantaged groups: (1) to sensitize other members of the profession to the needs, problems, and issues that affect each group, along with the social causes of their disadvantage and oppression; and (2) to interface with the larger socially disadvantaged populations. For example, the women's caucus of a professional social work association would communicate with women's groups in the community, the visible minority caucus would interact with the visible minority groups in the community, and so on. In this way, the likelihood of social work becoming ethnocentric is reduced and, conversely, it is more likely to develop a more meaningful anti-sexist, anti-racist, and anti-homophobic social work practice.

A progressive professional association should also have liaison committees as linkages to other social movement groups that seek the transformation of society – the peace movement, the environmental movement, the human rights movement. One other necessary committee, if a professional association is to avoid becoming a self-serving, status quo organization, is an active social action committee led by members who have a structural (as opposed to a reformist) outlook. This committee must be supported by the membership and the executive in carrying out analyses of social programs, policies, legislation, government actions, and corporate interests. In sum, the indigenous caucuses and the social action committee preserve the social conscience of social work in the face of its professionalization.

Electoral Politics

Little social work literature addresses electoral politics as an arena for struggle for social workers. A great deal has been written on lobbying and influencing governments, but almost nothing exists on supporting a particular political party as a way of dealing with social problems, let alone as a way of transforming our current liberal-capitalist society.

The reasons for this lack of attention to electoral politics are partly historical and partly methodological. Historically, social work has perceived involvement in party politics as unprofessional. To become involved in politics was to meddle in the preserve of the politicians. Not only is conventional social work emotionally neutral, it is also politically neutral. Involvement in party politics was considered to be a personal choice, certainly not a professional choice. Methodologically, conventional models of social work practice, such as systems theory and the ecological approach, preclude electoral political activity. One might assess the negative impact of government policy on people, but the social worker is limited to helping people adapt to the policy or to lobby government to ameliorate the policy. In view of the fact that governments ultimately decide on the nature, shape, size, and quality of social programs, it hardly makes sense for social work not to involve itself in attempting to get the political party most sympathetic to a progressive welfare state elected. If political decisions determine the fate of the welfare state and the nature of our social relationships, social work must involve itself in the political arena.

In political democracies, political parties constitute an important means by which social classes or social groups organize to pursue their collective interests.[44] In other countries, such as the Scandinavian nations, the working classes have been able to offset the greater power resources of capital by electing social democratic governments. These governments have, in turn, implemented policies that are favourable to the working class, such as full employment and the pursuit of a welfare state that promotes an equality of the highest standards.[45] Conversely, those countries that have elected mostly liberal or conservative governments, such as the United States and Canada, have developed political economies favouring the interests of capital over the working class, as evidenced by policies that accept high unemployment and a residual welfare state. Clearly, then, social work cannot remain at arm's length from electoral politics. Social work is not politically neutral; it is a political act or practice. If it does nothing politically it has removed itself as a force for change, which in effect supports the status quo. Given the inherent political nature of social work it must organize and declare its political hand. It must align itself with other groups and organizations that share similar goals. This includes supporting political parties committed to social, political, and economic justice for all and not just for a privileged minority.

American social workers committed to social transformation do not have a national socialist party to work with. In fact, the majority of Americans do not have the background and experience to allow them to discuss the nature of capitalism and socialism objectively and critically. Many people espouse an uncritical and unexamined commitment to the "free enterprise system" and to the "American way."[46] In the absence of a socialist or radical party, Wineman advocates radical activity at the local level as a means of building a "bottom-up approach to constructing a national radical presence in electoral politics."[47] Such activity not only pushes mainstream politicians to the left as they scramble for the votes of women, minorities, the poor, and so on; it also helps to mobilize and consolidate multi-constituency and multi-issue coalitions as "they begin to create a foundation for the eventual emergence of a national third party."[48]

In Canada there is a social democratic national party, the New Democratic Party. However, it is seldom mentioned in most Canadian social work and social welfare textbooks,[49] even in those books with a leftist perspective.[50] In Shankar Yelaja's widely used Canadian social policy text there is passing reference to the NDP as "the unequivocal advocate of social welfare ideals"[51] among Canada's political parties, but the potential relationship between social work and the NDP is not explored. Only Andrew Armitage pays tribute to the contributions made to the Canadian welfare state by the NDP and its predecessor, the Co-operative Commonwealth Federation.

> The New Democratic Party has been the most consistent advocate of social welfare in the Canadian political spectrum. The party's political statements have, more clearly than other parties', committed it to the welfare ideal of the redistribution of income, wealth, and power. When elected to office (only achieved in British Columbia, Saskatchewan, and Manitoba [and, more recently, Ontario]), New Democratic governments have shown a willingness to introduce social welfare programs not legislated anywhere else in Canada, or indeed in North America. . . . Long before Liberal or Progressive Conservative governments have introduced social welfare legislation, the spokesmen of the New Democratic Party and its predecessor, the Co-operative Commonwealth Federation, have brought the need of Canadians for such programs as pensions, medicare, housing, and income guarantees before the House of Commons.[52]

Very few major policy differences exist between Canada's other two national political parties, the Liberals and the Progressive Conservatives. Both parties are located near the centre of the political spectrum, with the Conservatives leaning more to the right. The Progressive Conservative Party has a tendency to disavow the progressive rhetoric of some of it leaders,[53] and the Mulroney Conservative government has been systematically retrenching the Canadian welfare state over the past decade through a policy of gradualism.[54] Although most of Canada's social programs have been legislated under Liberal governments, the motivation has often been to undermine the popularity of the NDP or to avert labour unrest. There have been periods of neglect and disinterest on the part of Liberal governments and, on occasion, Liberal spokespersons have appealed to the alienating aspects of welfare transfers in their quest for political support.[55] Both the Liberal and

Progressive Conservative parties accept liberal capitalism as the preferred socio-economic system, and both have a history of being more responsive to the needs of capital than to the needs of the working classes. This is the major reason for the persistence of residualism with respect to Canada's welfare state.

Given the history, ideology, and approaches of the three political parties to the welfare state, it makes no sense for structural social workers to support either the Liberals or the Progressive Conservatives. To do so would be no different from supporting an arsonist's bid to become fire chief. Social work is not above politics, it *is* a political activity. If it does not have a progressive agenda then it will automatically become part of the conservative forces in society. The warped professional notion of political neutrality must be rejected and replaced with the knowledge that electoral politics is a major arena where the struggle for social transformation occurs.

Making the Political Personal in Our Own Lives

This section focuses on the most important arena for radical change – ourselves. Moreau and Leonard contend that one of the central factors conducive to the practice of structural social work is to attain congruence between our personal/political beliefs and the way we live our lives.[56] Withorn states that socially committed social workers will need "to achieve harmony among their politics, their work, and their personal lives."[57] In other words, it is not enough to espouse structural ideology and to carry it out in our professional work – we must live it. To do otherwise is not only contradictory and hypocritical, it is self-defeating.

It was argued in the previous chapter that to avoid reproducing social relationships and behaviours that are part of our patriarchal, liberal-capitalist society, an anti-capitalist social work practice must be carried out. So, too, in our personal lives must we avoid reproducing social relationships and behaviours at the root of so many of our social problems – inequality, excessive competition, exploitation of people and resources, profit-driven production, distribution, and consumption, sexism, racism, homophobia, individualism, militarism, and so on. By carrying out our ideological beliefs in our daily lives we supplement our structural work by contributing to social transformation outside of our professional practice.

Our personal relationships represent one area for personal and social transformation. Just as we strive for egalitarian and participatory relationships in the workplace, so we should practice equality in our relationships. We must work at eliminating traditional roles and divisions based on gender in our homes and in our associations with others.

Structural social workers must examine their own lives and interactions with others to determine whether or not they are contributing to a social atmosphere of oppression, aggression, and even violence. Are sexist, racist, or homophobic jokes and slurs condoned or tolerated? Does violence in any form occur? Are environmentally harmful products purchased and used? Are war toys purchased for children or do we allow them to watch violent television shows? Structural social work requires more than a nine-to-five workplace effort; it requires a commitment to personal evaluation, challenge, and change.

Do our consumer patterns support capitalism or do we take advantage of the collective, more democratic, and non-exploitative alternatives that exist in the midst of our patriarchal, liberal-capitalist society? With respect to our personal finances, do we use private banks that make enormous profits for a few people, often have investments in countries with apartheid and oppressive labour policies, and often exploit their own workers, most of whom are women? Or do we join credit unions, which are collectively owned and operated by their memberships and invest their money in the local community? Do we purchase goods and services made or delivered by non-unionized companies or do we support the trade union movement by purchasing union-produced goods and services? Do we patronize profit-driven businesses when there are opportunities to support the development and expansion of the co-operative movement where, as with credit unions, the enterprises are membership-owned and operated in the best interests of its members and not for a few shareholders? Do we purchase environmentally friendly products and boycott products from establishments with poor environmental records? North Americans consume billions of dollars of goods and services yearly. The market is the heart of capitalism, but it also an area where the traditional capitalist principles of production-distribution and consumption can be altered.

To live structurally in a patriarchal, liberal-capitalist society is not easy, however. Most of the rewards – promotions, acceptance, respect – are given to those who conform to our present social order. By engaging in structural social work we run the risk of retaliation from the status quo. This retaliation can take the form of people being nervous in our presence or of overt efforts to discredit us by applying labels such as "troublemaker." Galper[58] and Withorn[59] have written about the risks involved in radical work and some of the ways of coping with and reducing the risks – avoid adventurism and martyrdom; be competent in your work; work collectively; realize that all radicals experience some degree of ambivalence about their radicalism by virtue of having been socialized into a patriarchal, liberal-capitalist society. The greater risk, however, is to capitulate to the status quo and not carry out our structural ideology in our work and in our personal lives. The risk in this case is that we do nothing to bring about progressive radical change and, thus, fail the people we serve and fail ourselves. We become part of the problem and not the solution as we join the conventional social work group delivering services and practising in ways that blame victims for their troubles. And we run the risk of cynicism, despair, and burnout because we know that in the long run what we are doing is simply perpetuating the system that causes people troubles in the first place.

In sum, to be effective as structural social workers we need a political analysis that distinguishes the causes and consequences of social problems. We need a vision of a humanized society to give us direction in our efforts. We need knowledge to enable us to work effectively both inside and outside of our social agencies. We need to have harmony between our political beliefs and our personal lives. And we need a commitment to carry out the difficult task of social transformation. Structural social work is more than a technique or a practice modality. It is a way of life.

Notes

Chapter 1

1. See, for example, Ian Gough, *The Political Economy of the Welfare State* (London: The Macmillan Press, 1979); Ramesh Mishra, *The Welfare State in Crisis* (New York: St. Martin's Press, 1984); Graham Riches, *Food Banks and the Welfare Crisis* (Ottawa: Canadian Council on Social Development, 1986).
2. Dennis Guest, *The Emergence of Social Security in Canada* (Vancouver: University of British Columbia Press, 1980).
3. Mishra, *The Welfare State in Crisis.*
4. For fuller and more elaborate explanations of this "legitimation crisis," see Vic George and Paul Wilding, *The Impact of Social Policy* (London: Routledge & Kegan Paul, 1984); Mishra, *The Welfare State in Crisis*; Gough, *The Political Economy of the Welfare State*; Riches, *Food Banks and the Welfare Crisis.*
5. Gough, *The Political Economy of the Welfare State*, p. 132.
6. Riches, *Food Banks and the Welfare Crisis*, p. 105.
7. James Midgely, "Introduction: American Social Policy and the Reagan Legacy," special issue on the Reagan Legacy and the American Welfare State, *Journal of Sociology and Social Welfare*, XIX, 1 (March, 1992).
8. D. Lee Bawden and J.L. Palmer. "Social Policy: Challenging the Welfare State," in J.L. Palmer and I.V. Sawhill, eds., *The Reagan Record* (Washington, D.C.: The Urban Institute, 1984).
9. *Ibid.*, p. 92
10. P. Riddell, *The Thatcher Government* (Oxford: Basil Blackwell, 1985), and P. Taylor-Gooby, "The Future of the British Welfare State" (mimeo, Canterbury: University of Kent, 1987), cited in R. Mishra, *The Welfare State in Capitalist Society* (Toronto: University of Toronto Press, 1990), pp. 23-24.
11. "Jobless figure a record again," *Manchester Guardian Weekly,* 17 March 1985, p. 3, cited in Mishra, *The Welfare State in Capitalist Society*, p. 29.

12. "The Starving of the NHS," *Manchester Guardian Weekly,* 13 March 1988, p. 12, and "The NHS: A Suitable Case for Much Better Treatment," *Manchester Guardian Weekly,* 31 January 1988, p. 6, cited in Mishra, *The Welfare State in Capitalist Society*, p. 24.
13. Gough, *The Political Economy of the Welfare State*, p. x.
14. Riches, *Food Banks and the Welfare Crisis.*
15. Jane Jenson, "Different but Not 'Exceptional': Canada's Permeable Fordism," *Canadian Review of Sociology and Anthropology*, 20, 1 (1989), pp. 69-94; E. Lightman and A. Irving, "Restructuring Canada's Welfare State," *Journal of Social Policy*, 20, 1 (1991), pp. 65-86; Mishra, *The Welfare State in Capitalist Society.*
16. Editorial, "A Bleak Year for Social Progress," *Perception,* 15, 2 (1991), pp. 4-6.
17. George and Wilding, *The Impact of Social Policy*, p. 256.
18. Mishra, *The Welfare State in Capitalist Society.*
19. *Ibid.*, p. 12.
20. Denis Bracken and Christopher Walmsley, "The Canadian Welfare State: Implications for the Continuing Education of Canadian Social Workers," *The Social Worker*, 60, 1 (1992), p. 23.
21. Michael Reisch and Stanley Wenocur, "Introduction," *Journal of Sociology and Social Welfare*, X, 4 (1983), p. 546.
22. See Robert Mullaly, "Social Welfare: Vigilante Style," *Perception*, 8, 2 (1984), for an example of this type of investigation.
23. Terry Hunsley, "Future Directions and Challenges in Social Development," discussion paper (Ottawa: Canadian Council on Social Development, 1987).
24. Michael Simpkin, *Trapped Within Welfare* (London: The Macmillan Press, 1983), p. 25.
25. See *ibid.*, and Jeffry Galper, *The Politics of Social Services* (Englewood Cliffs, N.J.: Prentice-Hall, 1975), for elaborations of this point.
26. Galper, *The Politics of Social Services.*
27. Steve Bolger, Paul Corrigan, Jan Docking, and Nick Frost, *Towards Socialist Welfare Work* (London: The Macmillan Press, 1981).
28. Chauncey A. Alexander, "Social Work in the 80's: Issues and Strategies," presented as the Plenary Address, 1982 Biennial Conference, Canadian Association of Social Workers, June 18, 1982, Winnipeg, Manitoba, cited in *The Social Worker/Le Travailleur*, 50, 2 (1982), pp. 63-67.
29. Ramesh Mishra, "Riding the New Wave: Social Work and the Neo-Conservative Challenge," *International Social Work*, 32, 3 (1989), pp. 171-82.
30. Steve Burghardt, *The Other Side of Organizing* (Cambridge, Mass.: Schenkman, 1982).
31. Karen Haynes and James S. Mickelson, "Social Work and the Reagan Era: Challenges to the Profession," *Journal of Sociology and Social Welfare*, XIX, 1 (1992), pp. 169-83.

32. Howard Jacob Karger, "Ideology and the Crisis of the Welfare State," *Quarterly Journal of Ideology: A Critique of Conventional Wisdom*, 11, 1 (1987), pp. 3-11.
33. Vic George and Paul Wilding, *Ideology and Social Welfare* (London: Routledge & Kegan Paul, 1976); P. Leonard, "Explanation and Education in Social Work," *British Journal of Social Work*, 5 (1975); C.R. Dykema, "The Political Economy of Social Welfare: A Perspective," *Journal of Sociology and Social Welfare*, 4, 3-4 (1977), pp. 439-69; P.G. Findlay, "Theories of the State and Social Welfare in Canada," *Canadian Journal of Social Work Education*, 14, 1 (1978), pp. 109-28; Colin Pritchard and Richard Taylor, *Social Work: Reform or Revolution?* (London: Routledge & Kegan Paul, 1978); G. Room, *The Sociology of Welfare* (Oxford, 1979).
34. Burghardt, *The Other Side of Organizing*, p. 19.
35. Howard Jones, ed., *Towards a New Social Work* (London: Routledge & Kegan Paul, 1975), pp. v-vi.
36. Paul Corrigan and Peter Leonard, *Social Work Practice Under Capitalism: A Marxist Approach* (London: The Macmillan Press, 1978), p. 90.
37. Findlay, "Theories of the State and Social Welfare in Canada," p. 109.
38. Simpkin, *Trapped Within Welfare*, p. 25.
39. See, for example, Frank M. Lowenberg, " Professional Ideology, Middle Range Theories and Knowledge Building for Social Work Practice," *British Journal of Social Work*, 14 (1984), pp. 309-22; William DeMaria, "Fumbling with the Kaleidoscope: World View Clashes in Social Work," *Canadian Journal of Social Work Education*, 8, 1 and 2 (1982), pp. 31-44; Ben Carniol, "Clash of Ideologies in Social Work Education," *Canadian Social Work Review* (1984), pp. 184-99; Pritchard and Taylor, *Social Work: Reform or Revolution?*
40. Angela Djao, *Inequality and Social Policy* (Toronto: John Wiley & Sons, 1983); G. Drover and D. Woodsworth, "Social Welfare Theory and Social Policy," *Canadian Journal of Social Work Education*, 4, 1 (1978), pp. 19-41; George and Wilding, *Ideology and Social Welfare*; Mishra, *The Welfare State in Crisis.*
41. Pritchard and Taylor, *Social Work: Reform or Revolution?*; Galper, *The Politics of Social Services*; De Maria, "Fumbling with the Kaleidoscope"; Carniol, "Clash of Ideologies"; Patrick Kerans, "Social Science and Ideology in Policy Analysis," *Canadian Journal of Social Work Education*, 4, 1 (1978), pp. 129-41.
42. Lowenberg, "Professional Ideology, Middle Range Theories and Knowledge Building for Social Work Practice"; Carniol, "A Critical Approach in Social Work," *Canadian Journal of Social Work Education*, 5, 1 (1979), pp. 95-111.
43. DeMaria, "Fumbling with the Kaleidoscope."
44. Thomas S. Kuhn, *The Structure of Scientific Revolutions* (Chicago:

University of Chicago Press, 1962; second edition, with postscript, 1970), pp. ix-x.

45. M. Masterman, "The Nature of a Paradigm," in I. Lakatos and A. Musgrave, eds., *Criticism and the Growth of Knowledge* (Cambridge, Mass., 1970), pp. 59-89.
46. Robert D. Leighninger, Jr., editor of the *Journal of Sociology and Social Welfare*, states that writers often use Kuhnian terms to give their work borrowed legitimacy, and if the concept "paradigm" is not applied carefully the legitimacy is bogus. Kuhn was dealing with the physical world and physical sciences, not the social world and social sciences. Leighninger does admit that one can apply the concept outside of the physical sciences and talk about multiple-paradigm sciences and paradigm shifts rather than single-paradigm social sciences and revolutions. Social work is, of course, well acquainted with borrowing concepts and knowledge and with the dangers inherent in this practice. Personal correspondence, June 11, 1990.
47. Julienne Ford, *Paradigms and Fairy Tales: An Introduction to the Science of Meanings* (London: Routledge & Kegan Paul, 1975).
48. Håkan Tornebohm, *Paradigms in Fields of Research* (Gothenburg: University of Gothenburg, Dept. of Theory of Science, Report No. 93, 1977).
49. P. Bandopadhyay, "One Sociology or Many: Some Issues in Radical Sociology," *The Sociological Review*, 19, 1 (February, 1971), p. 8.
50. Tornebohm, *Paradigms in Fields of Research*, p. 19.
51. Kuhn, *The Structure of Scientific Revolutions*, p. 37.
52. *Ibid.*, pp. 52-53.
53. *Ibid.*, p. 6.
54. DeMaria, "Fumbling with the Kaleidoscope," p. 33.
55. Carniol, "Clash of Ideologies," p. 185.
56. Mishra, "Riding the New Wave," pp. 180-81.
57. Burghardt, *The Other Side of Organizing*, p. 20.
58. *Ibid.*
59. Peter L. Berger and Thomas Luckmann, *The Social Construction of Reality* (New York: Doubleday, 1966); Mishra, "Riding the New Wave"; Maurice Moreau and Lynne Leonard, *Empowerment Through a Structural Approach to Social Work* (Ottawa: Carleton University School of Social Work, 1989); Steve Wineman, *The Politics of the Human Services* (Montreal: Black Rose Books, 1984).
60. DeMaria, "Fumbling with the Kaleidoscope," p. 34.
61. *Ibid.*, p. 35.

Chapter 2

1. There exists, of course, a plethora of various perspectives, models, theories, and so on within social work. With respect to our present social

order, however, two basic views are held by social workers. There are those who believe our present society is basically okay and that it is capable of righting any social wrongs that may occur. Others believe that our present society is not okay, that it is not capable of righting social wrongs because the social order itself produces these wrongs, and that limited reform of the system will do nothing to resolve social problems. The first group of social workers, called here conventional workers, seek to make our social order work better. The second group, progressive workers, seek to transform our present social order into one that works better for larger numbers of people. Another term for progressive social work is radical social work, which is discussed in some detail in Chapter 7.

2. Ben Carniol, "A Critical Approach In Social Work," *Canadian Journal of Social Work Education*, 5,1 (1979), pp. 95-111.
3. Jeffry Galper, *The Politics of Social Services* (Englewood Cliffs, N.J.: Prentice-Hall, 1975).
4. All social science disciplines and professions have witnessed the development or extension of critical or radical branches since the seventies. For a recent overview of the radical social work literature, see Robert Mullaly and Eric Keating, "Similarities, Differences and Dialectics of Radical Social Work," *Journal of Progressive Human Services*, 2, 2 (1991), pp. 49-78.
5. Ben Carniol, *Case Critical* (Toronto: Between the Lines, 1990).
6. Galper, *The Politics of Social Services*, p. 140.
7. *Ibid.*, p. 142.
8. Neil Nevitte and Roger Gibbins, *New Elites in Old States: Ideologies in the Anglo-American Democracies* (Toronto: Oxford University Press, 1990), p. 147.
9. Galper, *The Politics of Social Services*, p. 141.
10. Steven Wineman, *The Politics of Human Services* (Montreal: Black Rose Books, 1984), p. 159.
11. D.E. Woodsworth, "Social Work Forum: Dialogue on Ethics," *The Social Worker/Le Travailleur*, 52, 2 (Summer, 1984).
12. Colleen Lundy and Larry Gauthier, "Social Work Practice and the Master-Servant Relationship," *The Social Worker/Le Travailleur*, 57, 4 (Winter, 1989), p. 192.
13. Preamble (Section on "Philosophy"), "Canadian Association of Social Workers Code of Ethics (1983)," p. 2.
14. *Ibid.*
15. According to the *Encyclopedia of Social Sciences*, vol. 7, E. Selizam, ed. (New York: Macmillan, 1944), pp. 544-48, humanism proposes that people have two natures, good and bad, and that there is constant tension between the two. Humanitarianism, on the other hand, denies this inevitable dualism within the individual and believes that people are innately good and reasonable.

16. *Webster's New Collegiate Dictionary* (Springfield, Mass.: G. & C. Merriam, 1980).
17. This definition of humanism is taken from Murad Saiflan and Richard W. Dixon, eds., *Dictionary of Philosophy* (New York: International Publishers, 1984), p. 178. Another source, Dagobert D. Runes, ed., *Dictionary of Philosophy* (New York: Philosophical Library, 1960), pp. 131-32, cites five different meanings of humanism: a) the Renaissance revolt against religious limitations on knowledge, and a stress on people enjoying their existence; b) a twentieth-century philosophy of religion that rejects belief in all forms of the supernatural; c) an outmoded form of pragmatism emphasizing subjective elements; d) academic humanism, which was a short-lived movement in the 1930s urging a return to the classics in education; and e) any view in which the welfare and happiness of people in this life is primary. It is this latter usage of humanism that is adopted in this book.
18. J. Hardy, *Values in Social Policy: Nine Contradictions* (London: Routledge & Kegan Paul, 1981), p. 29.
19. David G. Gil, "Resolving Issues of Social Provision," in Gil, *The Challenge of Social Equality* (Cambridge, Mass.: Schenkman Publishing Co., 1976), p. 65.
20. Galper, *The Politics of Social Services*, p. 142.
21. Norman Goroff, "Humanism and Social Work Paradoxes, Problems, and Promises," *Journal of Sociology and Social Welfare*, VIII, 1 (1981), p. 1.
22. For a few American examples, see Galper, *The Politics of Social Services*; Gil, *The Challenge of Social Equality*; Ann Withorn, *Serving the People: Social Service and Social Change* (New York: Columbia University Press, 1984); Michael Harrington, *The Other America* (New York: Macmillan, 1962).

    For a few Canadian examples, see Keith G. Banting, *The Welfare State and Canadian Federalism* (Montreal: McGill-Queen's University Press, 1982); Allan Moscovitch and Glen Drover, eds., *Inequality* (Toronto: University of Toronto Press, 1981); M. Patricia Marchak, *Ideological Perspectives on Canada*, 3rd edition (Toronto: McGraw-Hill Ryerson, 1981); A.W. Djao, *Inequality and Social Policy* (Toronto: John Wiley & Sons, 1983).
23. See, for example, C.L. Clark and A. Asquith, *Social Work and Social Philosophy* (London: Routledge & Kegan Paul, 1985); C. Rojek, G. Peacock, and S. Collins, *Social Work and Received Ideas* (London: Routledge & Kegan Paul, 1988).
24. Nina Biehal and Eric Sainsbury, "From Values of Rights in Social Work," *British Journal of Social Work*, 21 (1991), pp. 245-57.
25. For example, Harrington's *The Other America* is often cited as the major work that brought to the attention of affluent America the fact that poverty was real and pervasive in the United States in the early sixties, and in 1964

President Lyndon Johnson instituted his war on poverty. In its *Fifth Annual Review* (1968) the Economic Council of Canada revealed disturbing evidence on the extent of poverty in Canada, which led to a special parliamentary committee to investigate poverty and make recommendations to remedy it. Biehal and Sainsbury state that poverty was rediscovered in Britain in the 1960s by non-social workers: "From Values of Rights in Social Work," p. 250.

26. The conventional social work view of egalitarianism is that of equal opportunity. This notion of egalitarianism and others will be discussed in the chapters focusing on the four different paradigms. See S.I. Benn and R.S. Peters, *Social Principles and the Democratic State* (London: Allen & Unwin, 1959), for an overview and discussion of different meanings of egalitarianism.
27. Gil, *The Challenge of Social Equality*, p. 3.; David G. Gil, *Unravelling Social Policy* (Cambridge, Mass: Schenkman Publishing Co., 1973).
28. Gil, *The Challenge of Social Equality*, p. 4.
29. *Ibid.*
30. For a fuller coverage of collectivism as an organizing principle for an idealized social work society, see Galper, *The Politics of Social Services*, pp. 140-52.
31. *Ibid.*, p. 151.
32. David G. Gil, "Implications of Conservative Tendencies for Practice and Education in Social Welfare," *Journal of Sociology and Social Welfare*, XVII, 2 (June, 1990), pp. 20-21.
33. Allen Pincus and Anne Minahan, *Social Work Practice: Model and Method* (Itasca, Ill.: F.E. Peacock, 1973), p. 39.
34. Daphne Statham, *Radicals in Social Work* (London: Routledge & Kegan Paul, 1978), p. 25.
35. *Ibid.*, p. 27.
36. Biehal and Sainsbury, "From Values of Rights in Social Work," p. 249.
37. This theme will be explored in more detail in subsequent chapters. See especially Chapters 4, 7, 8, and 9.
38. David G. Gil, "Social Policies and Social Development: A Humanistic-Egalitarian Perspective," *Journal of Sociology and Social Welfare*, 3, 3 (January, 1976), p. 242.
39. John Friedmann, "The Public Interest and Community Participation: Toward a Reconstruction of Public Philosophy," *Journal of the American Institute of Planners*, 39, 1 (January, 1973), p. 4.
40. *Ibid.*
41. *Ibid.*, p. 6.
42. *Ibid.*, p. 5.
43. *Ibid.*, p. 4.
44. Robert Mullaly, "A Calculus for Social Planning: Rawls' Theory of Justice," Working Papers on Social Welfare in Canada (Toronto:

U. of T. Faculty of Social Work Occasional Papers Series, 1980), p. 31.

45. Murray Ross, *Community Organization: Theory, Principles, and Practice* (New York: Harper & Row, 1967), p. 85.
46. Galper, *The Politics of Social Services*, pp. 142-46.
47. *Ibid.*, pp. 142-43.
48. *Ibid.*, p. 143.
49. C. Pateman, *Participation and Democratic Theory* (Cambridge: Cambridge University Press, 1970), p. 14, cited in Jean Hardy, *Values in Social Policy: Nine Contradictions* (London: Routledge & Kegan Paul, 1981), p.17.
50. See, for example, Hardy, *Values in Social Policy,*; Ray Lees, *Politics and Social Work* (London: Routledge & Kegan Paul, 1972); Galper, *The Politics of Social Services.*
51. Lees, *Politics and Social Work*, p. 39.
52. Hardy, *Values in Social Policy*, p. 19.
53. Lees, *Politics and Social Work*, p. 41.
54. *Ibid.*.
55. Maurice Moreau and Lynne Leonard, *Empowerment Through a Structural Approach to Social Work* (Ottawa: Carleton University School of Social Work, 1989), p. 235.
56. John Coates, "Putting Knowledge for Practice Into Perspective," *Canadian Social Work Review*, 8, 1 (Winter, 1991), pp. 82-96.
57. Norman Furniss and Timothy Tilton, *The Case for the Welfare State* (Bloomington: Indiana University Press, 1977).
58. Harold L. Wilensky and Charles N. Lebeaux, *Industrial Society and Social Welfare*, 2nd ed. (New York: Russell Sage Foundation, 1965).
59. Ramesh Mishra, *Society and Social Policy* (London: The Macmillan Press, 1981).
60. Furniss and Tilton, *The Case for the Welfare State*, pp. 15-16.
61. *Ibid.*, p. 18.
62. Mishra, *Society and Social Policy.*

Chapter 3

1. Roger Scruton, *A Dictionary of Political Thought* (London: The Macmillan Press, 1982), p. 90.
2. Geoffrey K. Roberts, *A Dictionary of Political Analysis* (New York: St. Martin's Press, 1971), pp. 46-47.
3. Clinton Rossiter, "Conservatism," in David L. Sills, ed., *International Encyclopedia of the Social Sciences,* vol. III (New York: Macmillan and The Free Press, 1968), pp. 290-94.
4. Mark O. Dickerson and Thomas Flanagan, *An Introduction to Government and Politics: A Conceptual Approach* (Agincourt, Ont.: Methuen, 1986).
5. Rossiter, "Conservatism," p. 294.

6. Dickerson and Flanagan, *Government and Politics,* p. 104.
7. *Ibid,* p. 105.
8. Ramesh Mishra, "Riding the New Wave: Social Work and the Neo-Conservative Challenge," *International Social Work*, 32, 3 (1989), p. 172.
9. *Ibid.*
10. *Ibid.*
11. Vic George and Paul Wilding, *Ideology and Social Welfare* (London: Routledge & Kegan Paul, 1976). Chapters 3-6 of the present book incorporate many of the ideas and insights found in George and Wilding's book.
12. A.W. Djao, *Inequality and Social Policy* (Toronto: John Wiley & Sons, 1983).
13. Ramesh Mishra, *The Welfare State in Crisis* (New York: St. Martin's Press, 1984).
14. Graham Riches, *Food Banks and the Welfare Crisis* (Ottawa: Canadian Council on Social Development, 1986), p. 154.
15. P. Resnick, "The Ideology of Neo-Conservatism," in Magnussen *et al.*, eds., *The New Reality* (Vancouver: New Star Books, 1984), cited in Riches, *Food Banks and the Welfare Crisis*, p. 106.
16. Dickerson and Flanagan, *Government and Politics*, p. 105.
17. Mishra, "Riding the New Wave," p. 173.
18. *Ibid.*
19. Rossiter, "Conservatism," p. 293.
20. Mishra, "Riding the New Wave," p. 171.
21. Stoesz and Karger, "Welfare Reform: From Illusion to Reality," *Social Work* (March, 1990), pp. 141-47.
22. Several conservative American writers have attributed the growth of the underclass to the welfare programs of the War on Poverty. The welfare poor were lured away from self-sufficiency by these programs and lost the capacity to live independently. See, for example, Stuart Butler and Anna Kondratas, *Out of the Poverty Trap: A Conservative Strategy for Welfare Reform* (New York: The Free Press, 1987); George Gilder, *Wealth and Poverty* (New York: Basic Books, 1981); and L. Mead, *Beyond Entitlement* (New York: The Free Press, 1986).
23. Stoesz and Karger, "Welfare Reform," p. 142.
24. Robert Mullaly, "Social Welfare and the New Right: A Class Mobilization Perspective," in Andrew F. Johnson, Stephen McBride, and Patrick J. Smith, eds., *Continuities and Discontinuities: The Political Economy of Social Welfare and Labour Market Policy in Canada* (Toronto: University of Toronto Press, forthcoming).
25. George and Wilding, *Ideology and Social Welfare*, p. 22.
26. M. Friedman, *Capitalism and Freedom* (Chicago: University of Chicago Press, 1962), cited in Djao, *Inequality and Social Policy*, p. 13.
27. M. Patricia Marchak, *Ideological Perspectives on Canada*, 2nd ed. (Toronto: McGraw-Hill Ryerson, 1981), p. 71.

28. Mishra, *The Welfare State in Crisis*, pp. 37-39.
29. Colin Pritchard and Richard Taylor, *Social Work: Reform or Revolution?* (London: Routledge & Kegan Paul, 1978), pp. 10-11.
30. George and Wilding, *Ideology and Social Welfare*, pp. 32, 38.
31. Gilder, *Wealth and Poverty*, pp. 114-39.
32. Earl Rubington and Martin S. Weinberg, eds., *The Study of Social Problems*, 2nd ed. (New York: Oxford University Press, 1989). The authors make the point that although the social pathology perspective of social problems is still alive and well, it has, to some extent, shifted its emphasis from pathology of people to pathology of society and its institutions.
33. *Ibid.*
34. John Coates, "Putting Knowledge for Practice into Perspective," *Canadian Social Work Review*, 8, 1 (Winter, 1991), pp. 82-96.
35. George and Wilding, *Ideology and Social Welfare*, p. 125.
36. H.L. Wilensky and C.N. Lebeaux, *Industrial Society and Social Welfare* (New York: Russell Sage Foundation, 1958).
37. Norman Furniss and Timothy Tilton, *The Case for the Welfare State* (Bloomington: Indiana University Press, 1977).
38. Mishra, "Riding the New Wave," p. 174.
39. Demetrius Iatridis, "Neo-conservatism Revisited," *Social Work* (March-April, 1983), p. 101.
40. Mishra, *The Welfare State in Crisis*, pp. 53-64.

Chapter 4

1. Geoffrey K. Roberts, *A Dictionary of Political Analysis* (New York: St. Martin's Press, 1971), pp. 113-14.
2. David G. Smith, "Liberalism," in David L. Sils, ed., *International Encyclopedia of the Social Sciences*, vol. III (New York: Macmillan and The Free Press, 1968), pp. 276-92.
3. For example, one heir of Jeremy Bentham and Adam Smith (two classical liberals) was John Stuart Mill, one of the pioneers of reform liberalism, and another was Herbert Spencer, a promoter of the ultra-conservative ideas of social Darwinism.
4. Smith, "Liberalism," p. 280.
5. Mark O. Dickerson and Thomas Flanagan, *An Introduction to Government and Politics: A Conceptual Approach* (Agincourt, Ont.: Methuen, 1986), p. 79.
6. The post-war welfare state in Britain developed from an amalgam of liberal and social democratic beliefs, values, and ideals and was based on the twin liberal pillars of Keynesian economics and Beveridge social policy. The Labour (social democratic) governments were responsible for the development of much of Britain's welfare state.
7. Vic George and Paul Wilding, *Ideology and Social Welfare* (London: Routledge & Kegan Paul, 1976), p. 21.

8. A.W. Djao, *Inequality and Social Policy* (New York: John Wiley & Sons, 1983).
9. George and Wilding, *Ideology and Social Welfare.*
10. Howard Jacob Karger, "Ideology and the Crisis of the Welfare State," *Quarterly Journal of Ideology: A Critique of Conventional Wisdom*, II,1 (1987), p. 8.
11. Vic George and Paul Wilding, *Ideology and Social Welfare*, 2nd ed. (London: Routledge & Kegan Paul, 1985), pp. 48-49.
12. *Ibid.*, 1976 edition, pp. 44-50.
13. *Ibid.*, p. 54.
14. David Gil, *The Challenge of Social Equality* (Cambridge, Mass: Schenkman Publishing Co., 1976), p. 57.
15. M. Patricia Marchak, *Ideological Perspectives on Canada*, 2nd ed. (Toronto: McGraw-Hill Ryerson, 1981), p. 46.
16. "Pluralism," in Sills, ed., *International Encyclopedia of the Social Sciences*, vol. XII.
17. Ray Lees, *Politics and Social Work* (London: Routledge & Kegan Paul, 1972), p. 30.
18. Colin Pritchard and Richard Taylor, *Social Work: Reform or Revolution?* (London: Routledge & Kegan Paul, 1978), p. 93.
19. George and Wilding, *Ideology and Social Welfare*, 2nd ed., pp. 62-63.
20. Ben Carniol, "Clash of Ideologies in Social Work Education," *Canadian Social Work Review* (1984), p. 188.
21. Earl Rubington and Martin S. Weinberg, *The Study of Social Problems*, 4th ed. (New York: Oxford University Press, 1989), pp. 55-61.
22. Carniol, "Clash of Ideologies," p. 188.
23. Carel B. Germain, ed., *Social Work Practice: People and Environment: An Ecological Perspective* (New York: Columbia University Press, 1979).
24. Bill Lee, *Pragmatics of Community Organization* (Mississauga, Ont.: Common Act Press, 1986), pp. 12-13.
25. George and Wilding, *Ideology and Social Welfare*, 2nd ed., p. 10.
26. *Ibid.*, pp. 62-64.
27. Leonard C. Marsh, "The Welfare State: Is It a Threat to Canada?" *Proceedings of the Canadian Conference on Social Work, 1950* (Ottawa: Canadian Conference on Social Work, 1950), p. 35. Marsh, who wrote the Canadian equivalent ("Report on Social Security for Canada," 1943) to the Beveridge Report, was greatly influenced by Lord Beveridge's thoughts and liberal ideology.
28. Harold L. Wilensky and Charles N. Lebeaux, *Industrial Society and Social Welfare*, 2nd ed. (New York: Russell Sage Foundation, 1965), pp. 139-40.
29. Jeffry Galper, *The Politics of Social Services* (Englewood Cliffs, N.J.: Prentice-Hall, 1975).
30. John McCready, "The Context for Canadian Social Policy," Working

Papers on Social Welfare in Canada Series (University of Toronto, Faculty of Social Work, 1980).

31. For example, see David Bell and Lorne Tepperman, *The Roots of Disunity: A Look at Canadian Political Culture* (Toronto. McClelland and Stewart, 1979); William Christian and Colin Campbell, *Political Parties and Ideologies in Canada: Liberals, Conservatives, Socialists and Nationalists* (Toronto: McGraw-Hill Ryerson, 1974); Gad Horowitz, "Conservatism, Liberalism and Socialism in Canada: An Interpretation," *Canadian Journal of Economics and Political Science,* 32, 2 (May, 1966); and Marchak, *Ideological Perspectives on Canada.*
32. Bell and Tepperman, *The Roots of Disunity*, p. 232.
33. Marchak, *Ideological Perspectives on Canada*, p. 14.
34. *Ibid.*
35. See Djao, *Inequality and Social Policy,* for an overview of this shift; see Dennis Guest, *The Emergence of Social Security in Canada*, 2nd ed. (Vancouver: University of British Columbia Press, 1985), for a more detailed coverage of this shift from a residual to an institutional model of social welfare in Canada.
36. M. Patricia Marchak, *Ideological Perspectives on Canada,* 3rd ed. (Toronto: McGraw-Hill Ryerson, 1988).
37. See, for example, *ibid.*; James Curtis *et al.*, *Social Inequality in Canada: Patterns, Problems, Policies* (Scarborough, Ont.: Prentice-Hall Canada, 1988).
38. Marchak, *Ideological Perspectives on Canada*, pp. 42-43.
39. See Galper, *The Politics of Social Services*, for an insightful analysis of how and why the social welfare state reinforces liberal capitalism.
40. Gil, *The Challenge of Social Equality*, p. 60.
41. Andrew Armitage, *Social Welfare in Canada* (Toronto: McClelland and Stewart, 1975; 1988).
42. Guest, *The Emergence of Social Security in Canada.*
43. Frank McGilly, *An Introduction to Canada's Public Social Services* (Toronto: McClelland & Stewart, 1990).
44. Carniol, "Clash of Ideologies," p. 192.
45. McGilly, *An Introduction to Canada's Public Social Services*, p. 39. Emphasis in original.
46. *Ibid.*, p. 12. Emphasis in original.
47. Carniol, "Clash of Ideologies," p. 192.
48. The notable exception is Ben Carniol, *Case Critical* (Toronto: Between the Lines 1987; 1990).
49. Shankar A. Yelaja, *An Introduction to Social Work Practice in Canada* (Scarborough, Ont.: Prentice-Hall Canada, 1985).
50. Lawrence Shulman, *The Skills of Helping Individuals and Groups* (Itasca, Ill.: Peacock, 1979). Although this is not a Canadian text, it is authored by a prominent Canadian social work educator.

Chapter 5

1. At present (late 1992) there are three provincial NDP governments – British Columbia, Ontario, and Saskatchewan.
2. Roger Scruton, *A Dictionary of Political Thought* (London: The Macmillan Press, 1982), p. 435.
3. A. Nove, "Socialism – Why?" in H.B. McCullough, ed., *Political Ideologies and Political Philosophies* (Toronto: Thompson Educational Publishing, 1989), p. 170.
4. Mark O. Dickerson and Thomas Flanagan, *An Introduction to Government and Politics: A Conceptual Approach* (Agincourt, Ont.: Methuen, 1986), pp. 110-27.
5. Scruton, *A Dictionary of Political Thought*, p. 436.
6. I am indebted to M. Dickerson and T. Flanagan for their succinct chapter on "Socialism" in their *Government and Politics*, which provided much of the material for my overview.
7. Geoffrey K. Roberts, *A Dictionary of Political Analysis* (New York: St. Martin's Press, 1971), p. 38.
8. Dickerson and Flanagan, *Government and Politics*, p. 116.
9. Howard Becker and Harry Elmer Barnes make this argument in *Social Thought From Lore to Science*, vol. II (Gloucester, Mass.: Peter Smith, 1978).
10. Dickerson and Flanagan adopt this position in *Government and Politics.*
11. Becker and Barnes, *Social Thought From Lore to Science*, pp. 657-58. Revolutionary socialism developed in Cuba and China much later.
12. Dickerson and Flanagan, *Government and Politics,* p. 113.
13. Becker and Barnes, *Social Thought From Lore to Science*, p. 654.
14. This notion of a provisional government caused the anarchist wing of socialism to split from the international socialist organization that existed (1864-1972) because they feared that this transitional government might become permanent.
15. Scruton, *A Dictionary of Political Thought*, p. 435.
16. Ramesh Mishra, *Society and Social Policy: Theories and Practice of Welfare* (Atlantic Heights, N.J.: Humanities Press, 1981).
17. Gerry van Houton, "Socialism Today: Renewal or Retreat?" in Joseph Roberts and J. Vorst, eds., *Socialism in Crisis? Canadian Perspectives* (Halifax and Winnipeg: Fernwood Publishing/Society for Socialist Studies, 1992), pp. 117-46.
18. Martin Jacques, "After Capitalism: What Now?" *Social Policy*, 21, 2 (Fall, 1990), p. 16.
19. For example: Vic George and Paul Wilding, *Ideology and Social Welfare*, 2nd ed. (London: Routledge & Kegan Paul, 1985); Colin Pritchard and Richard Taylor, *Social Work: Reform or Revolution?* (London: Routledge & Kegan Paul, 1978); Robert P. Mullaly and Eric F. Keating, "Similarities,

Differences and Dialectics of Radical Social Work," *Journal of Progressive Human Services*, 2, 2 (1991), pp. 49-78.

20. George and Wilding, *Ideology and Social Welfare*, p. 69.
21. *Ibid.*, p. 70.
22. *Ibid.*
23. *Ibid.*, pp. 70-73.
24. David Gil, *The Challenge of Social Equality* (Cambridge, Mass.: Schenkman Publishing Co., 1976).
25. George and Wilding, *Ideology and Social Welfare*, p. 74.
26. *Ibid.*, p. 75.
27. *Ibid.*, pp. 80-81.
28. A.W. Djao, *Inequality and Social Policy* (Toronto: John Wiley & Sons, 1983), p. 27.
29. George and Wilding, *Ideology and Social Welfare*, p. 81.
30. *Ibid.*, p. 77. This method of radical change is called "radical structuralism." It is discussed in detail in Chapter 8.
31. *Ibid.*, p. 83.
32. Charles E. Reasons and William D. Perdue, *Ideology of Social Problems* (Scarborough, Ont.: Nelson Canada, 1981), p. 6.
33. John Horton, "Order and Conflict Theories of Social Problems as Competing Ideologies," *American Journal of Sociology*, 71, 6 (May, 1966), p. 705.
34. Reasons and Perdue, *Ideology of Social Problems*, pp. 13-14.
35. George and Wilding, *Ideology and Social Welfare*, p. 4.
36. J.B. Rule, "The Problem with Social Problems," *Politics and Society*, 2,1 (1971), pp. 47-56.
37. *Ibid.*
38. Mishra, *Society and Social Policy.*
39. *Ibid.*, p. 133.
40. *Ibid.*, pp. 134-35.
41. *Ibid.*
42. *Ibid.* Mishra refers to this perspective as the "Social Administration School" of social policy (welfare).
43. George and Wilding, *Ideology and Social Welfare*, p. 91.
44. Pritchard and Taylor, *Social Work: Reform or Revolution?*, pp. 96-97.
45. *Ibid.*, p. 96.
46. *Ibid.*, p. 4.
47. *Ibid.*, p. 95.
48. *Ibid.*, p. 67.
49. Even with respect to the British experience with social democracy there is disagreement as to whether or not social democracy has moved Britain closer to a socialist state. There are also some who believe social democracy was not given a fair chance. See *ibid.* for a discussion of these issues.
50. Ulf Himmelstrand *et al.*, *Beyond Welfare Capitalism* (London: Heinemann, 1981), pp. 26-27.

51. J. Hughes, "Nationalization and the Private Sector," in J. Urry and J. Wakeford, eds., *Power in Britain* (London: Heinemann, 1973).
52. The best known and most controversial reform is called "The wage-earners fund," which is intended to rectify the unequal distribution of wealth and influence created by private ownership of industry. For details on how this scheme works, see Himmelstrand *et al.*, *Beyond Welfare Capitalism.*
53. Pritchard and Taylor, *Social Work: Reform or Revolution?*, p. 51.
54. *Ibid.*
55. These commissions are somewhat similar to royal commissions in the Canadian sense but usually comprise one member who is an acknowledged expert in the field of inquiry. These studies last an average of two-three years.
56. Ramesh Mishra, *The Welfare State in Crisis* (New York: St. Martin's Press, 1984), pp. 22-23.
57. Pritchard and Taylor, *Social Work: Reform or Revolution?*, p. 65.
58. Norman Furniss and Timothy Tilton, *The Case for the Welfare State* (Bloomington: Indiana University Press, 1979).

Chapter 6

1. A.W. Djao, *Inequality and Social Policy* (Toronto: John Wiley & Sons, 1983), pp. 31-32.
2. Ramesh Mishra, *Society and Social Policy*, 2nd ed. (Atlantic Highlands, N.J.: Humanities Press, 1981), p. 69. For an excellent overview of the Marxist perspective on social welfare, see *ibid.*, Chapter 5.
3. *Ibid.*, p. 70.
4. *Ibid.*, p. 71.
5. *Ibid.*, p. 68.
6. Vic George and Paul Wilding, *Ideology and Social Welfare*, 2nd ed. (London: Routledge & Kegan Paul, 1981), p. 121.
7. *Ibid.*, p. 98.
8. H. Laski, *A Grammar of Politics* (London: Allen & Unwin, 1925), cited in George and Wilding, *Ideology and Social Welfare.*
9. J. Strachey, *The Theory and Practice of Socialism* (Gollancz, 1936), cited in George and Wilding, *Ideology and Social Welfare.*
10. George and Wilding, *Ideology and Social Welfare*, pp. 107-08.
11. For example, Laski.
12. For example, Strachey.
13. George and Wilding, *Ideology and Social Welfare*, p. 109.
14. *Ibid.*
15. *Ibid.*, 1st ed. p. 98.
16. *Ibid.*, 2nd ed. pp. 109-10.
17. *Ibid.*, p. 12.

18. *Ibid.*
19. Ed Finn, "Ontario's Bill 70 a Major Step in Workplace Safety: Unionist," *Toronto Star*, February 19, 1979, quoted by Howard Buchbinder, "Inequality and the Social Services," in Allan Moscovitch and Glenn Drover, eds., *Inequality: Essays on the Political Economy of Social Welfare* (Toronto: University of Toronto Press, 1981).
20. James O'Connor, *The Fiscal Crisis of the State* (New York: St. Martin's Press, 1973), p. 6. Emphasis added.
21. Ramesh Mishra, *The Welfare State in Crisis* (New York: St. Martin's Press, 1984), pp. 72-78.
22. Jeffry Galper, *The Politics of Social Services* (Englewood Cliffs, N.J.: Prentice-Hall, 1975), pp. 45-72.
23. Mishra, *Society and Social Policy*, 2nd ed., pp. 74, 87.
24. For a polemic discussion and critique of both the Marxist revolutionary and Marxist evolutionary approaches to radical social and political change and social work practice, see Colin Pritchard and Richard Taylor, *Social Work: Reform or Revolution?* (London: Routledge & Kegan Paul, 1978), especially Chapter 7.
25. *Ibid.*, p. 5.
26. *Ibid.*, pp. 89-90.
27. *Ibid.*, p. 85.
28. *Ibid.*, p. 109.
29. *Ibid.*, p. 107.
30. Mishra, *The Welfare State in Crisis*, p. 97.
31. *Ibid.*, p. 97.
32. *Ibid.*, pp. 98-100.
33. *Ibid.*; George and Wilding, *Ideology and Social Welfare*; O'Connor, *The Fiscal Crisis of the State.*
34. George and Wilding, *Ideology and Social Welfare,* p. 135.
35. Mishra, *The Welfare State in Crisis*, p. 81.

Chapter 7

1. As discussed in Chapters 5 and 6, both social democracy and Marxism fall within the socialist camp. Both want the same type of society, but they differ on the means to get there. This difference in means is dealt with in Chapter 8 when developing a transformational social work theory.
2. Chris L. Clark and Stewart Asquith, *Social Work and Social Philosophy: A Guide for Practice* (London: Routledge & Kegan Paul, 1985), p. 105.
3. Mary Langan and Phil Lee, eds., *Radical Social Work Today* (London: Unwin Hyman, 1989).
4. *Ibid.*, p. 4
5. Ann Davis, "A Structural Approach to Social Work," in Joyce Lishman,

ed., *Handbook of Theory for Practice Teachers in Social Work* (London: Jessica Kingsley Publishers, 1991), p. 70.

6. Cited in Ann Withorn, *Serving the People: Social Services and Social Change* (New York: Columbia University Press, 1984), p. xii.
7. David Wagner, *The Quest for a Radical Profession* (Lanham, Maryland: University Press of America, 1990), p. 6.
8. R. Bailey and M. Brake, eds., *Radical Social Work* (New York: Pantheon Books, 1975); Jeffry Galper, *The Politics of Social Services* (Englewood Cliffs, N.J.: Prentice-Hall, 1975).
9. Clark and Asquith, *Social Work and Social Philosophy*, p. 105.
10. For an expository discussion of the commonalities and differences contained in the radical social work literature, see Robert P. Mullaly and Eric F. Keating, "Similarities, Differences and Dialectics of Radical Social Work," *Journal of Progressive Human Services*, 2, 2 (1991), pp. 49-78.
11. Ben Carniol, "A Critical Approach in Social Work," *Canadian Journal of Social Work Education*, 5,1 (1979), pp. 95-111.
12. Paul Corrigan and Peter Leonard, *Social Work Practice Under Capitalism: A Marxist Approach* (London: The Macmillan Press, 1978); John Longres, "Marxian Theory and Social Work Practice," *Catalyst*, V, 4 (1986), pp. 13-34; Steven Wineman, *The Politics of Human Services* (Montreal: Black Rose Books, 1984).
13. Withorn, *Serving the People.*
14. Chris Jones, *State Social Work and the Working Class* (London: The Macmillan Press, 1983); G. Smid and R. van Krieken, "Notes on Theory and Practice in Social Work: A Comparative View," *British Journal of Social Work*, 14 (1984), pp. 11-27.
15. Bailey and Brake, eds., *Radical Social Work*; Galper, *The Politics of Social Services*; Langan and Lee, eds., *Radical Social Work Today*; Peter Leonard, "Towards a Paradigm for Radical Practice," in Bailey and Brake, eds., *Radical Social Work*, pp. 46-61; C. Pritchard and R. Taylor, *Social Work: Reform or Revolution?* (London: Routledge & Kegan Paul, 1978); Mike Simpkin, *Trapped Within Welfare: Surviving Social Work* (London: The Macmillan Press, 1979); D. Statham, *Radicals in Social Work* (London: Routledge & Kegan Paul, 1978).
16. Jeffry Galper, *Social Work Practice: A Radical Perspective* (Englewood Cliffs, N.J.: Prentice-Hall, 1980).
17. Steve Bolger, Paul Corrigan, Jan Docking, and Nick Frost, *Towards Socialist Welfare Work* (London: The MacMillan Press, 1981).
18. Davis, "A Structural Approach to Social Work"; Ruth R. Middleman and Gale Goldberg, *Social Service Delivery: A Structural Approach to Social Work Practice* (New York: Columbia University Press, 1974); Maurice Moreau, "A Structural Approach to Social Work Practice," *Canadian Journal of Social Work Education*, 5, 1 (1979), pp. 78-94; Maurice Moreau and Lynne Leonard, *Empowerment Through a Structural Approach to*

Social Work (Ottawa: Carleton University School of Social Work, 1989); Gale Goldberg-Wood and Ruth R. Middleman, *The Structural Approach to Direct Practice in Social Work* (New York: Columbia University Press, 1974).

19. Mullaly and Keating, "Similarities, Differences and Dialectics of Radical Social Work."
20. *Ibid.*
21. Middleman and Goldberg, *Social Service Delivery,* p. 26. Emphasis added.
22. Middleman and Goldberg discuss several skills and techniques that would be useful to structural social workers, but nowhere do they state as a goal the undermining of the system.
23. Davis, "A Structural Approach to Social Work," p. 71.
24. Moreau, "A Structural Approach to Social Work"; Moreau and Leonard, *Empowerment;* M. Moreau, " Empowerment Through Advocacy and Consciousness-Raising: Implications of a Structural Approach to Social Work," *Journal of Sociology and Social Welfare*, 17, 2 (1990), pp. 53-67.
25. Professors Jim Albert, Peter Findlay, Helen Levine, Roland Lecomte, and Allan Moscovitch, as well as visiting professors from Britain – Mike Brake and Peter Leonard.
26. Professors Gisele Legault and Pierre Racine.
27. Professor Michele Bourgon.
28. Ben Carniol, "Structural Social Work: Maurice Moreau's Challenge to Social Work Practice," *Journal of Progressive Human Services*, 3, 1 (1992), pp. 1-20; Roland Lecomte, "Connecting Private Troubles and Public Issues in Social Work Education," in Brian Wharf, ed., *Social Work and Social Change in Canada* (Toronto: McClelland & Stewart, 1990), p. 38.
29. Moreau and Leonard, *Empowerment*, p. 1.
30. This concept of oppression is discussed in H. Sklar *et al.*, *Liberating Theory* (Boston: South End Press, 1986); and Steve Wineman, *The Politics of Human Services* (Montreal: Black Rose Books, 1984).
31. Carniol, "Structural Social Work," p. 19, Lecomte, "Connecting Private Troubles," p. 38.
32. Lecomte, "Connecting Private Troubles."
33. St. Thomas University in Fredericton, New Brunswick, has adopted the structural approach as its program focus, and the Maritime School of Social Work at Dalhousie University in Halifax acknowledges the major influence of a structural/feminist approach on its program.
34. Lecomte, "Connecting Private Troubles," p. 39; and Moreau and Leonard, *Empowerment.*
35. C. Pond, "The Changing Distribution of Income, Wealth and Poverty," in C. Hamnet, ed., *The Changing Social Structure* (London: Sage, 1989), p. 44, cited in Davis, "A Structural Approach to Social Work," p. 65.

36. The structural approach does not deny the need for individual change. Changing social structures will naturally affect individuals, both materially and psychologically. To think otherwise is to deny the connection between the personal and the political. Unlike conventional social work, however, structural social work does not believe that the resolution of social problems lies in individual change.
37. This particular approach to social change, which is called radical humanism, will be discussed in Chapter 8 and used as the theoretical basis for the structural social work practice described in Chapter 9.
38. This particular approach to social change, called radical structuralism, will be discussed in Chapter 8 and used as the theoretical basis for the structural social work practice described in Chapter 10.
39. The implications for structural social work of how we live our lives are discussed in Chapter 10.
40. Ben Carniol, *Case Critical*, 2nd ed. (Toronto: Between the Lines, 1990), p. 22.
41. M. Langan and P. Lee, "Whatever happened to radical social work," in Langan and Lee, eds., *Radical Social Work Today*, p. 13.

Chapter 8

1. Rosaline S. Barbour, "Social Work Education: Tackling the Theory-Practice Dilemma," *British Journal of Social Work*, 14 (1984), pp. 557-77.
2. See, for example, Barbour, "Social Work Education"; Jennie Pilalis, "The Integration of Theory and Practice: A Re-examination of a Paradoxical Expectation," *British Journal of Social Work*, 16 (1986), pp. 79-96; Ruth Reay, "Bridging the Gap: A Model for Integrating Theory and Practice," *British Journal of Social Work*, 16 (1986), pp. 49-64.
3. Barbour, "Social Work Education."
4. David Howe, *An Introduction to Social Work Theory* (Aldershot, England: Wildwood House, 1987), p. 17.
5. This simple but clear example was taken from Frank P. Williams and Marilyn D. McShane, *Criminological Theory* (Englewood Cliffs, N.J.: Prentice-Hall, 1988), p. 2.
6. Howe, *Introduction to Social Work Theory*, p. 2.
7. Robert Mullaly, "The Social Construction of Social Work Practice," unpublished manuscript.
8. Howe, *Introduction to Social Work Theory*, pp. 3-5.
9. Joel Fischer, *Effective Casework Practice* (New York: McGraw-Hill, 1978), cited *ibid.*, p. 5.
10. For a discussion of each of these functions, see Paul Davidson Reynolds, *A Primer in Theory Construction* (New York: Bobbs-Merrill, 1971), pp. 4-10.
11. Howe, *Introduction to Social Work Theory*, p. 17.

12. Use of the term "conflict" is problematic as it is used by different writers to refer not only to a perspective but to a theory or to a paradigm, as well as to other constructs that have a critical element to them. The term "perspective" is adopted here because many different conflict theories are based on the conflict perspective – structural social work being one of them – and to call the perspective a theory is to confuse the two. The position adopted in this book is that a perspective has descriptive and analytic qualities but no prescriptive component. Theory emanates from a perspective but includes a prescription.
13. John Horton, "Order and Conflict Theories of Social Problems as Competing Ideologies," *American Journal of Sociology*, 71, 6 (May, 1966), p. 703.
14. Charles E. Reasons and William D. Perdue, *Ideology of Social Problems* (Scarborough, Ont.: Nelson Canada, 1981).
15. Susan A. McDaniel and Ben Agger, *Social Problems Through Conflict and Order* (Don Mills, Ont.: Addison-Wesley, 1984), p. 14.
16. Horton, "Order and Conflict Theories," p. 703.
17. Howe, *Introduction to Social Work Theory,* p. 35.
18. Reasons and Perdue, *Ideology of Social Problems,* p. 7.
19. *Ibid.*
20. *Ibid.*, p. 8.
21. J. Philippe Rushton, "Race Differences in Behaviour: A Review and Evolutionary Analysis," *Personal Individual Differences,* 9, 6 (1988), pp. 1009-24.
22. Reasons and Perdue, *Ideology of Social Problems,* p. 9.
23. W. Ryan, *Blaming the Victim*, 2nd ed. (New York: Vintage Books, 1976), pp. 8-9, cited in A.W. Djao, *Inequality and Social Policy: The Sociology of Welfare* (Toronto: John Wiley & Sons, 1983), p. 171.
24. Howe, *Introduction to Social Work Theory,* p. 36.
25. McDaniel and Agger, *Social Problems,* p. 13.
26. Reasons and Perdue, *Ideology of Social Problems,* p. 10.
27. Horton, "Order and Conflict Theories," p. 704.
28. Howe, *Introduction to Social Work Theory,* p. 38.
29. Horton, "Order and Conflict Theories," p. 704.
30. *Ibid.*
31. Reasons and Perdue, *Ideology of Social Problems,* pp. 10-14.
32. *Ibid.*, p. 12.
33. *Ibid.*
34. *Ibid.*, pp. 13-14.
35. Howe, *Introduction to Social Work Theory,* p. 38.
36. On the history and development of the Frankfurt School, see M. Jay, *The Dialectical Imagination: A History of the Frankfurt School and the Institute for Social Research, 1932-50* (Boston: Little, Brown, 1973).
37. For an overview of the differences between modernist and post-modernist

critical theory and an attempt to reconcile the two, see Stephen T. Leonard, *Critical Theory in Political Practice* (Princeton, N.J.: Princeton University Press, 1990).

38. *Ibid.*, p. 3
39. *Ibid.*, p. 4
40. Leonard, *Critical Theory in Political Practice*, discusses these three critical theories in practice.
41. For a discussion of some internal contradictions of capitalism, such as the tendency of capitalism to over-produce and the fact that the majority of people actually produce the wealth but have no control over it, see Jeffry Galper, *Social Work Practice: A Radical Perspective* (Englewood Cliffs, N.J.: Prentice-Hall, 1980).
42. For a discussion of some internal contradictions of the welfare state and of social work, see Jeffry Galper, *The Politics of Social Services* (Englewood Cliffs, N.J.: Prentice-Hall, 1975).
43. M.L. Wardell and K.J. Benson, "A Dialectical View: Foundation for an Alternative Sociological Method," paper presented at the annual convention of the Midwest Sociological Society, Omaha, Nebraska, 1978, pp. 3-5, cited in Allan Rachlin, "Rehumanizing Dialectic: Toward an Understanding of the Interpenetration of Structure and Subjectivity," *Current Perspectives in Social Theory,* II (1991), p. 267. Emphasis added.
44. Robert P. Mullaly and Eric F. Keating, "Similarities, Differences and Dialectics of Radical Social Work," *Journal of Progressive Human Services*, 2, 2 (1992), pp. 49-78.
45. B. Frankel, "On the State of the State: Marxist Theories of the State after Leninism," *Theory and Society*, 7 (1979), pp. 199-242.
46. *Ibid.*, p. 237.
47. This does not mean that all oppressions are of equal intensity or prominence.
48. See, for example, Gail Kellough, "From Colonialism to Economic Imperialism: the Experience of the Canadian Indian," in J. Harp and J.R. Hofley, eds., *Structured Inequality in Canada* (Toronto: Prentice-Hall, 1980); Brad McKenzie and Peter Hudson, "Native Children, Child Welfare, and the Colonization of Native People," in K.L. Levitt and B. Wharf, eds., *The Challenge of Child Welfare* (Vancouver: University of British Columbia Press, 1985).
49. See, for example, Jim Albert, "Foreign Aid: The Welfare Function in Imperialist Relations between North and South," paper presented at the annual meeting of the Canadian Association of Schools of Social Work, Victoria, B.C., June, 1990; Hubert Campfens, "Forces Shaping the New Social Work in Latin America," *Canadian Social Work Review*, 5 (1988), pp. 9-27.
50. See, for example, H. Buchbinder, V. Burstyn, V. Forbes, and M. Steedman, *Who's on Top? The Politics of Heterosexuality* (Toronto: Garamond Press,

1987); R. Schoenberg and D. Goldberg, eds., *Homosexuality and Social Work* (New York: The Haworth Press, 1984).

51. Steven Wineman, *The Politics of Human Services* (Montreal: Black Rose Books, 1984), p. 163.
52. G. Burrell and G. Morgan, *Sociological Paradigms and Organizational Analysis* (London: Heinemann, 1979).
53. "Radical humanism is based on the ontological assumption that the human being is fundamentally set apart from everything else in existence because of its conscious and creative capacities. From this follows the epistemological assumption that the human mind does not receive objectivity from an external world. Rather it confers objectivity by imposing its own order on the world as it is perceived. What is 'known' or perceived about external reality is subjectively conferred by the knower.

    "Radical structuralism reflects the ontological assumption that the human person is merely one entity among many. While human conscious and creative capacities differentiate humanity, they do not set it apart from all else. From this follows the epistemological assumption that external reality is objective and as such tends to impose itself on our consciousness."

    From Mullaly and Keating, "Similarities, Differences and Dialectics of Radical Social Work," p. 66.
54. Howe, *Introduction to Social Work Theory.*
55. Burrell and Morgan, *Sociological Paradigms*; Howe, *Introduction to Social Work Theory.*
56. Howe, *Introduction to Social Work Theory.*
57. Ben Carniol, "Clash of Ideologies in Social Work Education," *Canadian Journal of Social Work Education* (1984), pp. 184-99; Howe, *Introduction to Social Work Theory.*
58. Mullaly and Keating, "Similarities, Differences and Dialectics of Radical Social Work," p. 67.
59. *Ibid.*, p. 71.
60. *Ibid.*, p. 72.
61. See, for example, L. Dominelli and E. McLeod, *Feminist Social Work* (Hampshire, U.K.: Macmillan Education, 1989); M. Langan and P. Lee, eds., *Radical Social Work Today* (London: Unwin Hyman, 1989); Peter Leonard, "Contesting the Welfare State in a Neo-Conservative Era," *Journal of Progressive Human Services*, 1, 1 (1990), pp. 11-25; F. Williams, *Social Policy: A Critical Introduction – Issues of Race, Gender and Class* (New York: Basil Blackwell, 1989).
62. See, for example, Carol Baines, Patricia Evans, and Sheila Neysmith, eds., *Women's Caring: Feminist Perspectives on Social Welfare* (Toronto: McClelland & Stewart, 1991); B.G. Collins, "Defining Feminist Social Work," *Social Work*, 31, 3 (1986), pp. 214-19; M. Eichler, *Families in Canada Today* (Toronto: Gage Publishing, 1988); N. Van Den Bergh and

L.B. Cooper, eds., *Feminist Visions for Social Work* (Silver Springs, Maryland: National Association of Social Workers, 1986).

63. Van Den Bergh and Cooper, *Feminist Visions for Social Work*; Ann Withorn, *Serving the People: Social Services and Social Change* (New York: Columbia University Press, 1984).
64. Van Den Bergh and Cooper, *Feminist Visions for Social Work*, p.x.
65. A. Jaggar and P. Struhl, *Feminist Frameworks* (New York: McGraw-Hill, 1978); A. Jaggar and P. Rothenberg, *Feminist Frameworks,* 2nd ed. (New York: McGraw-Hill, 1984).
66. Mullaly and Keating, "Similarities, Differences and Dialectics of Radical Social Work."
67. Langan and Lee, eds., *Radical Social Work Today.*
68. See, for example, E.M. Freeman, "Theoretical Perspectives for Practice with Black Families," in S.M.L. Logan, E.M. Freeman, and R.G. McRoy, eds., *Social Work Practice with Black Families: A Culturally Specific Perspective* (White Plains, N.Y.: Longman, 1990), pp. 38-52; M. Hutchison-Reis, "'And For Those of Us Who are Black?' Black Politics in Social Work," in Langan and Lee, eds., *Radical Social Work Today*, pp. 165-77; H. Shah, "Its Up to You Sisters: Black Women and Radical Social Work," *ibid.*, pp. 178-91; J. Small, "Towards a Black Perspective in Social Work: A Transformational Exploration," *ibid.*, pp. 279-91.
69. Mullaly and Keating, "Similarities, Differences and Dialectics of Radical Social Work," p. 57.

Chapter 9

1. Jeffry Galper, *The Politics of Social Services* (Englewood Cliffs, N.J.: Prentice-Hall, 1975), pp. 111-19.
2. For example, see J. Agel, *The Radical Therapist* (New York: Ballantine, 1971); William R. Caspary, "Psychotherapy and Radical Politics," *Catalyst: A Socialist Journal of the Social Services*, No. 7 (1980), pp. 27-36; David Forbes, "Counselling in Crisis," *Catalyst,* No. 20 (1986), pp. 53-84; F. Longres and E. McLeod, "Consciousness Raising and Social Work Practice," *Social Casework*, 61, 5 (May, 1980), pp. 267-76; Iris Vazala-Martinez, "Toward an Emancipatory Clinical Practice in Human Services," in D. Gil and E. Gil, eds., *Toward Social and Economic Justice* (Cambridge, Mass: Schenkman Publishing Co., 1985), pp. 55-62.
3. Ben Carniol, "Clash of Ideologies in Social Work Education," *Canadian Social Work Review* (1984), pp. 184-99; David Howe, *An Introduction to Social Work Theory* (Aldershot, U.K.: Wilwood House Publishers, 1987); Robert Mullaly and Eric Keating, " Similarities, Differences and Dialectics of Radical Social Work," *Journal of Progressive Human Services*, 2, 2 (1991), pp. 49-78.
4. Schools of social work have always had as one of their major curriculum

streams what was called the Human Behaviour in the Social Environment (HBSE) sequence.

5. Mullaly and Keating, "Similarities, Differences and Dialectics of Radical Social Work."
6. C. Wright Mills, *The Sociological Imagination* (New York: Oxford University Press, 1959).
7. Barbara G. Collins, "Defining Feminist Social Work," *Social Work* (May-June, 1986), p. 215.
8. Mullaly and Keating, "Similarities, Differences and Dialectics," p. 54.
9. The literature is too extensive to cite here, but since 1976, when *Social Work* published a "Special Issue on Women," there has been an avalanche of articles on "feminist counselling," feminist therapy," and "feminist social work."
10. See, for example, Joan Cummings, "Sexism In Social Work: Some Thoughts on Strategy for Structural Change," *Catalyst*, II, 4 (1980), pp. 7-34; Gillian Walker, "The Status of Women in Social Work Education." a brief prepared for the Canadian Association of Schools of Social Work (CASSW) Task Force on the Status of Women in Social Work Education (Ottawa: CASSW, 1977).
11. Marilyn Frye, *The Politics of Reality: Essays in Feminist Theory* (Trumansburg, N.Y.: Crossing Press, 1983).
12. *Ibid.*, p. 8.
13. *Ibid.*, p. 4.
14. Michael Albert *et al., Liberating Theory* (Boston, Mass.: South End Press, 1986).
15. Paulo Freire, *Pedagogy of the Oppressed* (New York: Continuum Publishing, 1970), p. 45.
16. S. Hall *et al., Policing the Crisis: Muggings, The State and Law and Order* (London: The Macmillan Press, 1978).
17. A recent Canadian example is the Free Trade Agreement (January 1, 1988) with the United States. This was a business concern taken up by a business-oriented Conservative government that presented it as a national issue to be passed in the public interest. No one had ever heard of the issue before the Mulroney government stated its intention to negotiate such an agreement with the United States. And, in spite of all public opinion polls showing that most Canadians were against the Agreement, it was imposed on Canada by the ruling class alliance of business and a Conservative government.
18. Freire, *Pedagogy of the Oppressed.*
19. Barry D. Adam, *The Survival of Domination: Inferiorization and Everyday Life* (New York: Elsevier, 1978).
20. Maurice Moreau and Lynne Leonard, *Empowerment Through a Structural Approach to Social Work* (Ottawa: Carleton University School of Social Work, 1989).

21. Jerome Agel, ed., *The Radical Therapist* (New York: Ballantine, 1971).
22. Freire, *Pedagogy of the Oppressed.*
23. Moreau and Leonard, *Empowerment.*
24. Michael Basch, "Toward a Theory That Emcompases Depression: A Revision of Existing Causal Hypotheses," in E. James Anthony and Theresa Benedek, eds., *Depression and Human Existence* (Boston: Little, Brown, 1975), p. 513, cited in Elaine B. Pinderhughes, "Empowerment for Our Clients and for Ourselves," *Social Casework* (June, 1983), pp. 331-38.
25. Sharon Freedberg, "Self-Determination: Historical Perspectives on Current Practice," *Social Work* (January, 1989), pp. 33-38.
26. Barbara Levy Simon, "Rethinking Empowerment," *Journal of Progressive Human Services*, 1,1 (1990), pp. 27-39.
27. Pinderhughes, "Empowerment for Our Clients and for Ourselves."
28. Yeheskel Hasenfeld, "Power in Social Work Practice," *Social Service Review* (September, 1987), p. 487.
29. Simon, "Rethinking Empowerment," p. 28.
30. *Ibid.*
31. Cummings, "Sexism in Social Work."
32. Simon, "Rethinking Empowerment," p. 34.
33. Hasenfeld, "Power in Social Work Practice."
34. Simon, "Rethinking Empowerment," p. 37.
35. Moreau and Leonard, *Empowerment..*
36. Hasenfeld, "Power in Social Work Practice."
37. Simon, "Rethinking Empowerment."
38. Moreau and Leonard, *Empowerment.*
39. Pinderhughes, "Empowerment for Our Clients and for Ourselves."
40. Peter Leonard, *Personality and Ideology: Towards a Materialist Understanding of the Individual* (London: The Macmillan Press, 1984).
41. John F. Longres and Eileen McLeod, "Consciousness Raising and Social Work Practice," *Social Casework* (May, 1980), p. 268.
42. *Ibid.*
43. J. Midgely, *Professional Imperialism: Social Work in the Third World* (London: Heinemann, 1982).
44. Peter Leonard, *Personality and Ideology*, pp. 210-11.
45. Scott Bock, "Conscientization: Paulo Freire and Class-Based Practice," *Catalyst*, II, 2 (1980), pp. 5-26.
46. John Longres, "Marxian Theory and Social Work Practice," *Catalyst*, V, 4 (1986), pp. 13-34.
47. Jan Fook, "Feminist Contributions to Casework Practice," in H. Marchant and B. Wearing, eds., *Gender Reclaimed: Women and Social Work* (Sydney: Hale and Iremonger, 1986), pp. 54-63.
48. Thomas Keefe, "Empathy Skill and Critical Consciousness," *Social Casework* (September, 1980), p. 389.

49. Longres, "Marxian Theory and Social Work Practice," p. 31.
50. *Ibid.*, p. 30.
51. Jeffry Galper, *Social Work Practice: A Radical Perspective* (Englewood Cliffs, N.J.: Prentice-Hall, 1980).
52. *Ibid.*, p. 149.
53. Longres and McLeod, "Consciousness Raising and Social Work Practice."
54. Richard A. Cloward and Frances Fox Piven, "Notes Toward a Radical Social Work," in Roy Bailey and Mike Brake, eds., *Radical Social Work* (New York: Pantheon Books, 1975), pp. xxiii-xxiv.
55. Galper, *Social Work Practice*, p. 146.
56. Longres and McLeod, "Consciousness Raising and Social Work Practice," p. 273.
57. Jeffry Galper, *The Politics of Social Services* (Englewood Cliffs, N.J.: Prentice-Hall, 1975), p. 213.
58. Leonard, *Personality and Ideology*, p. 208.
59. Longres and McLeod, "Consciousness Raising and Social Work Practice," p. 273.
60. Paul Corrigan and Peter Leonard, *Social Work Practice Under Capitalism: A Marxist Approach* (London: The Macmillan Press, 1978).
61. Galper, *Social Work Practice.*
62. *Ibid.*, pp. 140-42.
63. Ann Withorn, *Serving the People: Social Services and Social Change* (New York: Columbia University Press, 1984), p. 110.
64. Leonard, *Personality and Ideology*, pp. 211-12.
65. Maurice Moreau, "Practice Implications of a Structural Approach to Social Work," unpublished paper, Université de Montréal, n.d.
66. Moreau and Leonard, *Empowerment,* p. 124.
67. Stephen M. Rose and Bruce L. Black, *Advocacy and Empowerment: Mental Health Care in the Community* (Boston, Mass.: Routledge & Kegan Paul, 1985).
68. Roland L. Warren, Stephen Rose, and Ann Bergunder, *The Structure of Urban Reform* (Lexington, Mass.: D.C. Heath, 1974), cited in Rose and Black, *Advocacy and Empowerment*, p. 26.
69. *Ibid.*, p. 27.
70. *Ibid.*, p. 29.
71. *Ibid.*, p. 36.
72. Moreau, "Practice Implications of a Structural Approach."
73. Fook, "Feminist Contributions to Casework Practice."
74. G. Frayne, "Tape-Analysis Grid for the Action Research on the Structural Approach to Social Work," unpublished material, Université de Montréal, École de service social, 1987, cited in Moreau, "Practice Implications of a Structural Approach."

75. D. Gordon, *Therapeutic Metaphors* (Cupertino, Calif: Meta Publications, 1978).
76. Leon Festinger, *A Theory of Cognitive Dissonance* (Palo Alto, Calif: Stanford University Press, 1957).
77. Ruth R. Middleman and Gale Goldberg, *Social Service Delivery: A Structural Approach to Social Work Practice* (New York: Columbia University Press, 1974).
78. M.H. Erickson, *My Voice Will Go With You: The Teaching Tales of Milton H. Erickson, M.D.,* S. Rosen, ed. (New York: Norton, 1982).
79. Ronald L. Simons, "Strategies for Exercising Influence," *Social Work*, 27, 3 (May, 1982), pp. 268-73.
80. Michèle Bourgon, "How Feminism Can Take The Crazy Out of Your Head and Put It Back Into Society," in Geraldine Finn, ed., *Women's Studies: A Canadian Perspective* (Ottawa: Garamond Press, 1988).
81. This is not to imply that child abuse and neglect are only matters of class. It is recognized that physical abuse, emotional abuse, and sexual abuse each have their own distinct set of dynamics. The argument here is that class impacts on these dynamics and that an adequate material condition is often a more realistic solution than sending people to parenting courses when they may not know where their next meal will come from or if they will have a roof over their heads or even if they will still have children to parent.
82. Leroy H. Pelton, "Child Abuse and Neglect: The Myth of Classlessness," *American Journal of Orthopsychiatry*, 48, 4 (1978), p. 617.
83. Rose and Black, *Advocacy and Empowerment*, p. 45.
84. Freire, *Pedagogy of the Oppressed.*
85. Maurice J. Moreau, "A Structural Approach to Social Work Practice," *Canadian Journal of Social Work Education*, 5,1 (1979), p. 89.
86. Steve Burghardt, *The Other Side of Organizing: Resolving the Personal Dilemmas and Political Demand of Daily Practice* (Cambridge, Mass.: Schenkman, 1982), p. 215.
87. Moreau, "Practice Implications of a Structural Approach," p. 26.
88. Moreau and Leonard, *Empowerment,* pp. 82-87.
89. Galper, *The Politics of Social Services*, p. 45.
90. *Ibid.*, p. 46.
91. For an insightful and illuminating analysis of the control functions of social agencies and services, see *ibid.*, Chapter 4.
92. Withorn, *Serving the People*, p. 160.
93. Cloward and Piven, "Notes Toward a Radical Social Work," p. xii.
94. Withorn, *Serving the People*, Chapter 9.
95. *Ibid.*, pp. 160-61.
96. *Ibid.*, p. 200.
97. Raymond Scurfield, "An Integrated Approach to Case Services and Social Reform," *Social Casework*, 61, 10 (December, 1980), pp. 610-18.

98. Rino J. Patti and Herman Resnick, "Changing the Agency from Within," *Social Work,* 17, 4 (July, 1972), pp. 48-57.
99. Burghardt, *The Other Side of Organizing*, p. 191.
100. Galper, *Social Work Practice,* p. 198.
101. See, for example, the American book, Withorn, *Serving the People*; the British book, Mike Simpkin, *Trapped Within Welfare* (London: The Macmillan Press, 1979); and the Canadian book, Ben Carniol, *Case Critical,* 2nd ed. (Toronto: Between the Lines, 1990).
102. Most of the literature on democratic worker-run agencies focuses on alternative organizations and services. Very little has been written on democratizing the social agency as a workplace since Galper (1980) and Simpkin (1979). Most writings in the 1980s focused on stemming the tide of the deprofessionalization and/or the proletarianization of social work.
103. Moreau and Leonard, *Empowerment.*
104. *Ibid.*, pp. 152-53.
105. Peter Blair, "Orientation Towards Clients in a Public Welfare Agency," in Elihu Katz and Brenda Danet, eds., *Bureaucracy and the Public: A Reader in Official-Client Relations* (New York: Basic Books, 1973), p. 240, cited in Withorn, *Serving the People*, p. 202.
106. Withorn, *Serving the People*, p. 203.
107. Galper, *The Politics of Social Services*, p. 196.
108. Galper, *Social Work Practice,* pp. 198-200.
109. Withorn, *Serving the People*, pp. 200-01.
110. Galper, *Social Work Practice,* pp. 197-98.
111. Wendy Ruth Sherman and Stanley Wenocur, "Empowering Public Welfare Workers Through Mutual Support," *Social Work* (September-October, 1983), p. 377.
112. Moreau and Leonard, *Empowerment.*
113. Galper, *Social Work Practice,* pp. 253-54.

Chapter 10

1. Maurice J. Moreau, "A Structural Approach to Social Work Practice," *Canadian Journal of Social Work Education*, 5,1 (1979), pp. 78-94.
2. Ben Carniol, *Case Critical* (Toronto: Between the Lines, 1987), pp. 109-10.
3. Steven Wineman, *The Politics of Human Services* (Montreal: Black Rose Books, 1984), p. 20.
4. Moreau, "A Structural Approach to Social Work Practice," p. 87.
5. Carniol, *Case Critical*, p. 116.
6. *Ibid.*
7. Ann Withorn, *Serving the People: Social Services and Social Change* (New York: Columbia University Press, 1984).

8. Carniol, *Case Critical.*
9. *Ibid.*, p. 130.
10. Jeffry Galper, *Social Work Practice: A Radical Perspective* (Englewood Cliffs, N.J.: Prentice-Hall, 1980), p. 114.
11. David Sills, ed., *International Encyclopedia of the Social Sciences*, vol. 14 (New York: Macmillan and The Free Press, 1968), pp. 438, 445-46.
12. Robert L. Barker, *The Social Work Dictionary* (Silver Spring, Maryland: National Association of Social Workers, 1987), p. 153.
13. A recent publication that focuses on coalition-building within the human services from a practice point of view is Milan J. Dluhy, *Building Coalitions in the Human Services* (Newbury Park, Calif.: Sage Publications, 1990).
14. Douglas P. Biklen, *Community Organizing: Theory and Practice* (Englewood Cliffs, N.J.: Prentice-Hall, 1983), pp. 210-11.
15. Wineman, *The Politics of Human Services*, p. 159.
16. *Ibid.*, p. 163.
17. *Ibid.*, p. 182.
18. *Ibid.*, p. 169.
19. *Ibid.*, p. 167.
20. *Ibid.*, p. 221.
21. *Ibid.*
22. Galper, *Social Work Practice*, p. 157.
23. Neil Fraser, "The Labor Movement in the Explanation of Social Service Growth: The United States and Britain," *Administration in Social Work*, 3, 3 (Fall, 1979), pp. 301-12.
24. Ramesh B. Mishra, *Society and Social Policy*, 2nd ed. (London: The Macmillan Press, 1981).
25. Frances Fox Piven and Richard A. Cloward, *Poor People's Movements* (New York: Pantheon, 1977).
26. Peter Flora and Arnold Heidenheimer, eds., *The Development of Welfare States in Europe and America* (New Brunswick, N. J.: Transaction Books, 1981), Fraser, "The Labour Movement in the Explanation of Social Service Growth"; Norman Furniss and Timothy Tilton, *The Case for the Welfare State* (Bloomington: Indiana University Press, 1979); Mishra, *Society and Social Policy*; H.L. Wilensky, *The Welfare State and Equality* (Berkeley: University of California Press, 1975).
27. Mishra, *Society and Social Policy*, p. 113.
28. Carniol, *Case Critical*, p. 121; Paul Corrigan and Peter Leonard, *Social Work Practice Under Capitalism: A Marxist Approach* (London: The Macmillan Press, 1978), p. 144.
29. Galper, *Social Work Practice.*
30. Withorn, *Serving the People.*
31. Carniol, *Case Critical.*

32. Corrigan and Leonard, *Social Work Practice Under Capitalism.*
33. David Wagner and Marcia B. Cohen, "Social Workers, Class and Professionalism," *Catalyst*, 1, 1 (1978), pp. 25-55.
34. Corrigan and Leonard, *Social Work Practice Under Capitalism.*
35. Galper, *Social Work Practice.*
36. Robert Mullaly and Eric Keating, "Similarities, Differences and Dialectics of Radical Social Work," *Journal of Progressive Human Services*, 2, 2 (1991), pp. 49-78.
37. For example: Galper, *Social Work Practice*; Jean Hardy, *Values in Social Work* (London: Routledge & Kegan Paul, 1981); K. Laursen, "Professionalism," in H. Throssell, ed., *Social Work: Radical Essays* (St. Lucia, Queensland: University of Queensland Press, 1975); Wagner and Cohen, "Social Workers, Class and Professionalism"; P. Wilding, *Professional Power and Social Welfare* (London: Routledge & Kegan Paul, 1982); Withorn, *Serving the People.*
38. Ernie Lightman, "Professionalization, Bureaucratization, and Unionization in Social Work," *Social Service Review*, 56, 1 (1982), pp. 130-43.
39. L. Alexander, P. Lichtenbery, and D. Brunn, "Social Workers in Unions: A Survey," *Social Work*, 25, 3 (1980), pp. 216-33; G.L. Shaffer, "Labor Relations and the Unionization of Professional Social Workers: A Neglected Area in Social Work Education," *Journal of Education for Social Work*, 15, 1 (1979), pp. 80-86.
40. Linda C. Reeser and Irwin Epstein, *Professionalization and Activism in Social Work: The Sixties, The Eighties, and the Future* (New York: Columbia University Press, 1990).
41. Maurice Moreau and Lynne Leonard, *Empowerment Through a Structural Approach to Social Work* (Ottawa: Carleton University School of Social Work, 1989).
42. Leslie Bella, "The Canadian Social Work Profession, 1985-1989: Professional Self-Interest and Public Welfare," paper presented to the Canadian Association of Schools of Social Work, Laval, Quebec, June, 1989.
43. Paul Wilding, *Professional Power and Social Welfare* (London: Routledge & Kegan Paul, 1982).
44. David Wolfe, "The Canadian State in Comparative Perspective," *Canadian Review of Sociology and Anthropology*, 26,1 (1989), pp. 95-126.
45. Gosta Esping-Andersen, "The Three Political Economies of the Welfare State," *Canadian Review of Sociology and Anthropology*, 26,1 (1989), pp. 10-36.
46. Galper, *Social Work Practice,* p. 90.
47. Steven Wineman, *The Politics of Human Services*, p. 224.
48. *Ibid.*, p. 225.
49. For example: Dennis Guest's basic text, which is used by most schools of social work, *The Emergence of Social Security in Canada* (Vancouver:

University of British Columbia Press, 1980), makes no reference to the NDP or its predecessor, the Co-operative Commonwealth Federation, nor does Frank McGilly in his recent overview of Canadian income and health programs, *Canada's Public Social Services* (Toronto: McClelland & Stewart, 1990), except to mention that the provincial CCF government of Saskatchewan was the first socialist government in North America and the first government to enact and implement public hospital insurance. Similarly, neither Allan Moscovitch and Jim Albert, eds., *The Benevolent State: The Growth of Welfare in Canada* (Toronto: Garamond Press, 1987), nor Brian Wharf, ed., *Social Work and Social Change in Canada* (Toronto: McClelland & Stewart, 1990), makes any substantial reference to the NDP.

50. Angela Djao, a Canadian Marxist sociologist, makes no mention of the NDP in *Inequality and Social Policy: The Sociology of Welfare* (Toronto: John Wiley & Sons, 1983). Likewise, Ben Carniol, a radical social worker, says nothing about the CCF/NDP in his *Case Critical* (Toronto: Between the Lines, 1987; 1990).
51. Shankar A. Yelaja, ed., *Canadian Social Policy* (Waterloo, Ont.: Wilfrid Laurier University Press, 1987), p. 17.
52. Andrew Armitage, *Social Welfare in Canada: Ideals, Realities, and Future Paths* (Toronto: McClelland and Stewart, 1988), p. 91.
53. *Ibid.*, p. 93.
54. Ramesh Mishra, *The Welfare State in Capitalist Society* (Toronto: University of Toronto Press, 1990).
55. Armitage, *Social Welfare in Canada*, p. 92.
56. Moreau and Leonard, *Empowerment,* p. 238.
57. Withorn, *Serving the People*, p. 82.
58. Galper, *Social Work Practice.*
59. Withorn, *Serving the People*

Acknowledgements

To write a book such as this, which calls for a social paradigm and a social work approach different from those now dominant, requires a tremendous amount of angry energy. It is not enough to understand how our present set of social arrangements benefits a privileged minority (mainly white, upper-income, entrepreneurial males) at the expense of the majority (particularly the poor, visible minorities, women, immigrants, the disabled, and the working class), one must be angry enough to want to do something about it. So, I wish to thank all those individuals and groups and organizations who have fuelled and sustained my sense of indignation over acts and attitudes that unfairly and unnecessarily have denied so many people their essential human dignity and have blocked their human potential. Included among them are conservative politicians of all stripes; business organizations such as the Canadian Chamber of Commerce, the Canadian Manufacturers' Association, and the Business Council on National Issues; right wing think tanks such as the C.D. Howe and Fraser Institutes; the mainstream media, especially the Irving-owned sector that dominates Atlantic Canada; and all those conventional social work academics and scholars who should know better.

Of course, anger by itself is not enough to sustain one's writing. Support, encouragement, and assistance are also required. I wish to thank Sandy Wachholz and Eric Keating, who gave generously of their time to read several chapters in draft stage and to discuss the ideas contained in them with clarity of thought, and who supported me throughout most of this project. I owe a special debt to Jeananne Knox, who typed and proofed several drafts of the manuscript with speed, accuracy, and patience. Without her I would still be lost in a sea of pages full of hieroglyphics and unable to meet any of my deadlines. I am very grateful also to the many progressive social work writers who have gone before me, who have influenced my thinking, and who have inspired me to write this book: particularly Jeffry Galper, David Gil, and Ann Withorn in the United States; Roy Bailey and Mike Brake in Great Britain; Ben Carniol and the late Maurice Moreau in Canada; and Peter Leonard in Great Britain, now living in Canada. I am also deeply indebted to the many students who forced me to clarify my ideas and who provided critical (sometimes, very critical) comments during our classroom discussions of the material in the book.

My greatest debt is to my parents, Clement and Audrey Mullaly, who instilled in me a concern for the plight of others and a commitment to social justice. It is to them that I dedicate this book.

Index